A BIOGRAPHY IN NINE LIVES
LIMERICK

ARTHUR JAMES O'DEA

HEROBOOKS

PUBLISHED BY HERO BOOKS
1 WOODVILLE GREEN
LUCAN
CO. DUBLIN
IRELAND

Hero Books is an imprint of Umbrella Publishing
First Published 2022
Copyright © Arthur James O'Dea 2022
All rights reserved

9781910827543

Cover design and formatting: jessica@viitaladesign.com
Photographs: Sportsfile

★ DEDICATION ★

In memory of Anne and Eileen

★ CONTENTS ★

PROLOGUE

EPILOGUE

★ ACKNOWLEDGEMENTS ★

THERE IS ONLY one place to start. The prospect of my writing about Limerick hurling wouldn't have come about without Arthur O'Dea, hereafter known as my father. If my name was the first thing he passed down to me, an affinity for his native county and its hurling team was a close second. The greatest pleasure I took in writing this book was hoping how much he might enjoy reading it.

There are only two other people who fully understand what a largely frustrating, but recently joyous hold, Limerick's hurlers have had on our lives, and my mother Regina and my sister Helena have (as always) been a phenomenal source of support. Their excitement for this book from the very beginning motivated me to keep going on days where no end appeared to be in sight.

In a more practical sense, none of this would have come about without Liam Hayes and the brilliant people at Hero Books. When I first read Liam's remarkable memoir, *Out of our Skins*, it introduced me to a man for whom the satisfaction of winning a match had as much to do with how that match was won. From that Meath footballer to the editor I worked with, the same trait looms large. If I will miss anything from no longer having this book to write, it will be the discussions I had with Liam about how it ought to be carried out in the first place.

In their own way, I would also like to thank a number of friends who were there to listen when an idea needed figuring out, or, more likely, when my frustrations needed airing. Ciaran Bradley and Gavin Cooney bore the brunt of this superbly. Tommy Rooney – or the King of gaelic football podcasts as he's become – was the one who put me in touch with Liam Hayes initially. I cannot thank him enough for the support he showed this project from the very beginning. For listening to me as I excitedly relayed snippets of conversations I'd had with the book's contributors, I would also like to thank Ger Gilroy. It may not have been intentional, but his reactions gave me a good idea if I was on the right path.

Upholding a role he's played perfectly since we were in college together, Seán Fox ensured he was never too busy to read what I sent him along the way. A constant source of support, I urge anyone writing a book to find themselves a 'Seán'.

It has been my immense pleasure over the course of this book to speak with a great number of people for whom Limerick hurling has been a life's passion. I cannot thank them enough for giving me their time. I owe particular thanks to Breda Quaid, Éamonn Cregan, Ger Hegarty, Shane Dowling, Shane Fitzgibbon, Stephen Lucey and Tom Ryan, however. To a person, their generosity, openness and enthusiasm for what I was trying to do gave me a good clue that we were onto something worthwhile here. If this book has managed to get their collective passion for Limerick and hurling across to its readers, I will consider that a job well done.

Finally, I owe the greatest debt of gratitude to my partner Erica. From the very first call I made for this book through to its completion, she has been a rock of support and good sense throughout. Always there with an encouraging word, the keenest of critical eyes and a glass of wine when a day's writing was done, it doesn't go far enough to say that this book wouldn't have been written without her help. When she next finds herself cursing a referee's call or roaring encouragement at Limerick's hurlers from the stands in Croke Park, I hope she finds that it was all worth it.

Arthur James O'Dea
August 2022

The mind is its own place, and in itself
Can make a heaven of hell, a hell of heaven.
What matter where, if I be still the same,
And what I should be, all, but less than he
Whom thunder hath made greater? Here at least
We shall be free; the almighty hath not built
Here for his envy, will not drive us hence:
Here we may reign secure; and, in my choice,
To reign is worth ambition, though in hell:
Better to reign in hell than serve in heaven.

– John Milton, *Paradise Lost*

I've been burned before and I know the score
So you won't hear me complain

– Bob Dylan, *Is Your Love in Vain?*

I'm just absolutely delighted. What a place! I love this
place so much. What a day, what a day for Limerick
fans… Listen to Dolores here in Croke Park in front of
eighty-two and a half thousand people. It does not get
any better than that let me tell you.

– Gearóid Hegarty, 2022 All-Ireland final

★ PROLOGUE ★

I WAS THREE YEARS OLD when I first saw the Limerick hurlers. Sitting on the living room floor of our house in Sligo, the 1994 All-Ireland final was being played. My mother, only a few years older then, than I am remembering it now, was sat behind me. In her arms, my sister's age was still being measured in weeks. It would be a bit much to suggest that I was watching the match.

No more than the sun in the sky, I was aware of its being there without ever understanding what it was. I had been told, I am sure, that somewhere inside in the television was my father. I cannot imagine that I quite grasped that concept either, but nevertheless I craned my neck upward and looked for him.

In later years, as we sat together in Croke Park, he would point out to me the seat he had acquired high up in the Hogan Stand. Trying to spot him from the pitch itself would have been hard enough, let alone through the television. Yet I sat there long enough for it to lodge in my mind anyway.

Although most of what I must have witnessed does not remain, one outstanding feature of the event prompts me to believe that this memory is not a fabrication... the colour green.

It might be romantic to suggest that it was the greenness of Limerick's jerseys that grabbed me, but no, it was without question the viridescence of that pitch. The match itself was incidental. Like Gatsby, I was captivated by this green light luminating from the screen.

It took another seven years until I first saw Limerick hurling in the flesh. Old enough now to travel along with my father, we set off one Sunday morning for Thurles – by way of Tullamore. Not the most straightforward route from Sligo to Semple Stadium, our detour was not without good cause. My uncle, cousin, and a friend of his were coming along too.

Earlier that year, at a communion or confirmation or birthday party in Castlebar, the whole of my father's family had gathered on the same day Limerick travelled to Páirc Uí Chaoimh for the Munster Championship opener. There was too much excitement generally for the 10-year-old me to watch it carefully, but as Ollie Moran inspired Limerick to victory over Cork, I gathered from the reactions of those present that hurling had a strong hold over these people of mine.

As we set off on the final leg of our journey, the excitement I felt at finally attending my first game was matched by a similarly general enthusiasm. And how could it not? We were setting off to watch an All-Ireland final, after all. That these Limerick hurlers happened to be a team of under-21s was immaterial.

This was an All-Ireland final, nevertheless. Perched on my seat in a ground I have visited countless times since, Limerick's hurlers in their traditional colour came to resemble an extension of that green light from years before.

There was no going back.

II

Limerick fingers were trembling nervously near the end of yesterday's All-Ireland under-21 hurling final in Thurles, but the delicate brush strokes which had been applied earlier were enough to add a dramatic splash of colour to the county's rapidly expanding canvas. The disappointment of defeat by Wexford in their senior All-Ireland quarter-final evaporated on a glorious autumn afternoon as Limerick players created their own history by becoming the first team from the county to win consecutive All-Ireland under-21 titles.

– *Irish Independent*, September 17, 2001

III

A LITTLE OVER two decades have elapsed and I do not remember much of what occurred during this match either. The 'brush strokes' and 'splash of colour' Martin Breheny wrote about do not mean much to me. I remember Limerick winning though.

Indeed, the historical aspect of that win, captured in the general excitement surrounding this group of hurlers, remains vivid even now. There had been something approaching an expectation that our journey down would be rewarded with a victory. We knew they had been successful the year before, and word had already begun to spread of an even greater talent coming down the line.

'That's O'Shaughnessy down there,' I remember my uncle telling us, pointing to this unremarkable looking 16-year-old stood by the sideline watching the match much like ourselves. A young man for any under-21 panel, this sensation of schools hurling would be given a few minutes playing time at the end.

It may have been the first time I had actually seen him hurl, but we had already heard everything about him. A free-scoring forward with St Colman's College, he had already won an All-Ireland of his own earlier that year. *Fermoy had a brilliant match-winner in Kilmallock youngster, Andrew O'Shaughnessy,* one match report read from the school's Dr Croke Cup win in the summer of 2001. *[He] added to a rapidly growing reputation with a 2-8 contribution, seven of his eight points coming from deadly accuracy from frees in the style of a DJ Carey at his best.* Not simply compared to a Kilkenny hurling legend, O'Shaughnessy was being compared to that same legend 'at his best', no less.

And yet, as we sat there in Thurles watching the Limerick players celebrate, there was no sense that this was O'Shaughnessy's time yet. If the Kilmallock forward was all that we believed him to be, it was generally felt that he was going to be a jewel – albeit a big one, for sure – in an already decorated crown. The sense of anticipation and excitement was palpable even then. In much the same way that I had just left fourth class to take the natural step up into fifth class, I assumed that hurling worked in much the same way as primary school. As I kept progressing, so too would those Limerick hurlers.

So, when much of that same group of hurlers won a third successive All-Ireland as I made my way into sixth class the following year, senior success really seemed inevitable. Back then, my father had arranged for a copy of the *Limerick*

Leader to be delivered to the local newsagents. Although I cannot remember ever paying much attention to it, above my bed for a number of years after that third All-Ireland win was a pull-out image of the Limerick captain Peter Lawlor lifting that highly unusual Cross of Cashel trophy.

If this team could be so dominant underage, why would that dominance not continue, even once or twice? My logic was flawed, unfortunately. In those heady years of underage success, I had no concept of the frustration that typically associated itself with following this county team. Henry Martin's comprehensive portrayal of this sensation was still a few years away, but the unlimited heartbreak of Limerick hurling was not long making itself apparent.

IV

Son: 'Reeling in the Years is on… we'll watch that.'
Father: 'Fantastic. What year?'
Son: '1994.'
Father: '…'

V

TO ME, THE 1994 All-Ireland hurling final was initially understood through the match programme that my father had retained among his seemingly random – but carefully curated – collection of memorabilia. In excruciating circumstances, Limerick had managed to lose that game when it almost seemed easier to win.

Over breakfast before school, however, I would read and re-read that programme without much care at all for the match itself. Unlike some of the more arbitrary ones in his collection, this programme was full of the information and insight reserved for such a massive occasion. It was a little archive all of my own to wander around in. Untouched as I was by the disappointment, the programme also seemed so full of promise for the matches I might one day actually attend. And yet, in hindsight, I wonder now why my father held onto it.

Beyond my comprehension as a three-year-old watching from the living-room floor, he had been there in Croke Park when Offaly broke Limerick hearts. Although it served a purpose during the game, that match programme had truthfully been bought as a prospective souvenir should Limerick finally end what was then a 21-year wait for All-Ireland success.

For them to lose was one thing, but to lose like they did all in the space of about five minutes? What on earth possessed him to keep such a token of that devastating day about the house?

On the one hand, it offered proof, perhaps, that he could be mature enough to make decisions not entirely dictated by emotion and the fate of Limerick's hurlers. Instead of trying to run from this crushing defeat, he would meet it head on. It is a nice theory, but why then did we not have the match programme from 1996 around the house? An altogether different (but frustrating, nevertheless) final defeat to Wexford, he had been at that match too.

That second defeat always seemed a bit more acceptable though. It had been a cagey game and Limerick failed to make the most of their numerical advantage when Wexford were reduced to 14 men. That kind of thing happens in sport regularly enough. It makes sense.

The defeat in 1994 made no sense. It became a benchmark for what can – but ultimately almost never does – happen. It was a nightmarish realisation of the old adage that 'the game isn't over, until it's over'.

Realistically, before the eventual senior success of 2018 no amount of perspective or rational thinking could halt his damned disappointment when Limerick lost. To keep hold of that glossy, alluring and ultimately devastating memento from 1994 was to issue a subtle warning.

He was Limerick born and bred; following the hurlers was just what you did. I, on the other hand, had a choice. If I intended to follow him down this road with Limerick he wanted to make one thing clear: it rarely works out as you might like it to.

VI

2007 All-Ireland Senior Hurling Championship semi-final
Limerick 5-11 Waterford 2-15

Joanne Cantwell: 'It was supposed to be Kilkenny and Waterford in this final.'
Richie Bennis: 'We read the script, but all the pundits didn't read the script. We knew coming up today we were going to win. You wouldn't get a more honest

bunch of lads that were out there like. They'd die for you… they'd die for Limerick, and that's what it's all about.'

Joanne Cantwell: 'They say goals win games. Five of them you got today and so well taken as well.'

Richie Bennis: 'We got five… and Dan the Man got none!'

VII

IN THE YEARS that followed, as travelling to Thurles, Limerick or − if the championship had gone surprisingly well − Croke Park became a regular occurrence, we never made plans to meet family or anyone else along the way again. It had nothing to do with superstition (Limerick had won the time we tried it, after all), and it was most certainly not the result of any falling out. More than anything, my father and I found a shared fluency for saying nothing when there was nothing left to be said.

Unfortunately, for most of the 2000s, silence was about all we could muster on the way home from most Limerick matches. Contrary to any assumptions about manliness, masculinity and a wariness of wearing one's emotions clearly, such things had nothing to do with our stoic stillness. We just knew that talking about another defeat would do nothing to alleviate the disappointment.

And yet, there was something sufficiently special about setting off from Sligo on the Sunday morning of a match that continually gave us hope of having much to talk about on the journey home. This perseverance had been rewarded in 2007. In the Munster Championship, Limerick and Tipperary had gone toe-to-toe across a three-game epic.

On several occasions, Limerick appeared to be finished, but Tipperary, the county I have witnessed beating Limerick more than any other, could not finish them off for good.

The Munster final against Waterford that followed was a let-down, but we were back in Croke Park a few weeks later when Limerick got the better of Clare and qualified for an All-Ireland semi-final. The supreme confidence of Richie Bennis then, as he stood before the RTÉ cameras following Limerick's revenge defeat of Waterford, gave us all cause for hysterical hope.

'Are you afraid of Kilkenny,' he was asked, with Limerick fans thronged around him on the Croke Park sideline. 'No, no, no… no,' he replied, as if the very notion was preposterous.

As we departed for Dublin on All-Ireland final day in September 2007, the idea that Limerick might beat Kilkenny seemed possible, if not quite plausible. In hindsight, Brian Cody's team were only yet approaching their peak, and had already won a few All-Ireland titles. If fortunate is too harsh a word, Limerick were certainly unexpected and unfancied finalists.

No more than I had never seen a crowd of such magnitude as I sat within it that day in Croke Park, most of these Limerick hurlers had never played in such conditions.

'One hundred percent I thought we would win,' Andrew O'Shaughnessy told me years later when I worked for Balls.ie, no occasion too big in his mind. 'Even during the game after those two early goals for Kilkenny, I still felt we could have won, because despite the fact that Kilkenny had a fantastic team… we hurled particularly well, and I think that is often overlooked.'

He was only 22 years old in 2007.

I was by that stage a 16-year-old. All that excitement surrounding Limerick's young hurlers finally appeared to be bearing some fruit. Although the replayed games with Tipperary gave him an edge on Henry Shefflin, Damien Murray and Eoin Kelly, O'Shaughnessy would finish the year as the championship's top scorer. For good measure, he would also be named alongside Shefflin and Eddie Brennan in the full-forward line on that year's All Stars; one of only four Limerick players to win such an award across the whole of the decade (Mark Foley, 2001; Brian Murray and Ollie Moran, 2007.)

Unfortunately, it would be another six years until Richie McCarthy won Limerick's next All Star, and that in itself tells a story of 2007's false dawn.

VIII

The remaining 24 disaffected players in the Limerick hurling dispute last night issued a statement insisting that they will not be returning to the fold while the current management team remain in place and that the 'future of Limerick hurling' is the hands of delegates attending tomorrow night's meeting of the county board.

They believe that the board, management and backroom team are placing pressure on young players to come back and that others are being manipulated by officials. The odds would appear to be against them, however, given that Justin McCarthy has the backing of the county board, of its main sponsor JP McManus, and – most critically of all, and on the two occasions on which they've voted – of the club delegates.

In their statement, the 2009 squad claim: 'There has been a deliberate and concerted effort by members of the county board, the team management and the backroom team to influence the thinking of club delegates and the wider Limerick public. There has also been a deliberate and concerted effort by members of the county board, the team management and the backroom team to influence the younger players who have pulled out of the 2010 panel, with huge pressure being put on, using one player against another in trying to persuade them to change their minds.

'At this stage we feel the need to make our position crystal clear – we will not play under the current management; despite rumours, stories and spins to the contrary, most of that coming from the county board and the current management team.

'There will be no more players returning to training with the current management team. It is now up to the club delegates to address the matter with the county board executive on Tuesday night next – the future of Limerick hurling is in their hands.'

– Irish Examiner, March 8, 2010

IX

THE LIMERICK HURLING strike of 2009/10 was about as dramatic and conclusive proof there could be that the potential of those All-Ireland-winning under-21 teams was now never going to be realised. As the opening decade of the new millennium stretched out before them, Limerick reached the final of a National Hurling League, two Munster Championships and an All-Ireland. All four were lost.

'The same old heartbreak,' remarks O'Shaughnessy now, over a decade after he was diagnosed with multiple sclerosis and ultimately called a premature halt to his inter-county career. 'Limerick hurling is not all heartbreak, of course. But the losing always took precedence over everything else.'

A generational talent (although he balks at any such description), the two-year spell across which he made his diagnosis public, Limerick hurling fell into turmoil, and his ultimate retirement coincided with my own development out of adolescence into adulthood.

Good days were ahead, and Limerick finally ended their wait for senior success with a Munster Championship win in 2013. The sky-high expectations I had had as a 10-year-old were tempered now. At one time I could easily substitute in my mind the Liam MacCarthy Cup into Peter Lawlor's hands as he held the Cross of Cashel aloft over my bed. That was childish though. As Andrew O'Shaughnessy put it, the losing always takes precedence when you follow Limerick.

X

The distinctive Cross of Cashel will be awarded to the captain of the victorious Bord Gais Energy All-Ireland under-21 hurling team for the last time in Thurles tomorrow night… Wexford and Limerick go head to head in the decider, and either Eoin Conroy or Diarmuid Byrnes will be the last recipient of the trophy.

The GAA has already sourced a cup to replace it and it will be introduced for next year's championship. It is believed to have been procured in a London auction room as part of a drive to update some of the association's better-known cups. The Cross of Cashel was first introduced in 1967 when PJ Ryan was Tipperary's winning captain, three years after the competition's inception.

Some famous captains have lifted the Cross of Cashel over the last 51 years including Kilkenny quartet Jackie Tyrrell, Michael Fennelly, James 'Cha' Fitzpatrick and Ger Fennelly, and Cork's Martin O'Doherty, who all went on to lift the Liam MacCarthy Cup.

– *Irish Independent*, September 10, 2015

XI

LIMERICK AND WEXFORD in an All-Ireland under-21 final in Thurles. We've been here before. Amongst Limerick's starting XV that day were Sean Finn, Richie English, Mike Casey, Diarmuid Byrnes, Ger Hegarty, Darragh O'Donovan, Tom Morrissey and Cian Lynch. All eight would start for the seniors three years later in another All-Ireland final.

Many more besides in and around that team have similarly aided the county's resurgence thereafter. Losing took precedence in Limerick hurling until it didn't.

In 2001, Limerick's back-to-back champions edged out Wexford by a solitary point. Fourteen years later and the margin had extended out to 16 points. As Byrnes lifted the Cross of Cashel trophy for the last time, nobody had any idea of what was to come.

In 2007 it had seemed ambitious that Limerick might trouble what was becoming one of the sport's greatest ever teams. As we make our way through the third decade of this millennium, a new Limerick team looks set to challenge Kilkenny for the mantle of being the very best ever.

How Limerick have managed it is something that will be discussed throughout this book. Through the likes of Shane Fitzgibbon, it will explore how one former Limerick hurler fed up with the county's lot sparked a revolution. All-Ireland winners both, Éamonn Cregan and Shane Dowling will explore the different challenges they faced reaching the top, and those that only became apparent when they got there. Joe McGrath's relationship with Limerick hurling is a solemn lesson in the county's proclivity for shooting itself in the foot, while Tom Ryan and Ger Hegarty experienced the ultimate heartbreak of all without ever getting the credit a resurgent Limerick in the 1990s deserved. Stephen Lucey worked himself to the bone for Limerick GAA and offers us some insight into why that brilliant generation of the early 2000s ultimately fell short. All the while, the incredible Breda Quaid will keep everything in perspective with her own story of devastating human loss and resilience.

And then, of course, there is and ever shall be Mick Mackey. A triumphant hurler who became mythic while still mortal, his outstanding achievements gave every generation thereafter something to aspire to, and a weight be burdened down by.

This is not the story of Limerick hurling, nor is it a conclusive explanation of how unlimited heartbreak led to unparalleled joy. 'I cherish my hurling past and I would love to have my own time back,' Andrew O'Shaughnessy assures me, 'but that's not life. Imagine me saying to my son now "Don't you remember daddy used to play hurling?" He doesn't want to know about any of that. All he wants is for me to hit the ball back to him and give him a sweet. Life changes and your perspective changes.'

As with every former Limerick hurler spoken to for this book, the county's success has been entirely untainted by any selfish desire to be a part of it. When

Limerick started winning, whatever losses there had been seemed less important, and talking about it became that bit easier.

This book has been written for all the conversations that could not take place on the drives home from matches.

Limerick captain Declan Hannon lifts the Liam MacCarthy Cup in September 2018 as the county's supporters erupt with joy.

CHAPTER ★ ONE

2018 ALL-IRELAND FINAL

Oh, my life is changing everyday
In every possible way
And oh, my dreams
It's never quite as it seems
'Cause you're a dream to me
– The Cranberries, *Dreams*

Éamonn Cregan

I

ÉAMONN CREGAN DIDN'T watch the All-Ireland hurling final in 2018.

'I suppose it is hereditary,' he reasons, his father Ned an All-Ireland winner with Limerick before him. 'My father was in his early 60s and he stopped going to matches – the disappointment became too much.'

Following the landmark success of 1973, Éamonn lost two further finals with Limerick in '74 and '80. He was the disbelieving opposition manager when Limerick lost again in 1994. As a supporter, he sat watching in Croke Park as the 1996 and '07 finals went any way but Limerick's for the fifth time in succession. Kilkenny, Galway, Offaly, Wexford, and Kilkenny again.

Whomever the opponent, Limerick came up short. The measure of success in 1973 became entwined with all this heartbreak. He couldn't bear to see it happen again. So, as John Kiely's team were gearing up to face Galway, Cregan chose to hoover out the car instead.

II

2018 All-Ireland Senior Hurling Championship final
Galway 0-16 Limerick 2-15
(67:22)

Marty Morrissey: 'In 1994, Limerick looked like they had the game won. My commentary colleague was on the pitch and Offaly came back spectacularly. Limerick wouldn't want the same to happen.'

Michael Duignan: 'That's a great block down... Casey!'

Marty Morrissey: 'A great block down by Peter Casey who is heading towards goal. Will he pass... will he shoot? He tries the pass. It comes to Dowling... what's-he-going-to-do?! Back of the net! What a player! What a moment! Forty-five years is surely about to end.'

Michael Duignan: 'Well, that's it now Marty...'

III

'I GOT A call then from my daughter,' Cregan recalls vividly, his car now looking as new as when he bought it, 'and she was telling me that Limerick were well ahead, and the match was nearly over.' Against his better judgement, he chanced it.

'I turned on the television and sure there's Joe Canning scoring a goal from the '21'. Jesus, get me out of here!'

Back out to the driveway, he started work on his wife, Anne's car. It was all he could do not to think about 1994. After an unsatisfyingly brief spell in charge of Limerick in the late 1980s, Cregan had taken over Offaly's senior hurlers believing that the two counties were unlikely to meet in championship hurling. As fate would have it, neither county made it out of their province in his first season in charge.

The following year wasn't so straightforward. Under Cregan, Offaly got the better of Kilkenny, Wexford, and Galway to set up an All-Ireland final with Tom Ryan's resurgent Limerick. Teammates when the county last lifted the Liam MacCarthy Cup in 1973, he hadn't bargained for this.

A snapshot of his conflicted mind on the morning of the 1994 final: Cregan recalls dropping the same daughter who had called in 2018 off to the train station in town so she could head off with the other Limerick supporters for Dublin.

After spending the night in his own home, he then left Limerick to meet with his Offaly players. The opposition.

After devoting a lifetime to the betterment of Limerick hurling, he was pitched up against them at the most crucial juncture. As things went, it seemed that he need not have worried, however. Trailing by five points with as many minutes remaining, Limerick had been too good for his Offaly team. So be it.

He could live with this defeat at least.

IV

2018 All-Ireland Senior Hurling Championship final
Galway 2-17 Limerick 3-15
(75:44)

Marty Morrissey: 'What a recovery… Galway! What about this for character from the All-Ireland champions of 2017. A pass that should have been Limerick's goes astray.'

Michael Duignan: 'That ball should've been gone 90 yards up the field… what a championship! I thought we'd seen it all. It looked like Limerick were home and hosed… we've said it all year, nine points is a dangerous lead in hurling this summer and look at what Galway have done… back from the dead.'

V

THE DETAILS OF Offaly's miraculous recovery in 1994 need no retelling. It isn't really something Éamonn Cregan takes much pleasure talking about anyway. 'The cameras went on him when we won,' remembered Daithí Regan, one of Cregan's Offaly players, in a 2019 interview with *OTB Sports*, 'and he was devastated. Éamonn hated that we had won how we had won – playing rubbish for the bulk of the game and getting over the line.'

A momentous occasion for his players, conversations with Cregan about the 1994 All-Ireland final invariably turn back to those left sitting in the Limerick dressing-room. 'I couldn't talk to them because I felt their agony and pain,' he admits. 'I had a job to do, and Offaly won. Job done. But at the same time, I felt so much for Limerick, and I still do after all this time.'

It is little wonder he couldn't bear the thought of watching it unfold all over again in 2018. To be five points ahead in an All-Ireland final and lose was pure devastation… but eight? Unthinkable.

VI

2018 All-Ireland Senior Hurling Championship final
Galway 2-18 Limerick 3-16
(78:40)

Marty Morrissey: 'There's a free, dead straight in front of the Galway dugout and there's an opportunity for Joe Canning to level the match.'

Michael Duignan: 'This is definitely it now. There was eight minutes, and the Limerick crowd will be questioning James Owens for playing 40, 45 seconds more…'

Marty Morrissey: 'This is surely the biggest free he's ever taken in his career. It's up to Joe…'

VII

ÉAMONN WAS WORKING his way through Anne's car when Tom Condon burst forth from the melee of bodies with sliotar in hand.

Limerick had won the All-Ireland after a 45-year wait and he was none the wiser. 'Anne eventually came out to me at around half-five,' he remembers.

'The match is over!'

'I just said, "Yeah?… Yeah?"'

'"Limerick won!" she told me.

'By how much?'

'"A point."'

'I nearly died.'

★ ★ ★ ★ ★

Shane Dowling

I

DAMIAN, YOU KNOW me, and anyone who knows me knows I'm not short of words, but I just can't believe it. I honestly can't believe it. It's all I've ever wanted since I was a young fella and we eventually got there. I don't know how many prayers I said there when Joe was hitting the last ball, but I just can't believe it. This means the world to me and more importantly to my family and friends and my club… I stood here three weeks ago and pleaded with the fans to give us space and to allow us focus. I now say to the fans, can ye please go absolutely mental for the next couple of weeks!

II

BEFORE THE PITCHSIDE reporter Damian Lawlor found him, Shane Dowling had run into Mike Casey. Clubmates with Na Piarsaigh, two years earlier they had achieved what felt like the ultimate accolade. The first Limerick club to win an All-Ireland senior title, there are players who would trade in any medal won at county level to experience that high.

Embracing Casey after Limerick had won this All-Ireland, however, it didn't feel like a moment to be dispensed with at any cost. "We actually did it," was all I could say to him,' Dowling remembers. 'Those four words. After that, it is carnage really.' Bouncing from person to person, the amazement of realising a life's ambition played out again and again.

We actually did it.

Once Dowling had spoken to Sky Sports and the initial euphoria settled somewhat, the emphasis switched to finding his parents. He had done the hurling, but this was the realisation of a family effort.

This group of Limerick hurlers are bound by a familial closeness. Unscathed by the county's hurling trauma, an All-Ireland win always seemed to them a reasonable ambition. Buoyed by underage success, most of these players represented the fruition of an academy system that revolutionised how the county cultivated its hurlers. At 25, Dowling had come through at a slightly less sophisticated time.

The effectiveness of Limerick's capabilities to develop young talent only started working on an industrial scale with the next few years' worth of hurlers. It meant he was something of a veteran by 2018. Of the 15 players that started against Galway in the final, only three were older than Dowling – Nickie Quaid, Declan Hannon and Graeme Mulcahy.

Admittedly, only a few years separated him from even the youngest starters. Yet, his education in senior hurling took place in a different era entirely. When he first played county in 2012, Limerick had recorded just one win in 10 years of Munster Championship hurling. There had not truly been much underage success to speak of since the early 2000s and the final vestiges of their unfulfilled potential were all but gone as Dowling started making his way.

All-Ireland success was the ambition even then, but it had far less footing in reality.

The makings of Limerick's All-Ireland winning team developed year-on-year as Dowling, Hannon, Mulcahy, Quaid and a scattering of similarly experienced panel members stuck it out. He remembers still how these stars of the underage scene arrived at senior training looking all the world like senior hurlers. Once introduced, their acclimatisation was brief. Before long they were playing like senior hurlers too.

From a personal standpoint, this became a problem. With the exception of Mulcahy, five of the six attacking positions were soon occupied by younger men who had already experienced playing together on successful underage teams. Up until the end of 2017, Dowling's standing as a regular starter seemed unshakeable. In 2018 he had to be content with two starts and three further appearances off the bench across Limerick's seven championship outings.

'I only started against Waterford because Aaron Gillane was sent-off against Cork,' he notes, 'and I got dropped for the Carlow game after starting against Clare. That was a fierce low time in my life.' Relief awaited him in the All-Ireland semi-final. It didn't make the limited playing time any easier to accept, but without Dowling's 1-4 against Cork there would likely have been no All-Ireland final at all. His struggles in Limerick's most memorable year only endeared him further to the people he played for.

When Damian Lawlor made a beeline for him after the final whistle had been blown, the reporter knew that Dowling would capture the magnitude of this moment. Furthermore, Limerick supporters would want to see what it meant to him. 'It's all I've ever wanted since I was a young fella,' he admitted, the essence of Dowling's dream something everyone understood. He had idly wondered in the weeks building up to the final what it might be like to actually win.

Overwhelmingly, his mind returned to the enjoyment it would bring Limerick people. In many ways, they are one and the same, Dowling and the county's supporters. He wears their emotions well. They recognise something of themselves in his honesty.

As this new generation of Limerick hurlers progressed without the gnawing sense that something will go wrong, Dowling was a reminder of those leaner years. A winner in spite of all that baggage, he embodied the emotional depths of a moment when Limerick hurling changed forever.

★ ★ ★ ★ ★

Breda Quaid

BREDA QUAID HAD been contemplating the worst as Joe Canning's last-ditch attempt started falling short. *What if a Galway hurl flicked the ball into the net? How would this Limerick team deal with the heartbreak?* As she stood gratefully hugging her son Nickie by the sideline only moments later, that sense of dread had not entirely subsided. It never really does when you are the parent of a goalkeeper.

'Those last couple of minutes in a game,' Breda explains, 'when you know that if a goal goes in they'll be beaten, I find them very, *very* hard.' In an All-Ireland final, they become almost intolerable. Then again, you might think she had grown used to it at this stage. Breda has spent no small portion of her life keeping a close eye on the Limerick goalkeeper.

Thirty-eight years before Nickie become an All-Ireland winner in Croke Park, she attended a final there between Limerick and Galway as Tommy Quaid's special guest. She was still Breda Grace then, but that would change soon enough. Until Tommy's inter-county retirement in 1993, there were only ever a handful of Limerick games played that she did not attend. Hurling had been a passion that pre-dated Tommy to her upbringing in Kilkenny and she found that life being married to the Limerick 'keeper had its perks.

'When I met Tommy, the conversation came so easy to us with hurling to talk about,' she remembers. 'It was brilliant then getting to go to all of these matches across the country.' The partner's perspective didn't quite prepare her for what the parent experiences, however.

'They are one hundred percent more nervous than we are,' Shane Dowling reckons. 'My mother would've watched very few games when I was playing. She would go to the stadium alright, but she had to take out her phone because she got so nervous.' Gearóid Hegarty's parents occupy two opposing positions when Limerick are playing.

'Gearóid is just another player as far as I'm concerned,' Ger Hegarty explains, his long inter-county career with Limerick reason for the detached outlook. 'His mother would find it more difficult though because she only sees one fella playing… her child.' When it comes to playing in an All-Ireland final, the intensity and nerves are ratcheted up further still.

'It is a big difference being a sister-fan and a mother-fan,' Valerie Lynch explained to *OTB Sports* the morning after the 2018 final, the experience of watching her brother Ciaran Carey play no real preparation for watching her son Cian. 'Saturday was the worst, longest day of my life waiting for it. Cian's going around cool as a breeze focused and we don't know our heads from our elbows.'

Breda never found Limerick's losses easy to deal with when it was her husband playing, 'but he was a separate person,' she stresses. 'I know Nickie is his own man too, but when it is your child out there this rearing thing within just kicks in.' As that late, late Canning shot dropped short in front of Nickie's goal, she may as well have been standing down there beside him.

The nervousness hasn't anything to do with her faith in Nickie's capabilities, of course. She trusts him implicitly and knows more than anyone, bar perhaps Nickie himself, how hard he has worked to prepare for every eventuality. Trouble is, she knows how hard his father Tommy had worked too. His time as Limerick's goalkeeper had been spread across three decades; such was his stranglehold on the position. Even the most dominant goalkeeper remains prone to the unexpected occurring though.

In 1987, Limerick appeared to have Cork beaten in a Munster Championship semi-final before Kieran Kingston sent the game to a replay with a late point. The following day in Semple Stadium, Cork's John Fenton scored a goal of improbable genius that hastened Limerick's championship exit. 'A brilliant goal,' Breda admits, stunned as everyone else watching on in Thurles by the distance and speed of Fenton's shot, 'but it was a freak, you know. That's what can happen.' Supporters do not tend to be quite so forgiving, however, and Breda has had to listen on from her seat as barbs were thrown at Limerick 'keepers.

It was Tommy's cousin Joe Quaid who occupied the Limerick goal in the 1994 All-Ireland final. A noted shot-stopper, whatever confusion occurred on the goal-line as Offaly's Johnny Dooley lined up his late free ultimately fell back on Joe to explain. 'All I could picture was someone getting a touch to it, back of the net, game over,' he told Kieran Shannon, physically unable to watch Joe Canning's free descend on Nickie's goal 24 years later. He knows, as Breda does, that an eternity of damage can be done in those last few minutes.

★ ★ ★ ★ ★

Stephen Lucey

I

THE DREAM OF winning an All-Ireland final has occupied countless young Limerick minds. Although Stephen Lucey came closer than most to making it a reality, his dreams weren't always what they might have seemed. 'I grew up a Cork supporter,' the former county Limerick hurler and gaelic footballer of 17 years admits. 'I still have the red and white headbands that I got when I was eight or nine years of age at home – I use them for Liverpool matches!'

At an impressionable age, this dual player in the making was in his element with a Cork team that was winning on both fronts. Taken along to games by his father Mick, who was a Cork native, Stephen's All-Ireland ambitions as a young boy had a red tint to them. For a while, anyway.

'It was only around 1990, '91 that I thought to myself… *Hold on, I'm from Limerick,*' he recalls.

It was the beginning of a fruitful and frustrating relationship.

II

SITTING ABOUT 20 rows back from the sideline in the Lower Hogan Stand on All-Ireland final day in 2018, he had made this journey three times before. Twice as a fan, and once as a player in 2007, Stephen had been confident of a Limerick victory each and every time. Alas, it never arrived.

Cruelly enough, Cork's hurlers had won the Liam MacCarthy Cup on three occasions since he had abandoned the Rebel faithful. Good news for his father Mick at least. 'Ah no, he was a Limerick man by then too,' Stephen explains. Indeed, Dr Mick Lucey had spent the guts of 20 years working as team doctor for the county's footballers; a role Stephen assumed after his father stepped away. The pair of them were joined by Fiona, Stephen's wife, and her father in Croke Park. 'It was really important to me that my wife and my dad were there,' he explains, 'because I just had this gut feeling that we were going to win this time. I wanted that moment when the final whistle went… and Limerick had won. I wanted to be able to have that embrace with them.'

Right at last, as the final whistle was blown and Limerick won the All-Ireland final, a tearful Stephen Lucey got what he had been waiting for. 'It was just pure happiness. Elation, happiness… just pure joy,' he confirms.

'Even now, I get perked up thinking about it.'

III

'YEAH, I WAS there in 1994,' he remembers, a 14-year-old cheering on Limerick against Offaly in Croke Park. 'We were in the Hogan Stand that day too and I'd already left my seat and ran down to the gate to invade the pitch with a few minutes to go. I was surrounded by other Limerick people. In the blink of an eye then it was all Offaly people around me… and they were invading the pitch.'

Disbelievingly, Lucey returned back to where he had been sitting beside his father and began sobbing. His first All-Ireland final as a Limerick supporter, it was a devastating way to lose. It hardly helped that the industrious young Lucey had been up working half the night with balls of green and white wool. 'I decided to make a load of headbands and stayed up until about four the morning before,' he explains, still bewildered by whatever possessed him.

'I didn't know how to plait though, so I ended up just sort of tying them in knots to keep the wool in place.' All that work for nothing. Two years later, as Limerick travelled to Croke Park, again intent on beating Wexford this time around, his enthusiasm for looking the part had jumped a few notches. 'I had a straw hat, as you did back in those days,' he notes. 'The *Limerick Leader* had the headshots of all the players in the paper and I cut them all out.' Making use of a Corn Flakes box, the 16-year-old cut the cardboard into little rectangles that his headshots could be glued to. 'I used pieces of string then to put them on the hat,' he explains, 'and I wore that to the All-Ireland final.' Had things gone differently, it may have become a lucky charm for years to come. Unfortunately, it was not Limerick's day. Again.

It was hardly all doom and gloom for Limerick supporters though. There was some consolation to be found in the many games Limerick won along the way. A team of immense quality, the likes of Lucey enjoyed plenty of great days to keep the fires burning. 'My greatest day as a Limerick supporter was in 1996 when Ciaran Carey scored that point,' he states with absolute certainty; Carey's solo effort seeing off the reigning All-Ireland champions Clare in the Gaelic Grounds.

'I was standing under the scoreboard, and it was really chock-a-block. When the point was scored, I found myself about 15 yards away from where I'd started because the crowds were just heaving. It was brilliant!' Head-to-toe in Limerick green as was his wont in those days, he successfully managed to hitch-hike his way back home, nevertheless. 'I'll take those memories to the grave,' he insists, the joy he took from playing for Limerick only a few years later greatly enhanced by this immense pleasure he received from supporting his county. 'Unfortunately, we didn't get over the line in 2007 – or any other year – and that hurt,' he admits. 'To be there though when Limerick did finally win it. That was really... *really* special."

★ ★ ★ ★ ★

Shane Dowling

I

SHANE DOWLING HAD promised himself that he would make the most of Limerick's celebrations. After watching one of his closest friends, Declan Hannon lift the Liam MacCarthy Cup, and having a go of it himself, it was back to the dressing-room again. For what would be the final time, this panel of players could sit together as teammates.

To a man, they had each realised a lifetime's ambition. The remainder of their days would be lived as All-Ireland winners. 'I'd always wondered what it must be like in the dressing-room after winning an All-Ireland,' he admits, every player acutely aware of the effort that has been put in to get there. The reality surprised him.

'I just remember sitting there thinking, God, this is not what I had thought it would be,' he recalls. 'It is literally just fellas sitting down drinking cans and listening to a bit of music.' As the commotion of bodies in and out of the room continued, his mind drifted off beyond the four walls. 'I couldn't help thinking to myself that while we were here chilling out, what the hell must be going on down in Limerick. All I wanted to do was split myself up into 10 and be in loads of different places experiencing what was going on.'

He surely wasn't alone. No sooner had Sean South and The Cranberries entered the musical rotation, things became a bit wound up again.

The outside world couldn't be kept at bay for long though. He nipped off at one point to the bathroom for a bit of quiet. Though they had spoken only a short while ago on the sideline, he wanted to touch base with his parents again. Despite this glorious conclusion, it had been a difficult year.

When he struggled with the setback of being dropped, they had struggled with him. Although Dowling didn't rate his own performance in the final too highly, he had still scored another goal coming off the bench. To whatever extent he hurled for himself, Dowling got a great kick out of what it meant for his family too. Before Galway almost mounted a successful comeback, that goal had appeared to be the winning of the game.

A quick call to fill them in on the latest, and he was back again. The arrival of JP McManus into the dressing-room captured the magnitude of their achievement once more. 'It was a very special moment,' he remembers of McManus' quiet – and Dowling suspects reluctant – arrival. 'He is who he is, he has what he has… but at the end of the day he is the man who has backed Limerick hurling for a very long time.'

Dowling's phone rarely left his hand throughout the celebrations. 'I took a load of videos and photos,' he remembers, 'for no other reason than I wanted to have them for the memories.' Before he took the time to back them up (and send them all on to his mother's phone, just in case), these memories turned his phone into a prized possession. 'I remember saying to myself, *God help anyone who tries to steal it*,' he says now with a laugh, the retribution awaiting any such attempt no joke all the same. 'They mean a lot to me.'

His determination to chronicle the celebrations seems a bit prophetic in hindsight. Almost a year to the day after Limerick's All-Ireland win, Dowling picked up an innocuous enough knee injury in a club game against Adare. The situation deteriorated and he soon had to come to terms with a reality that no longer involved this Limerick team.

At 27, he wasn't really sure if he would ever hurl again. For one who embraced so heartily what John Kiely, his backroom team and the players had created together, the devastation is permanent.

II

TRADITION DICTATED WHAT would happen next as Limerick eventually left their dressing-room in Croke Park. The usual banquet and post-match traditions would play out in the Citywest Hotel later that night. The triumphant journey home to the waiting crowds would follow.

Generations of Limerick hurlers had looked on and wondered what this might be like, to no avail. The county's supporters had been equally envious as seemingly everyone else but them got to experience it at least once. Shane Dowling hadn't forgotten the sting of both sensations. As he headed for the bus that would carry them through streets still thronged with the green of Limerick jerseys and flags, he spotted the Liam MacCarthy Cup just sitting there on the dashboard.

'I just couldn't believe it,' he explains, the sight of the trophy taking him back to a time when playing for Limerick was still just a dream. 'We were coming home from some All-Ireland final when I was just a young lad and I remember spotting the winning county's bus getting the Garda escort out of the stadium. I just looked at them wondering what it must be like.'

All those years later, he found out.

He even has the pictures to prove it.

★ ★ ★ ★ ★

Ger Hegarty

I

GER HEGARTY MIGHT not match Éamonn Cregan for All-Ireland finals won, but he certainly has the same devastated grasp of what losing them feels like. 'I happened to meet Éamonn coming out of the 2007 All-Ireland final in Croke Park,' he recalls, accompanied that day by his son Gearóid, who had recently celebrated his 13th birthday. 'I'd say within 15 minutes of the final being over we were standing on the same platform waiting for the connecting train back to Maynooth to collect the car and go home.'

Thirty-four years had passed since Cregan won his medal, and this was the fifth final Limerick had lost since then. Hegarty had lined out against Offaly in 1994 – a rare day he and Cregan were on opposite sides. Injury kept him out of the final against Wexford two years after that. On the field or off it, however, his disappointment was much the same.

For all but those Limerick players for whom 2007 was their one and only All-Ireland final appearance, the eventual defeat to Kilkenny occupied a different psychological realm to what had happened Limerick in the 1990s. Yes, they were going to Croke Park under the impression that they could defeat the reigning champions Kilkenny. However motivated Richie Bennis had his players though, it was understood that a monumental performance would be required to upset a Brian Cody team that would go on to win six further All-Irelands in the coming eight years.

That had not really been the case in 1994 and '96 when Hegarty and his teammates knew success was within closer reach. 'Same old heartbreak, though,' Ger concedes, no defeat so easily explained that it does not hurt… 'coming back to Limerick with our tail between our legs.'

II

THIS HAD NOT been what he imagined for himself starting out.

An All-Ireland winning hurler with Limerick at minor level in 1984, that he would not be part of a winning team at senior level legitimately surprised him. 'We saw our team as being as good as many and better than most,' he insists, their inability to show it over one entire season an unshakable sore spot. 'Ultimately, we failed.' By that team's own standards, perhaps. Realistically, Limerick's hurling past from the post-Mackey era through to that point demonstrates how this team of the 90s were surpassed only by the 1973 All-Ireland winners. It does not make up for a medal, but they did achieve more in a few short years than most Limerick teams have ever managed.

'We failed!' he reiterates, whatever way one wants to look at it.

'Sport is about competing. You can look back with rose-tinted glasses, but I don't get sucked into that at all. We failed in the 90s to bring home the bacon. Colour the waters any way you want to, sport at that level is about winning.'

III

THIS RUTHLESSNESS HINTS at a fixation with winning at all costs. Hegarty's lived experience of winning as a teenager and, by his own admission, losing the games that mattered as an adult, have left him dissatisfied with his career. 'The dressing-room became like a glass cage,' he remembers now. 'When you're inside it, it is an adrenaline rush, 100 mph, pumped-up... all energy. But you can't see that when you're in there. You need to step outside and look from the outside-in.

'When you do that and you realise the time that it takes, the injuries, the disappointment, you say, *What am I doing going in there?!*' Yet, Hegarty's brutal assessment of that team's failings conceals an acute awareness of how one should best prepare hurlers for success at the highest level. Around the time that he was walking away from Croke Park after another All-Ireland final defeat for Limerick in 2007, Hegarty was already beginning to see things more clearly.

When a call came in from a former teammate of his about getting involved with the county's development of young hurlers, he jumped at the chance. He could not have known it then, but Shane Fitzgibbon had the makings of a plan that would change everything. Across the county of Limerick and even in Hegarty's own home, the next time he travelled to watch Limerick in an All-Ireland final, that 13-year-old son of his would not be sitting beside him.

★ ★ ★ ★ ★

Shane Fitzgibbon

WHAT SUCCESS GER Hegarty did have with Limerick, Shane Fitzgibbon missed out on entirely. Born only a few years apart, he was a 21-year-old already hurling senior for Limerick when Hegarty was in a thriving minor outfit. Teammates throughout the remainder of the 1980s and early 90s, Fitzgibbon opted out for good in 1993.

The Munster Championships and All-Ireland finals that followed would escape him. 'I retired in frustration,' he admits, the payoff for his efforts no longer justifiable as a 31-year-old with a demanding job and young family. 'I said to myself, *This isn't going anywhere*. Of course, I couldn't have been more wrong because they're playing in an All-Ireland final 12 months later.'

The solitary National Hurling League medal he did win over a decade hurling with Limerick was nice, but not nearly enough. He is familiar with the gnawing sense of regret many former Limerick hurlers experience for what they did not get out of the game. 'It probably fuelled my desire to become involved in the hurling academies and development squads, though,' he explains, Fitzgibbon's dedication to moving Limerick onto a different path a jolt the county so desperately needed.

Working from the bottom up, the problem Fitzgibbon sought to address was simple… 'Limerick were producing inter-county hurlers, but just not enough of them'. So long as that was the case, he knew they could never seriously rival counties like Kilkenny, Cork or Tipperary, where an abundance of talent could be typically counted on to keep coming through. He believed that if the proper structures and practices were put in place at a young age, Limerick hurling could develop a fruitful conveyor belt of talent for themselves. The first call he made was to a highly agreeable Éamonn Cregan. More than happy to do his bit, Ger Hegarty was keen also and soon took over the county's under-16s.

'I just felt Limerick had a great passion for hurling,' Shane explains. 'The whole element of that passion we brought to the game, that competitiveness, the desire, the hunger… and the toughness that was innately in Limerick, that was a great thing. But it needed to be alloyed to something else to bring success.

'We needed to develop more players with the technical ability of striking, first touch, control, and then alloy that in time to tactical ability to understand the game and how it is played… rather than just getting it and hitting it. We could become competitive then and win.'

Over the course of the decade that followed, Fitzgibbon's fundamental plan launched Limerick toward achieving both a healthy competitiveness and a winning team.

Although he does not entertain any suggestion that what he did was revolutionary, or that he even deserves much credit for doing anything at all, Fitzgibbon kick-started a new era for Limerick hurling. He mobilised a body of experienced hurling people in Limerick who wanted to help, but weren't necessarily sure how they could. He ensured that they first received the correct direction before trusting in their passion for the county and its young hurlers to do the rest.

Most of all, he had the doggedness to stick at it despite knowing how long it may take for the senior team to reap any benefit. 'I remember Ger saying when we started out with this, "We'll start it, but we won't finish it,"' Fitzgibbon recounted in the one prior interview he has consented to with Kieran Shannon. '"And if we're doing it in expectation of any thanks, we'll be disappointed."'

Adulation or praise is never something he was looking for. Talk about the work that was not done and Fitzgibbon will pepper the conversation with a point he cannot stress enough: 'It was never about one person'. All the same, this group of individuals would not have come together as they did, if not for him.

Eleven years after he had made that call to Éamonn Cregan, that hero of 1973 dialed Fitzgibbon's number the evening after Limerick's breakthrough.

'Congratulations!' Cregan said to Fitzgibbon. 'That's what you started!'

★ ★ ★ ★ ★

Breda Quaid

I

TOMMY QUAID WAS only 23 when Limerick were beaten in the 1980 All-Ireland final. Breda was a little younger as she watched on alongside his family in Croke Park. Although 13 more years of travelling together to games followed, this was the one and only time Limerick featured in the deciding fixture during Tommy's tenure.

'I got speaking to Éamonn Cregan the morning after the game,' she recalls, an ABBA song about to hit top spot in the Irish singles chart playing in the background. 'He just kind of said, "Isn't that song so apt... the winner takes it all."'

There is no doubting that the Green Isle Hotel had an air of devastation about it that morning, but hurling has given far more to Breda Quaid than it has taken away. In the car early for every matchday with Tommy, his father and occasionally his uncle, she cherished the Sundays spent driving around the country. 'You would go into Hayes Hotel in Thurles, and I might have known nobody in there,' she recalls, 'but sure everyone would be there for the same reason.' After the match was over, the journey back could generate as much fun.

For better or worse, Tommy's performance would become the primary source of discussion on the drive home. 'His father or uncle would say, "As big as the field was, you pucked the ball over the sideline,"' she remembers with a laugh. 'But sure, all of those things would be dealt with then over the journey home and I think Tom valued their contributions.'

When the first two of their three children was born, his county career was winding down, but unfinished. Although pregnancy occasionally interfered with her match-going, it was not long before Breda had their first two children attending Limerick matches to watch their dad. 'I had them with me for the National Hurling League final in 1992,' she recalls, the year Tommy Quaid won his All-Star, 'and I had Thomas sitting beside me and Nickie up in my arms. My mother used to be afraid of her life that I would lose them in the big crowds, but I had them warned… "There's no point looking for mammy if you get lost, so if somebody asks you for your name tell them that your father is playing inside in goals for Limerick."'

II

WHEN TOMMY DID finish up and his cousin Joe took over from him in goals, Limerick contested two All-Ireland finals across the next three years. Neither was won, but nothing new there as far as followers of Limerick hurling were concerned. It was just as Breda was growing familiar with having her husband sat beside her on matchdays, that Tommy Quaid tragically died in October 1998.

Only 41, his passing brought the GAA world to a standstill – no more so than where Tommy and Breda had made their home in the parish of Effin. 'The funeral was massive,' she recalls, an estimated 20,000 mourners flocking to pay their respects. An incomprehensible loss to their young family, Breda and her three sons, Thomas, Nickie and the newest addition Jack carried on as best they could.

Without the need to say so, Tommy was not far from anyone's mind as they met on the sideline with the All-Ireland final won in 2018. A strange serendipity that it was Galway they had overcome. The same opponents that Tommy's Limerick faced 38-years earlier, she knew how proud he would have been of this latest Quaid standing in goal.

As she quickly hugged Nickie and fell back into the crowd, Breda wanted her son to soak in this experience with someone else. 'I wanted him to be with his partner Orlaith,' she explains. 'I had had my time with Tommy, and this was their moment.

'You don't get many of them.'

★ ★ ★ ★ ★

Stephen Lucey

I

'TO ALL THE past Limerick managements, Limerick players… you're the guys who drove us and inspired us when we were young lads looking up to all of ye. So, I hope that all ye here today enjoy this as much as we are… and are going to enjoy the next few days as much as we are.'

II

DECLAN HANNON SPOKE directly to Stephen Lucey's heart as he began his acceptance speech on Limerick's behalf from the Hogan Stand.

Before anyone else got a mention, the captain highlighted those players, managers, coaches, and backroom figures that had come before. Nobody on the

36-man panel had seen the county win an All-Ireland before – manager John Kiely wasn't long born when Limerick did it in 1973. Far from being exclusively the pleasure of those players that did eventually get over the line, however, Hannon wanted all those who had tried and failed to know that this was their All-Ireland too.

'Declan really couldn't have said it any better,' Stephen insists. 'This was a win for everybody associated with Limerick.'

As Hannon carefully made his way through the county hurling team's extensive backroom grouping, he struck upon those most dear to all involved. 'To all our families,' he announced, 'to the wives, partners, girlfriends who've seen the good and bad I suppose when we bring training home. They're there for us every single night and there to pick us up. So, for all the love and support you've shown us throughout, we really, really appreciate it.'

For most of his adult life, the dual player-cum-team doctor, Lucey has been involved one way or another in a Limerick team. While only the most fortunate make it as far as looking up at their captain on All-Ireland final day, the time given over to inter-county commitments remains significant, nevertheless. 'My wife Fiona calls herself a 'GAA widow',' he says half-jokingly, 'because I'd have been gone most nights of the week with something.'

Although Lucey wasn't a part of this team, Hannon made their win feel like a vindication for past players' loved ones too. 'I just really wanted her there,' Stephen explains, a tangible payoff for the countless time they had surrendered chasing his dream.

III

THE PARTY WAS in full flow by the time they had left the stadium and headed towards the Croke Park Hotel across the road. Bumping into people he recognised and a whole lot more that he didn't, the prevailing mood of 'utter elation, pure joy' seemed universal. 'I met Eamonn Rea,' he remembers, one of the 1973 team who had travelled to the game. 'He was walking on air... we all were.' A guest on RTÉ's *The Marty Squad*, he sat alongside Ciaran Carey, Damien Hayes and Aislinn Connolly as Marty Morrissey and Damien Lawlor peppered them with questions about a match that seemed the least of their concerns at that stage. 'I became very concerned,' he admits now, the memory of 1994 not enough to dissuade Lucey that Limerick had surely won the final before Galway launched their attempt at a comeback.

'It was just happening bit by bit… by bit and I was sitting there thinking, *Oh, Jeeeeesus*… I felt it wouldn't be right though because we had done all the hurling. If we had lost it would have been a calamity.'

From the hotel to the Palace Bar in Dublin and off out to the team banquet in Citywest shortly after midnight. The opportunities to celebrate Limerick's success were plentiful. 'I went to see the team coming back then on the Monday,' he recalls. 'I was outside Colbert Station waiting for Declan to come out with the cup.'

Across the nights that followed, any fear that winning an All-Ireland might not be all that it is cracked up to be quickly fell away. 'No… God, no!' Shane Dowling responds when that prospect is put to him. 'From the Monday in the train station, to my singing with Nathan Carter on the Friday, the reality exceeded all expectations.'

Stephen Lucey had briefly entertained the notion of following the procession to Adare on the Tuesday night, but ultimately decided he had to draw the line somewhere. Back to work and a new kind of reality, there aren't many patients who have since met with Dr Lucey and not discussed those unforgettable days.

Ger Hegarty

WITHIN ONE MONTH of Limerick's All-Ireland triumph, it was the turn of Gearóid Hegarty to bring the Liam MacCarthy Cup back to his primary school. His teammate Sean Finn and two members of the backroom team, Paul Kinnerk and Brian Geary, were a part of this visit to Milford National School in Castletroy too.

Together, they walked into an assembly hall full of children and teachers delighted to welcome them. A sea of green to mark the special occasion, it remains one of Ger Hegarty's fondest memories from the days and weeks that followed Limerick's win.

'It was a fabulous occasion, and there was just an exhilarating atmosphere at the school that day.' The school where he had sent Gearóid as a young child, Ger was joined on the sidelines by a grandfather to some of the excited young pupils, Éamonn Cregan.

Sitting in the staff-room having a quiet coffee away from all the excitement, Hegarty recalls the conversation turning back toward 1973 again. 'Éamonn told me that himself and the rest of the team from back then were thrilled that the mantle had finally been passed on,' he remembers.

'They were a team that we all admired, but they never wanted to carry that mantle for 45 years.'

A weight of expectation on subsequent Limerick hurlers that never managed to break the unhappy streak, Hegarty's career bears the distorted marks of that pressure. 'Every year that we didn't win that elusive All-Ireland... that cement block of 1973 became heavier and heavier.'

★ ★ ★ ★ ★

Joe McGrath

I

IN 1973, THE enjoyment Limerick's players took in their All-Ireland success was quickly regarded as reason for their undoing in the years that followed. Although they reached the final again in 1974, Cregan is not alone in believing that they should have won the Liam MacCarthy Cup on more than one occasion. 'The idea with winning one All-Ireland was that you could go on then and win two,' he argues. 'We wanted to be able to compete with Cork and Kilkenny and Tipperary in the long-term.

'When we reached the top of the mountain in 1973 though, subconsciously, it was almost like we had done our bit and that was it. *We can take it easy now.*'

Good a team as Limerick had been, every county in Munster (and often enough the country) quickly had its hands full with a Cork team in full bloom. Provincial winners five years in-a-row after Limerick's Munster success in 1974, they achieved what Limerick couldn't and won three All-Ireland finals along the way.

Bolstered by great players from across the county's traditional hurling powerhouses, a strong Blackrock contingent of players was central. Cork county champions on five occasions across the 1970s, Ray Cummins, Cork's captain for the 1976 All-Ireland win, believes that a man with recent ties to Limerick hurling played a significant part in the successes at both club and county level. 'Joe McGrath was the bane of my life for two or three years before he joined Blackrock,' Cummins explains. 'Every time Cork played Limerick, Pat Hartigan used to be marking me and Joe would spend a lot of time standing in behind the goal. I'd slip away from Pat and there'd be a roar from Joe. "On your right, Pat... he's gone to your right!"

'I didn't dislike him or anything, but he annoyed the shit out of me.'

II

JOE MCGRATH WAS a GAA coach from County Down with little practical hurling experience. After work brought him to Limerick, he started out as a physical trainer with Claughaun GAA club. The positive impression he made there ended up with McGrath taking over the same role with the county team in 1969.

A disagreement with Limerick's County Board in 1972 eventually signalled the end of that relationship. Pitching up with Blackrock GAA club in Cork shortly thereafter, multiple county, provincial and All-Ireland titles were won under his stewardship. 'Despite the fact that we had a strong county team,' Cummins acknowledges, 'we would not have won what we won in the 1970s without Joe McGrath.'

Indeed, Bernie Hartigan, a teammate of Cregan's in 1973, believes their own All-Ireland win with Limerick owed something substantial to McGrath's influence in the preceding years. 'We would always say to Joe,' Hartigan recalls. '"Thanks Joe, for playing your part, we'd never have got there only for you."'

If nothing else, the dismissal of McGrath by Limerick's county officials demonstrated a streak for self-punishment that would play out many, many times in the years to come.

★ ★ ★ ★ ★

Éamonn Cregan

IT IS BELIEVED that Limerick's 1973 All-Ireland win prompted Mick Mackey to utter, 'That's a weight off my shoulders now'. A teammate of his own father's back in the 1930s, Éamonn Cregan would not have believed then that he would soon feel Mackey's burden himself.

He grew to despise the 'last Limerick team to…' tag, and that All-Ireland with Offaly in 1994 had only made things worse. 'It's just,' he begins, giving himself a moment to think, 'Limerick had been down for so long.' In the days and weeks that followed the breakthrough success for John Kiely's team, conversations inevitably came back to a shared sense of relief. 'Eamonn Rea stayed sitting down in Croke Park for a long while after the match,' he reveals of a conversation had with one of his former teammates, 'just absorbing the fact that we had won.'

Slowly, Éamonn felt the weight lift from his shoulders, as it did from Mackey's before him. That being said, he couldn't bring himself to watch the All-Ireland final in 2020, either.

'Ah, I was lying down on the couch about to turn it on, but I found an old western to watch instead,' he admits. In the warmth of his living room on that cold December evening, it was not long before he dozed off.

A man at peace, almost.

The statue of Mick Mackey created by Seamus Connolly in the legend's home village of Castleconnell.

CHAPTER ★ TWO

MICK MACKEY

Mick Mackey

I

He gave the world far more than it ever gave him but he didn't worry too much about that.

– Con Houlihan

II

THE POPULARITY OF Kerry's senior footballers hit fever pitch in 1981. Having won four of the last six All-Ireland titles and vanquished a formidable foe in Kevin Heffernan's Dublin, they possessed an aura that almost transcended the sport itself. The GAA's All Blacks, Yankees or Manchester United, it was in 1981 that they equalled the record of four national titles won in-a-row, set by Wexford over 60 years earlier.

For 1982, some were already planting a green and gold flag on the unchartered ground Kerry were soon to surely conquer. Five in-a-row… immortality.

With Mick O'Dwyer as team manager (and commercial director), unprecedented deals with Adidas and Bendix washing machines were struck. Modest by modern standards, these were revolutionary steps that demonstrated the untapped financial potential of the GAA's appeal, nevertheless. A county making and chasing history on the field with each passing year, O'Dwyer's Kerry captivated public interest quite unlike any team before them. Hardly short of gaelic football icons to begin with, Jack O'Shea, Pat Spillane, Mikey Sheehy and the like were elevated into the pantheon of Kingdom greats while still wearing the jersey. Through the prism of modern marketing, Kerry's senior footballers were a brand anyone with something to sell would be happy associating themselves with.

The *sean-nós* singer, Ann Mulqueen found this out to her dismay. With plans to release an album of Irish songs in the thrust of 1981's 'Kerrymania', her record company insisted that they would be catering to the hype. So it was that her recording of *Kerry's 25th*, a song written to celebrate the county's landmark All-Ireland win the previous year, would lend its name to the album itself.

Related through marriage to one of the team's star players, Páidí Ó Sé, Ann appreciated the practical sense of leaning into Kerry's current success. A resident of the Waterford Gaeltacht of Ring for over a decade by then, she remained a proud Limerick woman first and foremost, however. If she had had her way, GAA stars of an earlier era would have been given space to shine again.

For Ann Mulqueen, the album ought to have been called after a song that meant a great deal more to her. *Kerry's 25th* would have been *Mick Mackey and his Men* instead.

Mick lived before the era when commercialism began to invade even hurling and gaelic football, wrote Con Houlihan the day after Mick Mackey died in September 1982. *Nobody ever offered him money to wear a certain brand of boots – if they did, he would more than likely have gone onto the pitch in his bare feet, such was his sense of humour.*

Mackey's playing career with Limerick had wound down by the time Ann Mulqueen was born in Castleconnell. Yet, this quietly confident figure Houlihan celebrated was a man she knew well. Raised in a house owned by the Mackey family, the back field of her childhood home looked out on where Limerick's finest hurler had learned the game's basic skills years earlier. Before she knew anything of that though, Ann simply knew Mick Mackey as her neighbour.

'Growing up, I didn't know they hurled at all,' she admits, 'that they were these heroes. It wasn't until I started listening to the songs that I thought these guys must have been something special.' Indeed, in his stirring obituary, Houlihan explained how Mackey's legend was not even bound by parochial limits:

In our part of Kerry, we had a special love for Mick Mackey because we looked on Limerick as our hurling county. And we loved him for another reason – because he played with such obvious enjoyment.

He took his craft seriously but not solemnly.

He could laugh and joke on the field… [Nobody could] ever coax him to give up his status as a human being and become a representative… Nor did he worry about the endless debate that raged around himself and Christy Ring.

He was a modest broadminded man who liked honest praise but was embarrassed by adulation.

Ann similarly recalls this embarrassment and Mackey's own sense that he wasn't worthy of the ever-escalating plaudits that came his way. How strange then it must have been for Mick Mackey as he became the focus for so many adulatory songs and poems.

III

IT WAS THROUGH her grandmother and uncle that Ann first learned of songs celebrating Mick Mackey, his brother John, father 'Tyler' and often a few eras' worth of beloved Limerick hurlers from the first few decades of the 20th century.

An accomplished young singer, she was an All-Ireland champion three times over – something Mackey himself could relate to. Growing up in Castleconnell and meeting Mick occasionally when he travelled in to visit the family home, there was always a clear difference between this man she came to know and the hero of those songs. 'He wasn't one at all for talking really or taking praise,' Ann recalls. 'He never thought himself to be as good as he was… a very humble man.' To those who had watched him play, however, Mick Mackey was a hurler you dared not miss.

We followed you through Munster and we shouted for your fame,
In Dublin's far-famed pitch we stood, that bears a glorious name.
We jumped for joy each man and boy, each maid and matron when

We saw the sheen of the white and green for Mick Mackey and his men.
Now t'was well we knew that it would be both a fierce and stormy day
When the Noreside men came on the pitch all eager for the fray.
Resolved were they to win the day and gain the crown again,
But we said 'no' it will surely go to Mick Mackey and his men.

The opening verses to *Mick Mackey and his Men*, the song served as a celebration of Limerick's All-Ireland win in 1940. The fifth and final time that this generation of players would contest an All-Ireland final, their victory against 'the Noreside men' of Kilkenny prompted in the songwriter a moment for gratitude.

Be it some sense that Limerick were already beyond their peak, or an awareness of the coming Cork team featuring one Christy Ring that would win the next four All-Irelands, this well-known song does not overly concern itself with the future either way. Of what is considered for the time to come, the songwriter seems mostly concerned with hours that will be spent happily looking back at what has been achieved.

I'll go out to Castleconnell and I'll spend an hour or two.
I'll call out Tyler Mackey to some cosy rendezvous.
We won't talk of County Councils, Board of Health, or things akin
But make no boast we will drink a toast to Mick Mackey and his men.

Mick Mackey was only 28 years old when that final All-Ireland was won. A young man by any ordinary measure, there is curiously no place for him in the Power's imagination. Where is he when this visit to the Mackey household takes place? Why can the songwriter not foresee conversations with Mackey himself about what has been achieved? As if assumed body and soul into that realm where he and his men were at their hurling best forever more, little thought is spared for the great sportsperson's life thereafter.

It becomes a recurring theme in the many tributes made to Mackey that he must remain forever young, forever victorious in the minds of Limerick's hurling supporters.

He did have a few years left in him despite the song's celebration of what feels like the end, however. While his inter-county days ran on into the mid-1940s, he continued playing for his club, Ahane for over another 10 years. Albeit on a smaller stage, the pressure remained intense. A significant portion of those who followed Mackey's Limerick through Munster and on up to Dublin were drawn in by the prospect of club action also.

'When my brother Martin was about seven or eight, he was walked all the way from Castleconnell to Newport in Tipperary for a match,' Ann recalls, the five-mile trek over the border a journey worth making for Ahane. 'When he got to the gate there was a fella there with his leather bag collecting money to get in and watch the game. Sure, Martin hadn't a penny and your man wouldn't let him in.'

Agonisingly, Ann's brother stood outside unable to avoid the commotion and shouts coming from within.

'Good man, Mick!'

'Good man, John!'

'Up Ahane!'

When the noise quietened and the match was at its midway point, Martin tried again and this time the gatekeeper relented. He was in! 'Martin was standing by the sideline and Mick must have seen him anyway,' Ann explains. 'He came over to where Martin was while the game was being played. "How did you get here, Martin?" he asked him, and Martin told him he had walked.'

Surely enough, Mick Mackey wasn't going to have the young boy walking five miles back home again on his own. 'Mick and John had two bikes with them, and Martin came home across the bar on Mick's bike,' she remembers. 'Sure, Martin said it was better than being at the match itself listening to the two of them talk through everything that happened. He never forgot Mick's kindness that day.'

The dominant club team in Limerick hurling throughout the 1930s and 40s, three county titles in 18 years is the measure of what Ahane left behind them. For all that they were loved and adored, however, the best teams are naturally there to be beaten. As the former Limerick captain Fr Liam Ryan explained to Henry Martin for his comprehensive study of Limerick hurling, however, efforts to stop Ahane could appear Machiavellian at times:

Canon Punch was chairman of the county board and he had a great dislike of Ahane, who had won several championships in succession. He thought that Limerick hurling would go nowhere until he removed Ahane as county champions. In 1949, Canon Punch allowed Croom and Young Irelands to join and introduced divisional teams – City Gaels, East Geraldines, Western Gaels, and Emmets – which prevented Ahane from picking hurlers from junior clubs. That was the reason for the long-term decline of Ahane

On the field of play, there was no shortage of dirty strokes pulled either – depending on your outlook. Although the game in question had happened years before she was born, Ann Mulqueen's voice still lowers ever so slightly when *The Wet Day in Croom* is mentioned. A song likely written in response to Ahane's defeat by Young Irelands in the 1932 county championship, it cast the victorious opponents of Mackey & Co. in a fairly unflattering light.

> *But I was not surprised when Ahane did not win*
> *For the umpires were clever and they never gave in.*
> *On the Young Ireland team they had heavy bets down*
> *With Bookies and shop-boys all over the town.*
> *Now t'is hard to beat Young Irelands but the Ahane boys are quick*
> *But was it Young Irelands or an All-Ireland pick.*
> *They had some men from Limerick and more men from Clare*
> *From Cork and Tipperary and the devil knows where.*
> *But I'd love to see that game played over again*
> *With different umpires for the same thirty men*
> *And not for to have it all a one-sided play.*
> *I saw Ahane get two wides for two overs that day.*
> *So now to conclude and finish my rhyme*
> *Three cheers for Ahane in the height of their prime.*
> *Three cheers for Young Irelands though they're not the best team*
> *They blackguarded our Ahane boys in their gold, white and green.*

A defeat to the eventual county champions Young Irelands, it would be another eight years before Ahane failed to win the county title again. As Ann assuredly informs, singing that particular song could cause all sorts of bother depending on your audience.

The All-Ireland winning Tipperary goalkeeper Ned Maher once attempted to establish Mick Mackey's place in the hierarchy of hurlers. 'He was the greatest hurler ever and I saw them all,' Maher claimed, not allowing much room for debate. It is difficult to imagine given our modern conveniences how relatively few people would have seen the likes of Mackey play with any kind of regularity, however.

Playing largely in an age before even the most modest form of video footage became available, poems and songs served an important purpose. A means of celebrating victorious players and teams on the one hand, they also allowed for important details to be transmitted and committed to memory. Although the majority of those familiar with Mackey's legacy never had an opportunity to witness him at play (let alone playing at his best), his characteristic style has been helpfully recorded in verse.

> *In Lim'rick's fair County – not far from that city –*
> *Was born a hero if ever was one.*
> *He was cordial and jovial, an 'artist' at hurling,*
> *His name is Mick Mackey from far-famed Ahane.*
> *Sure he showed all how scoring was 'easy'*
> *By crashing his was through every defence,*
> *He adopted the solo, applied it with 'gusto,'*
> *And soon his opponents were 'taking offence.'*

Composed by Tadhg O Donnchadha of Doon to the tune of *The Bould Thady Quill*, this portrayal of the equal parts powerful and skilful Mackey incorporates as aura of invincibility around the hurler that has become commonplace. Reliably noted for his abundance of natural talent, the additional bonus of physical strength often makes Mackey appear unstoppable. *Those solo runs of Mick Mackey, yo-yoing the ball on his hurley, need some explanation other than to say that he performed them*, read a report of Limerick's 1936 All-Ireland final win, the journalist in question confused by Mackey's dominance over his opponents. *Why Kilkenny's defence always fled from him as the stunned spectators shrieked, 'Here he comes again!' will remain a mystery.*

The Cork poet Mick Barry put it as such shortly after Mackey's death in 1982: *Rare skill combined with brawn/Defenders reeled 'fore that man of steel*. Indeed, it was with his passing away that chroniclers of his era wilfully abandoned any pretence that Mackey was merely human at all. In *Centenary*, the poet Críostóir Ó Floinn's epic celebration of the GAA as it marked its 100th year, the outstanding icon of Limerick hurling is elevated into the realms of outright Irish folklore.

No curse of saint, no tale of woe
As we passed by the Treaty Stone
Could bother us on that summer's day:
We were going to see Mick Mackey play
In the Gaelic Grounds. The Thomond Feis
Brought thousands to enjoy the zest
Of hurling, music, dance and song,
But as our small feet trudged along
The Ennis Road we wondered where
That field could be. When we got there
With lemonade our lives were saved.
A father's solid shoulders gave
Each child in turn a grandstand glimpse
Of hurleys flashing in a green mist
Where red of Cork and Limerick's green
Darted like trout in mountain stream.
We gazed, engulfed by roaring faces
Under peaked caps. Afterwards voices
Cried, 'That's him, there's Mackey!'
Around the dressing-rooms the surging crowd
Like tidal wave swept us beside
Green jersey, black head bandaged white,
A laughing, sweating hero's face,
And then we were swept to open space.
We felt no weariness as home we strolled
Through Thomondgate, past the Treaty Stone,
Across the Bridge and by the Castle,
Shortening the road with childish prattle.
We told a mother pouring tea
That we had seem him, Mick Mackey.
So children of Eamhain must have come running
To tell that they had seen Cuchulainn.

Éamonn Cregan, son of Mackey's Limerick teammate, Ned in the 1930s, remembers the post-Mackey decades of the 1950s and 60s as a dour time for the county's senior hurlers. 'Mass disorganisation', is how he regards the set-up that was in place. Indeed, as much as O Donnchadha's poem is a celebration of Limerick's golden years, the yearning to celebrate times passed did not entirely mask the desperation of modern times: *From his inspiration may come restoration/ Of Lim'rick's proud honour and former glory!'*

In the immediate years after he finished hurling for Limerick, Mick Mackey must surely have felt the tremendous pressure of a superhero who had lost his powers. Either way, nobody was going to let him forget anyway.

III

THE RECORD COMPANY'S attempt at currying favour with fans of Kerry's senior footballers did not result in Ann Mulqueen having to overlook Limerick entirely, however. With their singer's native county in mind, she was encouraged to ask Mick Mackey himself if he would attend the launch of *Kerry's 25th* in Limerick city. Knowing him as she did and his reluctance to engage in such public events, Ann didn't hold out much hope for their suggestion. Furthermore, with around 12 months left to live, Mackey hadn't been in the greatest of physical health.

'But I went out to the house anyway and asked him,' she explains. 'To my great surprise he told me, "Ann, I'll go in with you".' Beside herself with excitement, this iconic figure she had first known as a neighbour went one further. 'He asked me then if I'd went and asked his brother John,' she recalls, another legendary hurler from the great Limerick team of the 1930s. 'I hadn't and he told me, "Go out now to his house and tell him I said he's to come in too". So, incredibly, I ended up with the two of them coming in.'

It was a testament to Mackey's kindness and warm feeling for Ann Mulqueen. The girl who had grown up next door to his family home releasing an album, it would have struck him as a privilege to be asked to partake in such an event.

The strength of feeling went both ways. Ann recalls when plans were being put in place to raise funds for the renovation of the Gaelic Grounds and the construction of the new Mick Mackey Stand. Living as she was in Waterford, she enthusiastically sought out known hurling people in the vicinity to see what additional funds she could raise in an alternative market.

'Funnily enough,' she explains, 'Mick had told me that he was nearly going to come and visit me in Waterford before, but he'd had a turn.' Crucially though, the former Limerick hurler had told Ann exactly what former opponents of his he would like to meet there. 'Tom Curran, Dec Goode… and Jimmy Mountain,' she remembers, three former Waterford hurlers. Located handily within reach of one another, Ann headed to Dungarvan with the hope that these men might be happy to help with the fundraiser.

It didn't quite pan out that way, however. She visited Tom Curran at his hardware store in the town first. 'A big, *big* man with a crop of black hair,' she begins, Ann laid out her pitch. '"Tom,' I told him, 'as you know I'm from the parish of Ahane and I'm a neighbour of Mick Mackey's…'"

She explained that there was a fundraising event coming up in Limerick and asked if he would like to buy a ticket for it. 'The first thing he did after I stopped talking was take the hair away from his forehead to show me this big scar,' Ann recalls. '"Look at that! That's all I ever got from Mick Mackey." Tom didn't give me anything.'

Deterred but still determined, she made her way to Jimmy Mountain next who had another shop in the town square. 'I told him my story,' she says, 'and he just showed me another scar that he had on his jaw thanks to John Mackey. So, that was two of the three that were no good to me.'

Onward to Declan Goode so in his shoe shop.

'The first thing he did was start crying,' Ann remembers, after telling him her story. 'He said Mick was a great hurler, no doubt about it, and he said he would certainly buy a ticket.'

It was in May 1981 that Ann launched *Kerry's 25th* in Limerick. Situated in Halla Íde on Thomas Street, the Mackey brothers, dressed in suit and tie, were Ann's guests of honour. Taking place during the county's first folk festival, Glor Ceoil Luimni, famed GAA commentator Mícheál Ó Muircheartaigh was among the large crowd that had gathered for the week long event.

Suitably enough, Ann opted to mark the event by singing *Mick Mackey and his Men*. Standing between the seated Mick and John as all three of them faced a captivated crowd, she put her hands on a shoulder of each man and began to sing.

'I thought I would never get to the end of that song,' she remembers. 'I was completely overcome and what upset me altogether was that Mick started crying. He wasn't that well really, and he got very emotional.'

Approaching the end of his life, Mackey, a man who was made legend before his 30th birthday, could still on presence alone enthrall a room of people. 'The crowd were just stunned seeing Mick and John on the stage,' Ann recalls, 'and I was really so proud because I never thought they would come.' Limerick hurling had redeemed itself in recent years and the All-Ireland success of 1973 had alleviated some of the burden surrounding what Mackey and his men had achieved decades earlier.

Nevertheless, heroes like these were not forgotten. After the emotional outpouring on stage, Ann was given cause to laugh by what her mother later revealed. 'She was there that night,' Ann remembers, 'and she just couldn't get over the feed that Mick Mackey had had. She said he nearly ate a whole loaf of bread!'

A king's appetite, no less.

★ ★ ★ ★ ★

Seamus Connolly

I

MICKEY MACKEY DIED in Limerick, but rose again in Clare.

A colossal figure in hurling folklore, it was the sculptor Seamus Connolly who brought him back to life. In 2012, the centenary year of his birth, a Mick Mackey Commemorative Committee was established by Ahane GAA club. Although the Mick Mackey Stand at Limerick's Gaelic Grounds, the Mackey roundabout and Ahane's own Mackey Park already paid tribute to him, it was felt that his captivating characteristics could not be conveyed in name alone.

They wanted something tangible, something to be seen and touched. A call was made to Connolly. The Olympian Paddy Ryan, writer John B Keane and gaelic footballer Dermot Early had already passed through his workshop and foundry. Bronze statues of great people that the living wanted future generations to keep in mind.

The committee tasked him with delivering the same for Mackey. Far out on the Irish coast, 'a mile from the Loop Head lighthouse… that far out,' Connolly went to work. He might have spent most of his life in Clare but the sculptor's father, Jim, a renowned sculptor in his own right, came from Foynes in Limerick. While he generally refrains from studying the lives of his subjects too closely, Connolly implicitly understood the significance of Mackey. A hurler 'who made the crowd come alive because of his swashbuckling style,' it was his challenge to communicate this sensation to onlookers, be it in a moment's glance or a lengthier stare.

'You're trying to capture the essence of this person,' he stresses, the pursuit of achieving a physical likeness identical to the subject's own a natural starting point for such projects. For the legendary Limerick hurler, however, this essence was forged decades earlier in his playing days.

A time before significant sportspeople were regularly filmed and photographed, Mackey, an athlete whose physical presence was renowned, posed an immediate problem. 'I was struggling with the one or two photographs there were of him,' he recalls, 'but then, out of the blue, somebody found a profile shot of him at play.'

A fortuitous find, the scarcity of such images speaks to the importance of the sculptor's work. However many ways people may attach Mackey's name to some object or other, a statue promises a far more substantial link to the very man and hurler himself.

II

THE SPORTSPERSON POSES distinct challenges for the sculptor. If, as Connolly decided with Mackey, the athlete's body is presented in motion a balancing act of two potentially opposing conditions must be struck.

Firstly, as Connolly achieved with Mackey, the hurler in action must look authentic. Although the commissioned statue would ultimately become the completed work of art that now stands in Castleconnell, it had to retain the qualities of a 'snapshot in time… like a photograph'. Planting the sliotar on the end of Mackey's hurley recreating one of his famous solo runs, Connolly's work urges onlookers to think of the Limerick legend at his most devastating.

Mick Mackey, the irrepressible, was off again on a dazzling run, reads one *Irish Press* match report from his playing days, *with the ball apparently glued to his caman, and the inevitable point followed.* This moment occurred in the 1936 All-Ireland final, but it could have been at any point throughout Mackey's career.

Connolly captures the 'irrepressible' Mackey running still… running forever.

Designed to communicate the high regard in which Mackey is held and his genius that informed this opinion, however, the sculptor understood that most onlookers – much like himself – had never seen Mackey play at all. To authentically portray Mackey in the heat of battle required an imaginative leap.

This is where Connolly had to concern himself with that second condition.

When commissioned to create this statue, the committee wanted a piece of work that resembled Mackey as they knew him. Or, as they believed they knew him, anyway. Be it through photographs, on the field of play, or as a friend and fellow clubman known personally, each individual assumed that upon seeing the finished statue they would confidently recognise Mick… *as Mick.*

With so few images or readily available footage from his playing days in circulation, however, how does the sculptor decide what Mick Mackey should look like? How could Seamus Connolly convey the intricate details of a life that meant so much to so many in a single moment in time? The images we share of Mackey the hurler vary. He is no doubt the man staring intently down the camera as he is presented with the Liam MacCarthy Cup in 1940 for some. Or the dapper gentleman in his trench coat with a steely gaze holding that same trophy only a few years earlier, perhaps.

'Mick Mackey was a hugely charismatic figure who hurled with a smile on his face,' suggested the Ahane GAA chairman, Turlough Herbert. A striking image most certainly, but the number of people to have seen Mackey hurl is ever dwindling. 'Ultimately, sportspeople's faces never look like their faces when you have a photograph taken in the middle of a match,' Connolly points out, further complicating things. 'They are contorted.'

Mackey the man or Mackey the hurler, Connolly's task was to bring something of both to his statue.

III

UNDERSTANDABLY THEN, IT was Mick Mackey's face that required the greatest amount of work. 'He was definitely a frowner,' Connolly remarks, the sight of something resembling a smile appearing once in Mackey's famous exchange with Christy Ring. The seriousness of his gaze was no indication of a dour personality, however. Less still did it reflect a playing style that was lacking in joyful enthusiasm and daring.

Hurling's first superstar, as Mackey has been described, his brooding revealed the cool remove of a Limerick hurler who was utterly adored and understood why. 'I stared at Mick Mackey's face more intently than anyone has ever stared at his face,' Connolly states matter-of-factly. In painstaking detail, he worked on recreating this 'great strong face' for months.

'You start to feel like you know the person,' he admits, the daily routine of greeting his ongoing subject in his workshop a curious sensation. 'The whole thing takes on a personality right away.' Off out on the west coast of Ireland, often listening to test match cricket on the BBC for its drawn-out entertainment, Connolly carefully crafted Mackey out of clay.

Before it was cast in bronze, the statue began as a kind of skeletal steel frame welded together. Covered in mesh, it stood waiting for what the sculptor could conjure. 'Something I learned from my father was not to be precious,' he explains, the process of creating such an intricate work laced with potential pitfalls. 'Even if you've spent ages on something, you can't be afraid to rip it all up and start again. You have to be ruthless.'

Given his reputation as a fearsomely strong and physical hurler, there was an onus on Connolly to transmit Mackey's power. Yet, here too stood *the greatest playboy and stunt artist in the game, dummying and swerving his way through, shooting goals and points with easy freedom,* according to PD Mehigan (Carbery), a leading journalist of the day. A skilful player well capable of looking after himself in the rough and tumble of 1930s and 40s hurling, Mackey's aura was hard to measure in feet and inches.

This sculptor has grown used to dealing with extraordinary people though. It is by now his specialty. After Mick Mackey, Páidí Ó Sé, Anthony Foley and President John F. Kennedy made their way through his workshop. 'I find the openings difficult,' he concedes, Connolly far more comfortable doing the six months work on his own than attending the public unveilings.

'I'm okay for about three minutes and then I have to go.'

The pressure was no more greatly felt than at Mackey's own unveiling in May

2013. While the statue bore an incredible physical resemblance to the hurler, one among those gathered raised a concern regarding the accuracy of other details. 'This person said to me, "He was left-handed, you know?"'… Connolly's Mackey carrying his hurley in the right hand.

'It was a joke! But it nearly put the heart crossways in me because I had researched those details so carefully.' It encapsulates the difficulty of the sculptor's task. For however he decided Mick Mackey to appear, someone is unlikely to recognise the hurler they thought they knew. The idea of Mackey, his name a byword for greatness in Limerick, has only so much to do with the man himself, however. It is this idea that Connolly attempted to translate – successfully, it should be said.

A hurler… *the* hurler at play, the statue reveals to onlookers more about their relationship with the game than anything else. Yes, it looks like Mick Mackey, but what does Mick Mackey represent in Limerick if not the love of hurling. 'Nobody remembers the sculptor,' Connolly states, not an ounce of regret in his voice as he reflects on a job exquisitely done.

★ ★ ★ ★ ★

Titan(ic):

I

The choir had sung 'Nearer My God To Thee' as the coffin draped in the number 11 jersey of Ahane and Limerick was carried from the Parish Church of St Joseph by members of his own family – his brother John among them – to the waiting house after the Requiem Mass had ended.

– Irish Independent, September 16, 1982

II

A LITTLE UNDER three months before Mick Mackey was born in July 1912, RMS Titanic, the largest ocean liner of its time, sank. Caught somewhere between its dreadful reality and James Cameron's Hollywood treatment of the story decades later is *Nearer, My God, To Thee*. A 19th century Christian hymn, as that mixture of panic and terrible acceptance settles on Cameron's passengers while the ship is swallowed up by the Atlantic Ocean, it provides the soundtrack.

The musicians, gripped by their powerlessness and ultimately awaiting death, turn to the song that it may provide some much-needed comfort. An incredibly poignant moment in the 1997 film, whether or not *Nearer, My God, To Thee* was played during the actual sinking remains debated and uncertain. Nevertheless, it sounded right in hindsight.

Any number of mourners at Mick Mackey's funeral years earlier must have been similarly struck by its suitability. The *Titanic* and the hurling Titan.

When the 'unsinkable' goes down, what other way is there to look, but up?

Ger Hegarty storms out of defence during Limerick's agonising loss to Offaly in the All-Ireland final in 1994.

CHAPTER ★ THREE

1990s

Tom Ryan

I

TOM RYAN IS adamant that he never really wanted the Limerick job in the first place. How he ended up managing the county's senior hurlers for four years owed much to stubbornness, and a mischievous streak. One of 18 nominees put forward for three selectors positions in the summer of 1993, Ryan, an All-Ireland winner on the field in 1973, had shown himself to be quite capable on the sideline also.

His own Ballybrown ('a small club that reached great heights') had made it all the way to an All-Ireland club final with Ryan serving as a selector only a few years earlier. Limerick's senior hurling champions in 1989 and '91, it was a feat the club had not managed before or since. No surprise then that the *Limerick Leader* talked up this candidate as a heavy favourite for the county's top job.

Indeed, it had been Ryan's club that put his name forward in the first place. It was not necessarily a sense of civic duty that motivated Tom Ryan to heed the call, however. 'The powers-that-be didn't want me at all,' he believes, Limerick's

County Board a source of consternation for Ryan then and in the years to come. 'So, my staying in was a kind of "f**k you" to them.'

As the list of nominees was whittled down to 13 by election night, it was decided after the 11th count of Limerick's PR voting system that Ryan, Liam Lenihan and Rory Kiely would fill the three vacant selectors roles. A former chairman of the county board, Kiely's selection came a remarkable 31 years after he had first been a selector for Limerick's senior hurling team. What's more, he had been serving as a Senator in the Seanad more or less consistently since 1977.

Meanwhile, Lenihan was chairman of the West Limerick GAA board (a future county and Munster GAA chairman in the making). Unsurprisingly, Ryan was left feeling isolated in this trio alongside what he considered to be two staunch county board men. 'I never had any problem at all with Tom,' Lenihan insists, his memories of their time spent working with Limerick overwhelmingly positive.

Truthfully, Ryan's suspicions may have had more to do with what – or who – he believed his fellow selectors were representing than anything else.

The morning after he was elected, Ryan, who had opted not to attend election night itself, received a visit at work from Gerard Bennis. Chairman of the county board, it was Bennis's brother Phil – a teammate of Ryan's in 1973 – who had most recently managed the Limerick hurlers. 'He said to me, "I'm going on my holidays, and I'll be back at the end of August,"' an incredulous Ryan insists. 'You wouldn't believe then what came next, this is unreal like. "Don't make any decisions until I come back."'

Although still only one of three selectors, Ryan did not fancy waiting around for six weeks to get this new era for Limerick hurling underway. 'I told Gerard, "I want to meet the county board tomorrow night in the Woodlands Hotel in Adare,"' he explains. '"If you can't be there, have someone there in your place that can make decisions."'

In later years, Bennis insisted that he had only vague memories of this encounter with Ryan and found the idea of his going on a six-week holiday fanciful. Nevertheless, both men would sit opposite each other the following night as the new selectors met the county board.

Arriving half-an-hour before that summit, Ryan, Kiely and Lenihan set about their first order of business: deciding which one of them would become the Limerick hurling manager.

II

BALLYBROWN HAD NEVER felt the need to appoint a singular figure of authority during their heyday. Between Ryan, John Loftus, Sean Bennis and Michael Lynch, the local schoolteacher, a club with no history of senior county success almost conquered all of Ireland, thanks in part to their collective effort.

As a group of selectors, their skills dovetailed nicely. The fervent Ryan and more equable Loftus would reliably keep the club's players on their toes. 'Tom would tell fellas exactly what he thought of them,' explains Loftus of a joined approach they mastered over time.

'Then I would put the arm around them and interpret what he had said. Good cop… bad cop.' Of course, any suggestion that Ryan would frequently fly off the handle is nonsensical.

In the years they served alongside him, both Loftus and Bennis testify to having witnessed a master motivator at work – even if his words did occasionally draw on questionable analogies.

Not so long after the Zeebrugge Disaster of 1987, when the MS *Herald of Free Enterprise* capsized off the coast of Belgium leading to the deaths of almost 200 passengers and crew, Ryan solicited meaning from this tragedy for what the Ballybrown hurlers were trying to achieve.

'He had all the players out in the middle of the training field on a Tuesday night,' recalls Loftus, 'and he was talking about a game we had coming up on the Sunday. "It is a bit like that ship," he told them. "That was a perfectly good ship, I'd say. But one f**ker who was supposed to close one door f**ked up and everyone went down."

'As Tom was saying this, he almost spun like a ballet dancer around on his heel so every player would see his face. "So, on Sunday… who's going to be that f**ker?"'

If these motivational messages could often sound slightly tyrannical, Ryan understood that success in sport was a game of component parts, nevertheless. 'He was very fair,' insists Bennis. 'It didn't matter if you were a brother, cousin or whatever… and Ballybrown is full of his cousins. Tom always had his ideas of course, but he would take on your ideas as well as his own.'

Downplaying his own role in things, Bennis points to the effectiveness of Ryan and Loftus particularly. Whereas Ryan could bring his players to where they needed to be mentally, he identifies the meticulousness of Loftus seeking out recorded videos of Ballybrown's opponents and studying them diligently. 'I still think to this day that if Tom had brought John with him to Limerick, he would have been a great help,' Bennis explains. 'John could spot a weak link in another team quicker than anyone else I've seen.' And yet, for all that Ballybrown's selectors and the special group of players they possessed brought to proceedings, only one figure is roundly acknowledged by all to have been indispensable to the club's success: Dave Mahedy.

A Dublin native who would notably go on to become Director of Sport and Recreation in the University of Limerick, Loftus jokes that he hardly knew one end of a hurley from the other in the late 1980s. Nevertheless, Mahedy had an aptitude for physical training that few clubs – and only a handful of county teams one could expect – in Ireland would have experienced at the time. 'I brought Mahedy in,' insists Loftus, the physical trainer later becoming the only member of Ballybrown's backroom team that would be drafted into the Limerick set-up by Ryan in 1993.

What Mahedy could deliver in terms of physical preparation relied heavily upon a culture of professionalism across the club's senior team. Unsurprisingly, this was something he had to help cultivate also. 'He had told everyone to be out on the pitch by 7pm,' Loftus recalls of a training session Mahedy had organised early enough in his tenure.

'By 7pm there were maybe 12… 13 players togged out on the field… four or five more in the dressing-room, and then seven or eight more just arriving in the gate.'

Unsatisfied, Mahedy sought to make his feelings clear. 'He just walked off down to his car and drove off,' Loftus remembers, unsurprised at the time, as he had been told by Mahedy that anything but total commitment from the players would not be tolerated. 'There was absolute mayhem then among the players. "Where's Mahedy gone?!" And I told them, "He's gone because you weren't all out on the pitch."'

With enough light left in the evening to not write it off entirely, new plans for the session were made. 'Tom took them for a run,' he recalls with a laugh. 'They must have done about seven miles that evening through bogs, up over walls… the entire thing. When Mahedy came back a few days later then for the next session, every player was out on that field by quarter-to-seven. That night changed everything.'

Given the circumstances in which Mahedy would ultimately walk away from Ryan's Limerick set-up years later, gravely insulted by the county board's tactless questioning about unaccounted "monies handed out to any member of the management team," Sean Bennis's recollection of the club's secret weapon are equally worth recalling. 'Mahedy did it all without every charging the club anything,' he explains.

'He was a brilliant man.'

And yet, brilliant men were exactly what Ballybrown required. Long before the club began to make its mark both in Limerick and further afield, they had to overcome an almighty hurdle within their own parish. If Ballybrown seemed like upstarts of the late 1980s, Patrickswell GAA club were already Limerick hurling royalty. Neighbouring clubs within a single parish, this dominance scarcely told the full story, however.

It had been decades after Ballybrown emerged in the late 19th century that Patrickswell first came into existence. Although Tom Ryan would go on to hurl with the parish's older club, his father Willie Ryan had been one of three men central to the founding of Patrickswell in the 1940s; one of numerous examples where the two clubs have always been inextricably linked.

Before Ballybrown claimed their maiden county senior title in 1989, Patrickswell had already won 11. Twice county finalists before that 1989 breakthrough, in both 1983 and '87 it had been Patrickswell that defeated Ballybrown in the decisive fixture. In 1988, when Ballybrown rightly fancied themselves to be one of the county's best senior teams, the championship draw pitted them against Patrickswell in the first round. Once more, they came up short.

Where both clubs were already as closely linked geographically as could be, both Ballybrown and Patrickswell just so happened to possess two fantastic senior teams in tandem also – if the former could just overcome the latter.

While Tom Ryan's paternal link to Patrickswell demonstrated the close alignment of their histories, fellow selector Sean Bennis contended with more pronounced links of his own. When Patrickswell started lifting county titles in the mid-1960s, this rare Ballybrown Bennis could only watch on and wonder. 'The first county title Patrickswell won,' he recalls, 'there were six Bennis' on the team.' The eldest of 13, Sean witnessed the likes of his younger brothers Phil and Richie achieve brilliant success with Limerick – and near domination of the county scene for a spell with Patrickswell.

Home had been where his siblings would make their name but Sean, through marriage, ultimately found himself living at the other end of the parish in Ballybrown. 'I was betwixt and between what I would do,' he admits, ultimately opting in the late 1950s to throw his lot in with Ballybrown. 'I wasn't too popular with the Bennis' down through the years, but I'd do it all the same again. I enjoyed every minute of my hurling here.'

When Bennis felt the legs going and brought his hurling days to an end in the late-1960s, Ryan, around 10 years his junior, was making a name for himself in senior hurling. 'He was a great hurler,' Bennis recalls, 'and he always led by example. When we won the 1967 Limerick Junior Championship, Tom was already the one who was training us.' As the county team went on to achieve All-Ireland success in 1973, Sean sat in Croke Park with his daughter, delighted as two of his brothers helped to end the 33-year wait.

No small amount of pride was reserved for his fellow clubmate too, however; Tom making an appearance off the bench as Limerick overcame Kilkenny. 'Tom was always the shining light in Ballybrown down through the years,' Bennis admits with a laugh. 'I'll let him have that.'

III
1989 Limerick Senior Hurling Championship final
Ballybrown 4-11 Doon 3-9

New champions, yes, but little to indicate that Ballybrown's breakthrough at domestic level could signal a new era on a higher plain for Limerick hurling… that was the unanimous verdict at the Gaelic Grounds on Sunday as Doon failed to measure up to expectations before a crowd which paid £15,100 at the turnstiles. What was meant to be the showpiece of the local hurling calendar turned into a major disappointment. As a spectacle it fell rather flat. There were precious few individual performances to excite neutrals and the overall standard was never more than mediocre.

– John O'Shaughnessy, Limerick Leader, September 11, 1989

1989 Munster Senior Hurling Club Championship final
Ballybrown 2-12 Sixmilebridge 1-8

Any question marks which may have existed about Ballybrown's pedigree in the domestic and provincial championships this season were well and truly buried at the Gaelic Grounds on Sunday when they had their finest hour in beating Sixmilebridge to claim their first Munster club championship... Sixmilebridge had to accept they were beaten by a superior side who, if delayed in swinging into top gear, won in the kind of fashion which stamps greatness.

– John O'Shaughnessy, *Limerick Leader*, November 20, 1989

IV

THANKS TO THE same kind of amateur filmmaking that allowed John Loftus to study Ballybrown's opponents before such practice was commonplace, one can still watch the 1989 Limerick county final back on YouTube. Shaky and lacking in the kind of production value most modern viewers have grown used to, it captures the exuberance of Ballybrown's breakthrough, nevertheless.

Pitted against Doon, Sean Bennis is quick to address how serendipitous a pairing this was. Years earlier, when Ballybrown had won the junior title for only the second time, it had been Doon they had defeated in the final. What he chose not to mention, of course, was that it had been his late goal which overturned Doon's two-point lead and gave Ballybrown the victory. Situated along the sideline, what the camera captures of the closing moments of the 1989 final does not tally with how John O'Shaughnessy saw things for the *Limerick Leader*. Dressed immaculately in a dark suit and tie, a beaming Tom Ryan is addressed by the man behind the camera.

'Are you happy now,' he asks Ryan, who with both thumbs turned up assures him... 'I'm very happy. We've been waiting for this day a long time.'

One of the county's oldest clubs, Ballybrown were perhaps unusual in not really being of the Limerick hurling establishment. A lack of success tends to ensure you remain an outsider though. If Ryan & Co. likely balked then at the leading local paper's assessment of their victory the following morning, O'Shaughnessy, who did not shirk revising his assessment somewhat months later as the same team took Munster, should nevertheless be viewed as a fair representative of what a portion of Limerick's hurling fraternity made of Ballybrown.

Two years later, as Ballybrown claimed their second county title, O'Shaughnessy was once more impressed only to a point, highlighting in his match report that *the attendance was little over 5,000 and gate receipts were £10,100, which was £3,000 short of last year's returns.* Between the broader assessment of their achievements and the nature of their highly competitive rivalry with neighbours Patrickswell (Ballybrown's 1991 triumph meant the parish's two clubs had now held the John Daly Cup between them for five consecutive years), it is unsurprising that Ryan would enter the county stage with some trepidation.

Gerry Bennis, the county chairman he found himself immediately at odds with, was a Patrickswell man. Phil Bennis, the man Ryan would ultimately replace as Limerick manager, had cut his teeth in management, breaking Ballybrown hearts with Patrickswell. Any hope of success with the county team would likely mean getting the best out of the likes of Ciaran Carey and Gary Kirby, two Limerick stars who also hailed from the 'Well.

In the melting pot of this small parish sprung a wild competitiveness between neighbours. He may have been an All-Ireland winner on the field with Limerick 20 years earlier, but as Tom Ryan looked set to walk through the establishment's 'open door' he would keep both eyes open.

V

TO ALL BUT Ryan himself then, the man who should take charge of Limerick after Phil Bennis was obvious. Yet, as he sat alongside Rory Kiely and Liam Lenihan at a trestle table waiting for the county board contingent to arrive in the summer of 1993, Ryan's recollection of his ascent is tinged with reluctance. 'I said to the two lads, "Right, who is going to be the manager?" I was at the bottom of the ladder here because of my inexperience,' he insists. 'So, I turned to Rory. "You would be the man. You have the experience, and you know all the people involved. You should take the manager's job." Well, he says he wouldn't be able for it, that he wouldn't have the time.'

Fair enough, Tom thought, before moving on to Lenihan. 'So, I turned to my right and there was Liam,' he explains. '"You're the next man Liam, you're the chairman of the West Board and you've an awful lot of experience with managerial matters in the GAA – you'll have to take it." The man nearly swallowed his tongue… so that was a no.'

Running short on candidates, Ryan knew what this meant for him. 'So, in the end it was left to this b*****x here to take the job,' he concludes. 'That was the appointment of the Limerick manager.' Lenihan's memory tallies with Ryan's (minus the tongue-swallowing, admittedly), but he dismisses the idea that Ryan was lacking in the necessary experience or preparedness for the role. 'Tom was a strong character and a very straight-talking man,' he insists, 'and a very good judge of people. He always listened and we ruled by consensus.' Gerard Bennis subsequently suggested that Ryan was the obvious choice too.

It will not have surprised Bennis then that he was dealing primarily with the forthright Ballybrown man when he entered the Woodlands Hotel at 8pm that night. Flanked by county secretary Jimmy Hartigan of Ryan's own club and treasurer Michael Fitzgerald, the new manager was in no mood for pleasantries.

'The only one they didn't have any respect for was me,' Ryan claims, 'a man who had soldiered out on the field for 10 years and spent his life hurling.' How this disrespect manifested itself is unclear (Lenihan recalls relations between the management team and county board being largely cordial – until they undoubtedly were not in later years), but Ryan remains certain. As a general chat ensued about the sorry state of Limerick hurling – on and off the field – Ryan took exception with what he felt was a passing of the buck. 'I agreed with Gerard that Limerick hurling was not in a good place,' he admits, 'but he was the chairman… he was the boss, and I didn't want any of that coming down on my shoulders.' For better and worse, Tom Ryan was starting off with a blank slate.

★ ★ ★ ★ ★

Ger Hegarty

I

1986 Munster Senior Hurling Championship
Clare 2-14 Limerick 0-14

As for Limerick, they paid the price of relying too much on inexperience. Ger Hegarty

found the task of playing centre half-back at this level of competition beyond him and
made one ask why Mossy Carroll was not started in the No. 6 jersey.

– Evening Press, June 5, 1986

II

GER HEGARTY WAS seeking a similar clarity of purpose to Tom Ryan by the
end of 1993. It had been seven years since he made his championship debut for
Limerick in a humbling defeat to Clare in Ennis. Although expected wins against
Kerry and Waterford had been picked up in the meantime, Hegarty's experience
of the Munster Championship was not all that he had hoped it might be.

Fresh out of Limerick's All-Ireland winning minor team of 1984, he was
making waves with the county's under-21s, when Noel Drumgoole drafted him
into the senior team in 1986. Absent through suspension when the under-21s
drew their Munster final clash with Clare in early May, the *Irish Independent*
praised the returning Hegarty for putting in a storming final 20 minutes as
Limerick eased to victory in the replay.

While the team ultimately fell short in their All-Ireland semi-final against
Galway, Hegarty and his teammates corrected things the following year, defeating
Galway in the under-21 final. Hegarty's second underage All-Ireland winners
medal, few match reports of this time failed to reference his towering height and
immense physical presence.

It is little surprise then that Hegarty was sure of himself. 'I wasn't there just to
play for Limerick,' he explains of making the transition to senior hurling. 'I was
joining to play for Limerick and win All-Irelands. That might sound arrogant,
and I don't mean it to sound arrogant, but we had had a great colleges career that
fed into Limerick's nursery system.'

Hegarty and his teammates would come about as close as possible to fulfilling
that ambition without ever fully making it in later years. In 1986, however, they
were far from ready. 'They were two teams in transition,' he remarks of a Limerick
team combining some stragglers from the 1973 All-Ireland-winning panel with
exciting youngsters, and a Clare XV still boasting seasoned pros like Seán Stack
and Ger Loughnane.

Ready to take on the world, Hegarty would have been forgiven for assuming he had senior hurling sussed following Limerick's initial burst when the ball was thrown in at Ennis. In the opening 15 minutes, with a slight breeze behind them, the visitors outscored their opponents 0-8 to 0-1; each of Limerick's points coming from play. To understand how Clare managed to win from this inauspicious starting-point, one goes looking for a decisive moment whereby the impetus Limerick had seized from the opening changed hands.

Unfortunately for the championship debutant Ger Hegarty, he played his part in the relinquishing of Limerick's control. Thirteen years earlier, John Callinan, a Clare midfielder playing his first game of championship hurling, was excoriated in the *Irish Independent* for failing to keep better tabs on the brilliant Richie Bennis. *Bennis hurled Pascal Russell and John Callinan into oblivion*, the report read, *and there will no doubt be many an 'inquest' why no attempt was made to contain the Patrickswell man.* Nevertheless, in a match that very almost ended Limerick's run to 1973 All-Ireland success before it got started, Callinan was also responsible for a goal that had briefly appeared to kick-start Clare's revival early in the second-half.

A two-time All Star in the years since his first appearance and one of his last for the county in 1986, Callinan gave Hegarty a headache the like of which Bennis had given him years earlier. Breaking through on the Limerick goal, Hegarty dragged Callinan to the floor giving away a penalty. 'I suppose I was very young and inexperienced,' Hegarty concedes, the resulting penalty converted by Gerry McInerney. 'That wasn't, as the saying goes, the start that I wanted.' It was only a start, at least. For Limerick manager, Noel Drumgoole, defeat to Clare in Ennis was ultimately the end of his spell in charge of the county's senior hurlers.

III

Ger Hegarty lost his battle to regain fitness for Limerick's championship battle against Clare at Ennis on May 23. Hegarty, out of action since he injured a leg against Tipperary in a challenge match last September, has had three operations already on his knee and there is a possibility he may have to have a fourth. 'I had hoped to be back for the game in Ennis but my doctor has advised me not to even attempt to go back into full training. Should I do further damage to my injury then my career could well be over,' said the 25-year-old Hegarty. He has not given up hope though of being available for

the semi-final against Cork should Limerick get over Clare in the opening round.
                                            – *Sunday Independent*, May 9, 1993

IV

FOLLOWING THE DEPARTURE of Drumgoole in 1986, Limerick struggled to find much stability on a managerial front. All-Ireland winners in 1973, Éamonn Cregan, Liam O'Donoghue and Phil Bennis were involved at different intervals in varying capacities across the next five years. The manager who had guided Limerick's minors and under-21s to All-Ireland successes in 1984 and '87 respectively, Bennis took on the senior job for a second time in the summer of 1991.

Morale is rather low just now, discipline has been called into question and expectations not very high, John O'Shaughnessy bluntly put it in the *Limerick Leader* before speculating that the arrival of Bennis may change all that. *There might yet be light at the end of the tunnel.* After only agreeing to join on a 12-month basis, Bennis must have seen enough in his Limerick team across 1992 to go again the following year.

'We lost the Munster final to Cork,' recalls Hegarty, Limerick's first appearance in the provincial decider since 1981. 'I was one hundred percent certain we would win it.' Although the difference between them was not great at full-time, the tone of Donal Keenan's match report in the *Irish Independent* was mirrored across most publications. *Only five points separated the two sides at the end but it is a false guide to the story of this game,* he warned. *It could, and probably should, have been double that figure to properly reflect the superiority of Cork.*

The following year, as Limerick once again came up short against Clare in Ennis, and Bennis suffered the same fate as Noel Drumgoole seven years earlier, the tunnel seemed dark beyond any hope of illumination.

Things may have been made somewhat easier, perhaps, had Limerick their full complement of inter-county stars available to them, of course. As Bennis' team crashed out of the 1993 championship, they had been without Ger Hegarty, who remained locked in a battle to save his hurling career. 'I'd had an injury-free run up until 1992,' he recalls, a summer of club hurling after their Munster final defeat to Cork passing by without much happening of note. 'Then I played a practice match against Tipperary around September in the run-up to the 1992/93 National Hurling League.'

The 25-year-old with no track record of injuries proceeded to sever the anterior cruciate ligament in his knee. Publicly quoted in the build-up to Limerick's defeat by Clare that he could possibly feature in the 1993 championship were the team to go deep enough in the competition, his next meaningful game for Limerick was almost another year away at that stage. 'This injury was only the beginning of my problems, really,' he grimly confirms.

★ ★ ★ ★ ★

Tom Ryan

I

A series of trials have been arranged, involving all four divisions. The west will play the east, at the Gaelic Grounds, on Tuesday, August 24, and one week later, the city and south clash at Bruff. The selectors will then pick two finals teams for another trial, on September 11.
– Limerick Leader, August 14, 1993

II

AS THEY QUICKLY found out, Tom Ryan arrived with certain expectations of his Limerick hurlers. Primarily, they were challenged to concern themselves with the here and now of a new regime – reputation counted for nothing.

'Tom had no interest where you were from or what club you played for,' Lenihan remembers. 'He was very democratic when it came to picking teams.' Confident that the county contained hidden gems and promising youngsters who only needed a chance and some good coaching, Ryan scoured Limerick looking for players. 'You'd be seeing Tom Ryan at a lot of club matches,' Mark Foley recalls, still only a 19-year-old yet to play under-21 hurling for Limerick, when Ryan called him up to the senior panel in 1994.

To the annoyance of some established county players, the new manager had decided from the outset that trials would be an effective way of unearthing talent (he suspected it might shake loose some of those no longer hungry enough to do what he needed them to do, also). 'There was a huge negative reaction within the squad to that and a number of prominent players refused to participate in the trials,' Ryan explains; those who did not play ball in these formative weeks discounted from consideration thereafter.

'Like, how dare we expect these county players who had lost in Ennis a few weeks before to even contemplate going on a trial!' Those who did make it through to Ryan's senior panel soon discovered that his rigorous approach to identifying players was nothing compared to the determination with which he sought to coach and condition them.

Along with Kiely and Lenihan, his backroom team consisted of 'the great physical trainer' Dave Mahedy, Dr David Boylan and Charles Hanley, a man who became Ryan's go-between with the players. Dissatisfied with elements of his own inter-county playing experience with Limerick years earlier, Ryan insists that he never had the benefit of being properly coached.

As had been demonstrated during Ballybrown's recent successes, however, he was determined to make up for this shortfall when his time came to oversee the county team. Taking great pleasure in the development of players, the ferocious intensity he chose to work within remains vivid for all involved. 'You would hear those stories about the Kilkenny training matches when they were going well,' Foley notes. 'Well, the matches we had that time were full-blooded.' Executing the game's basic skills at breakneck speed two or three nights a week, Ryan goes one further.

'Cody's training matches wouldn't hold a candle to the matches we had,' he asserts, no doubt in his mind.

★ ★ ★ ★ ★

Ger Hegarty

I

GER HEGARTY COULD only watch on from afar as Tom Ryan doggedly sought to instil a fresh determination and belief in a Limerick team that had endured a decade with precious little to get excited about. A dedicated trainer 12 months of the year, Hegarty's genuine enjoyment of physical activity only made his absence through injury all the more frustrating.

Immobility, or even impaired mobility, didn't come natural to him at all. 'I used to train every single day,' he recalls of his preferred routine. 'Whether it was physical training or skills training, I trained every day. I was just one of those freaks who loved even training on my own or with my brothers. A pure love for the game.' Playing inter-county hurling for Limerick was not something Hegarty ever took for granted. All that hard work was in aid of a singular goal: to win.

'I had this whole thing I used to do, and my parents would be giving out to me,' he explains. 'I used to do a training session on January 1 every year. It was a cyclical thing for me. The clock had turned to a new year, and this was a blank page. There were no league champions, no Munster champions, and no All-Ireland champions. Here was a new year and I was going to have a cut off it.' As he quickly identifies in hindsight, 'being a Limerick hurler took up a huge amount of my time.'

Rehabilitation was not his idea of using this time effectively. Nevertheless, in the year before Ryan's arrival it was all that he could do to help himself along. 'They sent me to Dr Fionan O'Carroll in Tralee,' Hegarty recalls, the ACL injury he'd sustained not entirely uncommon. 'He told me, "Your injury is the same as Pat Spillane's," before referring me to a surgeon in Dublin who carried out the procedure."'

The best treatment available to him in the country, it was a serious ordeal all the same in 1993. 'The operation now is key-hole surgery and non-invasive. The surgeon did a brilliant job for me, but there was a lot of cutting involved.' Aware that he faced a frustrating number of months waiting to return to the field, Hegarty set about making his life off it that bit more comfortable. 'I was in St Michael's Hospital in Dublin after my operation lying back on the bed,' he remembers, the uncomfortable uncertainty of when he would return settling in. 'So, I said to myself, *Right, I'm going to buy a house, settle down and get married.* And that is exactly what I did within the next couple of months. Just like that.'

The arrival of the married couple's first child Gearoid would come the following year, as Hegarty made a tentative return to hurling. By April 1994 he had finally made his senior comeback in a challenge game against Offaly. Although there would be another injury scare for him in the six or so weeks left before Limerick faced Cork in the Munster Senior Championship, Hegarty was named in the starting XV for his competitive return. It was as well. Before even that Munster final defeat in 1992, Hegarty had faced some of his sternest challenges taking on Cork hurlers.

II

LIMERICK'S ALL-IRELAND WINNING minor team of 1984 was inextricably linked to the Dr Harty Cup team of CBS Sexton Street. One of 11 players who featured on both panels, Hegarty's firm belief that senior success with Limerick was always within reach stemmed from these formative years. After all, a strong foundation in schools hurling had propelled the county forward not that long beforehand.

'What happened Limerick hurling in the 1970s was thanks to the secondary schools,' Éamonn Cregan explains, a past pupil of Sexton Street from an earlier generation. 'We won the Harty Cup in 1964 and that was the first time in 32 years. The school won it consecutively four times in total then.' CBS Sexton Street had lost the next four finals they featured in after the last of those wins in 1967.

By the time Hegarty and his teammates had a shot at ending that run in the early months of 1984, they had the bulk of a Limerick team that would beat Kilkenny in the All-Ireland minor final come September. 'I was playing great stuff at the time,' Hegarty remembers, 'I'd had a great colleges campaign right up to the final.' It was then that he was introduced to St Finbarr's of Cork and DJ Kiely.

A physically imposing player for schools hurling, Hegarty had had the run of midfield up to their meeting with Finbarr's in the 1984 Harty Cup final. 'This guy ran up to mark me… DJ Kiely,' he recalls, feeling completely unconcerned. 'I'd say he was probably up to my shoulder, and I was thinking to myself, *I'm going to go to town on this guy today.*'

Things didn't pan out that way, however. 'I ended up getting one puck of the ball and he gave one of the best exhibitions I've seen. In all of the games I've played in my career, I got one puck of the ball in that whole game.' Fortunately, this wasn't a one-man team Hegarty was on and though Finbarr's had put on a bit of a show, the Sexton Street lads had salvaged a draw.

'I remember Willie Moore, our manager and a former Limerick hurler, told us in the dressing-room afterwards,' Hegarty remembers, '"You have got a draw that you did not deserve but we will rectify this next weekend, and there will be a one hundred percent improvement." And there was.' Familiar now with the player he was up against in the replayed final, Hegarty didn't dare underestimate DJ Kiely again.

'Yeah, this time I was one hundred percent better,' he insists. 'I got two pucks of the ball! DJ gave me the mother and father of a beating over two Harty Cup finals, like I've never had before or since.' Another chastening experience, it was a fifth consecutive final defeat for Limerick CBS.

There would be some joy for Hegarty and his teammates when Limerick later knocked Kiely's Cork minors out of Munster in early May. Nevertheless, if he was at all ever tempted to take his hurling ability for granted beforehand, Ger Hegarty had learned a lesson he would never forget.

★ ★ ★ ★ ★

Tom Ryan

TOM RYAN WAS 'no social animal' by his own admission.

The idea of forging personal relationships with his players held no appeal for him. 'I don't think I ever phoned a player when I was manager... or that a player ever phoned me,' he asserts; Charles Hanley left to deal exclusively with communications. A lifelong Pioneer, he had no great reason to visit many pubs. 'You're considered an odd ball,' he suggests, the Irish tendency to consider non-drinkers as somehow suspicious something he is acutely aware of. The manager of a factory on Thomas Street in Limerick city by day, Ryan's professional life made demands on his time that required a strict demarcation between it and his inter-county responsibilities.

Distant to the point of indifferent about players' personal lives, he zealously stressed the importance of impartiality. For the period of time that they could be called his players, there would need to be some kind of a significant bond there, nevertheless. 'I brought them out into the middle of the pitch in the Gaelic Grounds,' he recalls of an early encounter, 'and I told them, "I can't guarantee that we'll win a match, but everyone sitting here tonight is of equal importance." I hated people having favourites.'

Mark Foley's unforeseen rise into the senior panel (and his ability to stay there) owed much to Ryan's philosophy of fairness. 'After a week or two training,' Foley remembers, 'Tom pulled me aside. "You're in here because you're good enough. Don't think you're here to make up the numbers."' Although his championship debut would not arrive until 1995, the Adare native was made to feel a part of things from the very beginning.

'Even though he was trying to win an All-Ireland with Limerick at that stage,' Foley explains, 'Tom was determined to help every individual player in what they could do to improve.'

Despite this determination to nurture players, however, Ryan remained most comfortable at a remove. 'I wasn't there to be loved. I didn't give a damn what they thought of me.' A master motivator from his days with Ballybrown, he was as happy if his players hurled well only out of a desire to spite him.

'Not one of my players ever invited me to their wedding,' he remarks, no ounce of regret or sadness in his voice. 'I'd be under no illusions what they thought of me.'

Married a few years after Ryan had drafted him into the Limerick panel, Foley is not convinced it was a lack of fondness for their manager that resulted in players often mirroring Ryan's indifference back to him.

'All I can say is that if I thought Tom Ryan would've enjoyed one second of being at my wedding,' he says with a laugh, 'I would have asked him.

Yes, he was the boss, but there was a huge respect there.

'He wanted to do everything that was possible to win for Limerick. You have to respect that.'

After all, at the root of everything for Tom Ryan was Limerick.

Perhaps he did not want the job when his name was put forward, but Ryan scarcely seems a man who will do what he does not want to do. The 'F**k You' he reserved for the county board would only have carried him so far. Whatever reluctance did exist disappeared.

Once in the door, it was his top priority to win an All-Ireland. Or second, maybe! 'You represent Limerick when you put on that jersey,' he states, the importance of that detail something he carried from his own playing days.

'I wanted us all to represent Limerick accordingly. I insisted on that first and foremost.'

*Éamonn Cregan lines up another point against Galway
in the All-Ireland semi-final in 1981.*

CHAPTER ★ FOUR

ÉAMONN CREGAN

Éamonn Cregan

I

THERE WAS A timelessness to Tom Ryan's core principle for his players. Little room for confusion was allowed: you were expected to treat your position as a representative of Limerick seriously. Train hard, play hard… and don't embarrass yourselves, the team, or the county. It was as pertinent in the 1990s as it had been for any team of Limerick hurlers up to that point and any group beyond.

And yet, even the simplest instructions will struggle to hold meaning if nobody is there to receive them. 'I went out training with the senior panel in 1965 before we played Waterford in a Munster quarter-final,' Éamonn Cregan recalls, the summer he celebrated his 20th birthday.

'Do you know how many people were training?

'We had four… *four* players. And we only trained for two weeks.'

It had been nine years since Limerick last contested a Munster final then, and a full decade since the team of 1955 had actually conquered the province. Before

Cregan and a crop of other promising young players brought the county back to hurling's top table in the 1970s, Limerick had already spent a good deal of time wandering through the wilderness. As Cregan remembers it still, 'This was Limerick hurling at its lowest ebb.'

The promise of this new generation was legitimate, nevertheless. Unfortunately, it would not be realised in time for Limerick's Munster Championship opener in early June 1965. *Bernie Hartigan [and] Éamonn Cregan, each produced brilliant patches,* the *Irish Press* explained, two alumni of Limerick CBS Sexton Street starting that day at the Cork Athletic Grounds, *but lacked the constructive approach of their Waterford counterparts.* Partnered together in midfield, Hartigan and Cregan, a half-forward and half-back respectively when Limerick would go on to win the All-Ireland final eight years later, were instrumental in Limerick's strong start to the game. *[Hartigan] and Cregan were so completely in command of midfield through the opening quarter that the Limerick forwards had a constant supply of ball,* the report continued, *which they used to such reasonably good effect that they led by 1-3 to nil after 16 minutes.* What's more, both young men proved themselves capable of contributing scores also.

Having *a whale of a game at centre-field* as the *Southern Star* put it, Hartigan contributed 0-2 of Limerick's 2-9. Meanwhile, with Limerick trailing by a point, Cregan pounced on an unlikely opportunity for a goal. *When [Limerick] were awarded a 21 the equaliser seemed certain,* the same report read, *but Cregan caught the defence napping with a quick shot to the net.* In addition to his own pair of points, the two midfielders contributed 1-4 of Limerick's tally. And yet, it would not be enough; a late rally by Waterford deciding the game in their favour.

For the Limerick senior hurling team, an early exit from the championship was not necessarily shocking at this moment in time. For the likes of Cregan and Hartigan, coming as they were from an all-conquering colleges career, it was not easily shaken off.

It is just as well then that they did not have to contend with the modern resistance to dual players, lest they felt a choice needed to be made. In the same summer that Limerick's hurlers came undone against Waterford, the county's footballers reached their first provincial decider in a little over 30 years. *Lowly Limerick, whose name has not appeared on the championship finalists' role since 1887, confounded the critics by scoring a decisive victory over Cork in the Munster Senior Football semi-final at Fitzgerald Stadium last Sunday,* the *Southern Star* reported under the unflinching headline: **Spiritless Cork Seniors Plumb Lowest Depths**. Two weeks after the hurlers had come predictably undone, Cregan and Hartigan found themselves in the middle of a most unexpected Limerick GAA success story.

Against the most dispiriting odds, the county's footballers overcame both Waterford and Cork to reach the 1965 Munster football final; a competition not won by the county since the final years of the 19th century. Although they would ultimately fall short, as Kerry progressed to win the county's eighth successive Munster Championship, Cregan and Hartigan, notably impressive as hurlers, nevertheless showed themselves quite capable of taking on the country's very best in gaelic football too. *Limerick's creditable performance in this final gives hopes for a brighter future for Munster football,* the *Kerryman* suggested in the aftermath of Kerry's 2-16 to 2-7 victory.

Alternately knocked out by Cork, Kerry, Tipperary and Clare across the next four championship summers, one could argue that the standard across the board did indeed improve. All the same, Limerick would not reach another Munster football decider until 1991. Even at its lowest ebb, hurling for Limerick retained a majesty that Éamonn Cregan could not easily disregard.

II
1932 Thomond Feis hurling final
Limerick 2-6 Clare 2-4

Hurling which can only be described as hectic, followed, Ned Cregan, in the Limerick back division, putting paid to a breathless Clare attack. Then Limerick moved up field, the ball travelling from wing to wing, and Timmy Ryan capped the attack with a point... Following a hold-up due to an injury to one of the players, Cregan, with hurley high up in the air, stopped a pile driver from the Clare right-wing. Gibbons – playing a stalwart game throughout – relieved the home county's lines immediately afterwards and, the ball going to the Limerick right, P. Clohessy relived and slammed it home for the sixth point.

– Limerick Leader, June 18, 1932

Ned's father played football in the years when the GAA was only establishing itself, but it was hurling which held the stage in the stirring years of Ned's upbringing. A big mistake

that must surely have been regretted in after years was the complete concentration then in Monegay on the senior side, and there were no organised games for the youngsters. Ned, consequently, had to paddle his own canoe in learning the rudiments of the game.
– Limerick Leader, September 2, 1972

III

A STURDY HURLER with a rugged style, one columnist named 'Green Flag' described Éamonn Cregan's father in the early 1930s. Upon Ned's passing in August 1972, a different columnist, 'Caman', explored the capabilities of that ruggedness in the *Limerick Leader*. *He shone as one of the best right full-backs*, it was written, *wonderfully clever in anticipation, able to use both hands dexterously, and with fine length in his rapid clearances*. An All-Ireland winner in 1934, Ned Cregan efficiently foiled the kind of attacking hurlers his son Éamonn later became.

As his obituary made clear, however, Ned, like his son after him, experienced a *do it yourself* introduction to hurling. The reverberation of Limerick's success throughout the 1930s was not readily apparent around the city when Éamonn was growing up there. 'I was born in 1945 and up until '57 we never even knew of what a GAA club was,' he explains, hurling as he first understood it an unstructured pastime that required keen young players such as himself to shape it as they saw fit. Had his own father not played in the last successful Limerick team alongside the likes of Mick Mackey, dreams of winning an All-Ireland for his county might not have come so readily to the young boy.

Neither one of his parents had been born in Limerick city. Ned was from the parish of Monegay to the west, while his wife – Éamonn's mother – Hannie had come down from Sligo. It was the family business that resulted in Cregan growing up a 'townie'. Hanratty's Hotel on Glentworth Street belonged to his mother, and it was in its vicinity that he grew up. In amongst the surrounding laneways, this was also where he learned to hurl.

More often than not accompanied by his brother Michael, a future Limerick hurler himself and the team's trainer during the 1973 All-Ireland-winning campaign, they created worlds of their own in small spaces. 'There was a lane with two walls about 10 feet apart,' he recalls. 'We hurled up and down the lane and we played "10 goals in". I often wonder now when I see fellas playing around in a field pucking the ball to each other, there's no purpose in what they're doing. They would be better off putting down two goals.'

When the family later left the city for Castletroy in 1957, 'Mac's field' replaced the laneways. 'There were two electrical poles in it about 80 yards apart,' he explains, 'and we used to still play "10 goals in"… but 80 yards apart.' No small distance for a pair of young boys, Cregan believes the greater distance between them only served to enhance their ball-striking skills. 'You might think from that distance you'd never score 10 goals, but Michael always scored 10 goals on me. The ball would hop or bounce to the right.

'Every time we played, he beat me.'

The People's Park had offered children in the city some chance to play on grass, while the Cregan boys had gained some experience of organised games of hurling and gaelic football at primary school in The Model. It wasn't the GAA alone that had a monopoly on their interest growing up, however. Rugby had its appeal, but Cregan found the rules unnecessarily complex and the inherent dangers of actually playing the game off-putting.

Soccer, on the other hand. 'There was the "Ban" then but that didn't mean anything to us,' he recalls, the GAA's infamous Rule 27 prohibiting members from playing or watching foreign games. Kicking a ball around in what was then known as the 'Bombin' field' in Limerick city, they caught the eye of a local soccer aficionado Jack Tuohy. 'He asked us if we would play for Reds United, but sure we had to tell him no because our father would kill us. That was on a Tuesday… but by the Friday evening Michael came to me and asked if he could have the lend of my boots.'

Curious as to what his brother might be up to, he soon found out. 'He told me that he was off to play soccer for Ballynanty Rovers on the Saturday,' he remembers, handing over his boots and opting to come along for a look himself. 'In the end Ballynanty only had 10 players so they asked me if I'd play as the outside-right… the right-winger now. I'd say within 24 hours our father had heard about it and he'd kicked us around the room for playing soccer. That was our first proper experience of the infamous ban anyway.'

It wasn't until they heard a rumour about some trial that was taking place at the 'Bombin' Field' that playing gaelic games for a team really took hold. 'It was a trial match for a club by the name of Claughaun,' he explains, that they were looking to field an under-16s team no deterrent for the 11-year-old Éamonn and his 12-year-old brother.

'I was the last player to be picked because I was so small, and they put me in goals.' It hardly dampened his enthusiasm, however. Two of about 30 eager young players to have turned up. Dermot Kelly, a modern hero of the Limerick senior hurling team was also present. The scorer of a remarkable 1-12 in the victorious 1955 Munster final, here was one of the famous 'Mackey Greyhounds' in the flesh.

'It went from there anyway... and my first match playing for Claughaun was as a goalkeeper,' he remembers. 'We went and won the county championship in the end because the club had gotten so many players from that trial.'

At both hurling and gaelic football, the diminutive Éamonn excelled. He didn't stay small for long, however. Nor would he remain a goalkeeper.

★ ★ ★ ★ ★

Stephen Lucey

IT WAS ALMOST 25 years after Dermot Kelly's Munster final heroics that Stephen Lucey was born. Yet, when the main protagonist in such a memorable game happens to be your uncle, you tend to hear about it from time to time.

A strong sporting link on his mother's side, there was no shortage of activity on the Lucey side of Stephen's family either. Born a few years earlier than Éamonn and Michael Cregan down in Cork, Stephen's father, Mick had his own run-ins with the GAA's 'Ban'. Unlike the two lads in Limerick indulging an interest in soccer though, it was hurling that he was trying to sneak in a game of undetected.

'He would have to play under an alias,' Stephen recalls his father explaining to him... "John Murphy" is what he called himself. He was telling me once about being recognised and having to edge up toward the corner... and just disappearing off into the crowd. Crazy stuff.' It was at rugby that he truly excelled, however. Fifteen years before Munster famously defeated New Zealand at Thomond Park, the Irish province came up short on a score-line of 6-3. Starting that day on the wing and earning his 10th cap for Munster was none other than Mick Lucey from Cork.

A speedy opportunist who by sheer opportunity and drive often works out his own chances, read the description of Stephen's father in the match programme that day. On a medical path that his son would follow after him, it was only atrocious bad luck that kept Mick Lucey from representing his country. 'He got picked to play for Ireland in what was then the Five Nations,' Stephen explains, 'but he broke his shoulder and missed it.'

Back for another crack the following year, Mick Lucey arrived in Dublin to participate in a trial match that would decide the Irish team for the tournament. 'Dad was staying in the Shelbourne Hotel with Tom Kiernan,' he notes, another Munster player from Cork who would amass 59 international caps. 'They opened up the curtains the morning of the trial and it was snowing. So, the trial was cancelled, and the organisers just went with the squad from the previous year again.'

The reality of being a young doctor frequently on the move brought the curtain down on Mick Lucey's rugby ambition. That being said, serving as the team medic for Limerick's gaelic footballers (and the hurlers, occasionally) kept him in the thick of things. 'Dad covered for Dr Dave Boylan with the hurlers for a pitch opening in Adare,' Stephen remembers being told by Ciaran Carey.

'They were standing on the sideline and the action was kind of boiling over. Didn't the players spill over… then crash into dad and break his nose! So, he was there lying on the ground with blood pumping out of him and Ciaran is just standing there laughing. "Jesus, who is going to look after you now?!"'

★ ★ ★ ★ ★

Éamonn Cregan

I

ÉAMONN CREGAN DIDN'T learn the rights and wrongs of how to prepare for hurling matches in any inter-county set-up. Two Christian brothers at CBS Sexton Street – Br Burke from Clonmel, and Br Hennessy from Waterford – were instrumental in grounding his generation of promising young hurlers in this best practice. 'When we were preparing for Harty Cup matches in Sexton Street,' he explains, 'we had proper collective training.'

A school devoted to hurling, the pair of trainers found a golden generation to work with in the mid-1960s. *Seamus Shinners, in goal, and Noel O'Gorman, full-back, are the foundations of a tough and capable defence,* the *Nenagh Guardian* proclaimed in the build-up to the 1964 Dr Harty Cup final between Limerick CBS and St Flannan's College of Clare. *Paddy Doherty is a good support for Cregan on the halfway and in a clever forward division Brian Cobbe, Pat Nash, Eamon Grimes and Tom Clohessy (a son of Paddy Clohessy, who starred for Limerick in the '30s) are the stars.*

Thirty-two years since a Limerick school had last won the competition, there was no shortage of excitement surrounding the final. Boasting an official attendance of 11,000 at the Gaelic Grounds, the *Limerick Leader* assured readers that an inestimable number of additional spectators had made their way in without going through the turnstiles. *The entire population of the city was out to watch Limerick,* as the *Irish Examiner* only half-jokingly put it. Indeed, so all-encompassing was the surrounding interest that the powers that be within the school opted to bus the players out of the city before it was time to return for the match itself.

And yet, as the Limerick school proceeded to hit 13 first-half wides, the thousands gathered may have had cause to revisit their optimism.

Of course, no small amount of what made Limerick CBS such an exciting team to watch came down to how they played. They had already scored an incredible 20 goals across the three games it had taken them to qualify for the Harty Cup final, and six more would follow against Flannan's. *Limerick threatened to run riot in that fifteen minute period after the break,* the *Irish Examiner* explained, the Limerick school leading by six points at half-time despite the wides. *When fed by the immaculate Eamonn Cregan, they were often in attack. Brian Cobbe in the left corner at last found his form and this pair were mainly the cause of boosting Limerick to 4-8 against 1-6.* Comfortable winners in the end, it was the beginning of a glorious run in the competition for Limerick CBS.

In 1965, it was Eamonn Grimes who shone brightest winning Man of the Match as the school retained their Harty Cup crown. In 1966 and '67, with their legendary trainer Br Burke gone owing to a transfer to Dublin, the competition was won twice more as the likes of Pat Hartigan and Sean Foley came to the fore. Winners all with Limerick in 1973, they were schooled in success at Sexton Street.

Before Éamonn Cregan finished up his secondary education, however, there was still the small matter of an All-Ireland schools final to contest in April 1964. As the *Sunday Independent* wonderfully captured it, this decider was not without controversy (before any ball was even thrown in):

Limerick CBS are displeased that they must come to Croke Park today for the Colleges' hurling final showdown with St Peter's, Wexford – and there is good cause for their displeasure. For first the game was for Thurles and then, without as much as a by-your-leave, it was switched to Headquarters. Ordinarily, this would be no handicap, but consider that when they lineout today, it will be before a king-size crowd, the vast majority of which will be howling themselves hoarse for St Peter's!

Indeed, the clash with Leinster's leading school was scheduled as the curtain-raiser for Wexford's National Hurling League semi-final against Cork.

And yet, all confidence was not lost. *But if they can take this loaded-dice in their stride,* the same column read, *the talented Shannonside squad have the equipment to succeed. In the young Eamonn Cregan, their captain, they have a top-rate leader, cool, intelligent and wonderfully versatile... [while] Eamonn Grimes, Paddy Nash and Brian Cobbe [are] Limerick minors, not new to the Headquarters sod.* In front of an estimated 26,000 spectators, the Limerick school ultimately overcame whatever distraction the partisan crowd may have created and defeated their Wexford counterparts by 6-7 to 4-5.

Widely celebrated as Limerick hurling's finest hour since the county's senior All-Ireland success of 1940, a civic reception followed along with dreams of what this success may mean in the years that followed. If the Liam McCarthy Cup would soon follow this arrival of the Dr Croke Cup, the only thing that seemed certain then was that Éamonn Cregan would be involved. *One lithe Limerick lad stood out above all in last season's Colleges campaign,* wrote Peadar O'Brien in his *Irish Press* review of the year's hurling. *That one Limerick lad was fair haired Éamonn Cregan, who with the power of a Mackey, the elegance of a Jimmy Doyle, and authority of a born hurler, steered his school, Limerick CBS, not only to the Munster Colleges Cup title, but also to an All-Ireland triumph as well. It was Limerick's first success in the All-Ireland championship, and Cregan's hurling feats are still being spoken of down South.*

II

AS ONE MIGHT have expected, success at schools level coincided with an upturn in form for the underage county set-up in Limerick as well. Although, as Cregan remembers now, Limerick's good fortune arrived almost in spite of the county board's lacklustre efforts. Before he captained his school to provincial and All-Ireland success in 1964, Cregan was elected captain of the Limerick minor team that reached an All-Ireland final in the summer of 1963.

Fittingly, they would play Wexford in the decider; a county similarly feeling the benefit of St Peter's imminent success in the Leinster Schools Championship. *The standard of hurling was poor, marking was loose on both sides, there were far too many misses and mistimed pucks, and the only factor which kept interest alive was the closeness of the scoring in the first fifty minutes,* wrote O'Brien of Limerick's eventual defeat to Wexford. Undoubtedly disappointed, Cregan could not help but wonder how they had made it that far in the first place.

Schooled in the necessity of good preparation in Sexton Street, the inter-county minor set-up was generally underwhelming. 'We came into the Gaelic Grounds two weeks before the Munster minor final,' Cregan remembers; Tipperary all that stood between Limerick and only the county's third triumph at this level. 'There were about six sliotars thrown down in front of us... "Puck around", we were told.'

A management team made up of a few selectors and no clear leader, the players themselves were better versed in how a modern team ought to be preparing. Indeed, as the *Limerick Leader* described things the morning after Limerick's defeat of Tipperary in the provincial decider, individual praise was reserved for the *great leadership of Éamonn Cregan.* One of the country's best young hurlers, it was dispiriting for Cregan that a county set-up should come with such frustrations. Furthermore, although the demands put upon county minors then are incomparable with modern standards, representing Limerick still required a certain degree of commitment from players.

A few years after the Cregan family had left Limerick city for Castletroy, it was around a six-mile trip back toward the Gaelic Grounds for one of those training sessions. Getting a lift was out of the question, but Éamonn considered himself fortunate enough that he didn't have to walk it.

'I had a bicycle,' he explains, albeit with a slight caveat, 'a boys bicycle really.'

Manageable for a young man who had celebrated his 18th birthday between Limerick's quarter-final and semi-final, he contrived to make things harder for himself by throwing one of his teammates into the mix.

'I used to collect Pa O'Brien from his house on the way,' he recalls, his friend and Limerick teammate living along the Dublin Road. 'He'd get up on the bar of the bike and I'd give him a lift into the Gaelic Grounds. When training was over then it was up on the bike and home again.'

For two teammates, it was certainly a unique way of building comradeship. As Cregan distinctly remembers though, it wasn't always a favour he provided in aid of a common goal. 'Pa played for St Patrick's and I was obviously playing for Claughaun,' he explains, the two clubs pitted against one another in a club final on one occasion. 'I collected him from his house as usual anyway and gave him a lift over to the Gaelic Grounds. Well, they beat the shite out of us… and I still had to give him a lift home on the bar of the bike!'

To whatever extent 1963 was a landmark year, provincial success and the experience of an All-Ireland minor final failed to assuage Cregan's concerns about the county's future. 'There was a feeling among younger people that the county board just wasn't interested even in winning championships,' he believes, 'or that it was too costly to prepare properly. When Mick Mackey took over the senior team in 1955 it gave the thing a bit of impetus and glamour, but even they were beaten in the end.'

After his own colleges success and the success he watched continue in his absence, Cregan unquestionably knew that Limerick had hurlers who could compete with the country's best. And yet, beyond the confines of one school in the city, he could see no cohesive plan or vision whereby this progress could be harnessed and brought county-wide.

In time, success and medals would arrive. The emergence of an effective strategy was still decades off, however.

The Limerick team which defeated Kilkenny in the
All-Ireland final in 1973.

CHAPTER ★ FIVE
JOE MCGRATH

Joe McGrath

I

An All-Ireland championship title for both Limerick hurlers and footballers within five years a pipe-dream? To most people it sounds like it. But to team-trainer Down-born Joe McGrath it's within their capabilities if he gets the co-operation from the players and officials. Joe, a native of the Downpatrick area of Co. Down, is at present General Manager of the Thomond Cabinet Factory, Ennis Road, Limerick. He came to Limerick early [last] year and was immediately approached by Claughaun to join their club. He enjoyed the atmosphere within the club and soon assumed the position of team trainer. The senior footballers, under his supervision, won the County Championship, and later he was appointed trainer of the Limerick senior hurlers and footballers. The teams have enjoyed much success since Joe took over in charge of the panel's fitness.

– Limerick Leader, January 3, 1970

II

THE EVENTUAL UNDOING of Joe McGrath has a certain familiarity to it. As Noel Drumgoole found out in 1986, and Phil Bennis seven years after that, nothing good comes from losing to Clare in the Munster Championship. For Drumgoole and Bennis, defeat in Ennis was the final straw and swiftly saw their managerial tenures come to an end.

Even after the back door allowed counties a second chance after provincial defeat, Joe McKenna, John Allen and TJ Ryan all similarly ceased to be Limerick manager directly after losing to the Banner. It was following Limerick's 1972 defeat in Cusack Park that McGrath was deemed dispensable. Of course, what he didn't share in common with those who would later fall in these circumstances was his title.

Drumgoole, Bennis, McKenna, Allen and Ryan were all Limerick hurling managers. McGrath was the physical trainer. 'My belief is that Joe forgot his job was trainer,' Éamonn Cregan suggests, the circumstances surrounding his departure not necessarily linked to his conditioning of the Limerick hurlers.

The concept of a singularly authoritative manager was still a few years off in Limerick by the early 1970s. To the chagrin of those who had to get on with the actual business of winning hurling matches, the committee was still king. Despite being neither manager nor selector, McGrath had strong thoughts on the issue. *'There should be a far greater streamlining of authority in decision making drawn up,'* the *Limerick Leader* reported him saying less than two months after the Limerick defeat to Clare in 1972.

'The farcical situation and system which allows for a "conclave" of selectors to be needed is outdated and should be got rid of. By the time the selectors get together, discuss the particular item, reveal their findings to the manager who in turn must convey to the player involved, a match could be won and lost… and has been in fact.'

A 3-11 to 2-10 result in Clare's favour, their undoing of Limerick was praised as the county's *greatest hour in many years… and something approaching a miracle* in one post-match report. Dogged by their own off-field controversies in the build up to the game, Clare's attacking approach put their opponents on the back foot, nevertheless. *In truth, Limerick were out-hurling, outmanoeuvred and unsettled from an early stage in the game,* the same *Irish Examiner* report read, *and they never played with the skill and confidence which could be expected of them.* Highlighting the urgency of McGrath's post-match concerns, it continued, *Undoubtedly, Clare's sensational start to the game went a long way towards deciding the issue... Limerick looked disorganised and dejected at the end of the first quarter.*

If those charged with managing the team had to speak over and back between one another before a decision could be made, it is unsurprising that guidance may have been missing when the team needed it most. Whatever sense McGrath's words held, however, within a month of his questioning the system, he had been notified by a letter in the post that his services were no longer required by Limerick.

A physical trainer who spoke above his station, or a pernicious county board that did not appreciate being publicly challenged, Joe McGrath's story tells us practically all we need to know about the proclivity for background senseless bickering that dogged Limerick hurling for so long.

III

HE WAS ONLY three years into a five-year-plan when Limerick got rid of him. Although nearly three decades had passed since Mick Mackey and his men had last won an All-Ireland, McGrath, a Co. Down native with minimal hurling experience to speak of, talked a good game. '*I made it quite clear that if I received the support I needed from the players and officials,*' he explained in that contentious *Limerick Leader* interview that would be his undoing, '*there was no reason why we should not lift the major trophies within any stipulated period.*'

Unquestionably well-versed in the modern trends of GAA coaching, any lack of specific hurling knowledge did not slow him down. As he put it himself, '*The majority of the panel could hurl extremely well anyway, the plan was to get them to do it faster and more often.*' For this, McGrath would ensure that the Limerick hurlers were physically fit and psychologically ready.

Indeed, anyone who has spent any time at all being coached by McGrath will primarily commend him for his ability to get players in the right frame of mind. 'He would have said himself that he didn't know a great deal about hurling,' the former Limerick hurler Bernie Hartigan explains, a close friend of McGrath's, 'but he was a great motivator. By far the best motivator I've ever seen.'

Éamonn Cregan can confirm, 'Joe could motivate you to climb up a wall after a fly'. In later years when he worked with Cork's senior footballers, Tadhg Murphy, scorer of a famous goal in the 1983 Munster final defeat of Kerry, attests to McGrath's undimmed enthusiasm. 'Joe was Mr. Positive,' he explains. 'He was brought in really to give us a gee-up, I think... to motivate us and give us something different. His biggest strength was to be able to get the very best out of fellas.'

This he achieved through a combination of words and actions. *'The County Board should be run on the same lines as a business concern,'* McGrath believed, it being his contention that Limerick's county board would have gone to the wall long ago. McGrath understood that any business should treat its primary assets with the greatest amount of care. In Limerick, as Cregan's recollection of his inter-county years prior to McGrath's arrival demonstrates, the players were treated with anything but such respect.

With – and often without – approval from above, McGrath went about trying to make things better for these players. As became a feature for seemingly every team he trained, he liked to ensure that there would be no scrimping when it came to the supply of balls. Be it hurlers or gaelic footballers, the sufficient provision of balls at training was something nobody spoken to for this book has forgotten about McGrath.

'We went out onto the pitch that first night and there were 30 footballs out there,' the former Cork footballer Denis 'Dinny' Allen recalls. 'We were all gaping at him because up until then we would only get around six footballs to play with and the county board were afraid of their lives that we might lose a few.'

Be it county or club, the demands put upon the administrators remained the same.

'When he came to Blackrock, he asked for 24 sliotars for training,' Ray Cummins explains. 'This is when we were lucky enough to have two or three... and he just sent shockwaves through the committee.' It had been the same story at Limerick in 1969.

While Bernie Hartigan cannot but commend McGrath for making greater demands of everyone involved in the inter-county set-up, he appreciates that some resistance was inevitable. 'He was rightly demanding,' the Old Christians clubman believes, 'but he was rubbing the county board up the wrong way... even if he had the best of intentions.'

IV

Dear Sir – At a meeting of the Limerick Hurling Club in Chicago held on August 30th, 1972, with approximately fifty members present, every member had in his possession a Limerick Leader *sporting the interview Cormac Liddy had with trainer Joe McGrath. The members praised the trainer for the fine job he is doing for Limerick hurling and agreed with him thoroughly on the points he made. They backed him 100% when he said a County Board should be run the same as a business and was convinced that the man who should make the decisions during matches should be the trainer – a man who knows what his players are capable of doing. We, as members of the Limerick Club and as officers, would like to make this final point: Why not give the power to a man who wants to bring hurling back to its best in Limerick? Why not give the wheel to the trainer, Joe McGrath?*

– Morty Scanlon, *Limerick Leader*, September 9, 1972

V

THE FIRST TANGIBLE success associated with McGrath's involvement came as Limerick won the National Hurling League in 1971. Beaten finalists the year before, Limerick saw off Tipperary in the final and provided McGrath's five-year-plan with one of the trophies it had promised.

Widely felt to be Tipperary's final to lose, there was no small sense of excitement in the local media that Limerick had managed to stick one in the eye of those who had written them off. *Those know-all Dublin Gaelic reporters – with one exception – got a rare kick in the teeth by the Limerick hurling team which rattled, bustled, but most important of all, out-hurled a highly rated Tipperary team to the National Hurling League title for the first time in 24 years,* the *Limerick Leader* proclaimed the morning after Limerick's 3-12 to 3-11 victory at the Cork Athletic Grounds. The game itself was played at a frenzied pace, in the balance until a late Richie Bennis free ensured victory for Limerick.

One of those among the Dublin media who had written Limerick off, perhaps, J. D. Hickey was quick to commend the magnanimity of the county's supporters gathered in Cork. *Limerick people, to their credit, did not strut,* he wrote, *they danced with pleasure when it was all over, and their exultation is understandable.*

Indeed, it was not the Limerick people alone who were delighted. This victory was a definite feather in Joe McGrath's cap.

Emboldened, perhaps, by the realisation of his ambitious talk, McGrath watched Limerick run the eventual All-Ireland winners Tipperary to within a point in the Munster final that followed that summer, before winning the now defunct Oireachtas Cup later that year. The Liam MacCarthy Cup may yet have remained elusive, but Limerick were unquestionably headed in the right direction.

They made it back to the National League final again in 1972, but were beaten by Cork. In the Munster Championship, a date with Clare in Ennis awaited them. 'I'd never played a Munster Championship match in Ennis before that,' Hartigan recalls, the venue only one bone of contention that Limerick had in the aftermath of the defeat that followed. (Limerick had faced Clare on four occasions (including one replay) in the decade up to that Munster Championship match in 1972. While the first three of those games had taken place in Nenagh (1964) and Thurles (1967, 1970), the replayed game in 1970 took place in Limerick's Gaelic Grounds.

The 1972 meeting of Limerick and Clare was the next match in that sequence. *The selectors were doing a lot of messing around with the team at that time*, another former Limerick hurler, Mickey Graham explained in *Unlimited Heartbreak*. Indeed, between the starting XV who were defeated by Cork in the 1972 league final, and those who lined out against Clare a little under two months later, six changes were made. 'Senseless changes,' as Hartigan describes them.

The situation was further clouded by the fact that only five players started the Clare game in the same position they had started against Cork. Another lasting image of the ill-fated match was the Limerick selector Rory Kiely making his way onto the pitch to take Éamonn Grimes out of the game. The man who would finally lift the Liam MacCarthy Cup for Limerick about 14 months later, Grimes refused to leave the field of play.

'It looked very bad,' Kiely subsequently claimed, but the player's frustration seemed closer to that which a powerless Joe McGrath felt looking on as Limerick suffered a shocking setback. As 1973 would demonstrate, this wasn't the end for Limerick. McGrath had reason to wonder why it should be the end for him, though.

The man charged with preparing Limerick's hurlers in training, McGrath had no say in team selection. Before he opted to publicly air his grievances with the whole operation weeks after the Clare defeat, it seemed unlikely that he would have borne the brunt of the fallout if he had kept quiet. 'There was a postmortem at the next county board meeting,' Kiely recalled. 'Joe McGrath used to speak a lot to the press at the time, and Matt Connell, who was chairman of the city board said, "The trainer said before the match that Limerick had a psychological advantage. I don't know what a psychological advantage is but coming home from the match they didn't have a hurling advantage anyway".'

After suggesting that a county board ought to be run like a business and critiquing the convoluted management set-up, McGrath had had no issue speaking at length about the psychological barriers holding Limerick hurling back. In an era when the procurement of anything more than five or six sliotars at training was regarded as revolutionary, it is little surprise that this kind of talk would be used against him when things went wrong. *'I remember (a County Board) official saying to me, "what went wrong, Joe?',"* McGrath recalled of a conversation he had following the team's league final defeat in 1970. *'I told him that as far as I was concerned it was psychological immaturity on the part of Management and Players.'*

He went on, *'I told him there were several things I couldn't understand about the set-up in Limerick. One was why could Limerick with the potential the county has – and must have had – not won an All-Ireland for thirty years and a National League for nearly as long. As far as I am concerned it was one of poor Management. A situation where no one person or group of persons could be blamed, but rather the system that allowed these things to happen. I told him that what must happen was to create a situation where the greats were encouraged to take a greater interest and give advice and encouragement to players, etc. He mentioned to me then that the system operating within the county would not allow this to happen. I told him that we had to make it happen'.*

There was no shortage of people deeply rooted in Limerick hurling who similarly acknowledged and felt McGrath's frustration with what he regarded as clear barriers to success. However, the veneration of a singular figure like Mick Mackey had proven an easier alternative over the years.

A hero to breathe life into Limerick hurling, the reluctance to act and bring about the widespread changes that were required left the county in a maddening limbo.

Éamonn Cregan had never been impressed with the workings of any Limerick

County Board, and it is perhaps no surprise that McGrath felt so at home in Cregan's own club of Claughaun. 'While you're fighting other counties trying to beat them,' he explains, Cregan's involvement with the Limerick County Board stretching from the early 1960s through to the 2000s in one capacity or another, 'you're also having to watch your back because you don't know what's happening behind you in your own county.'

It had been Claughaun's dissatisfaction with Limerick's standing that prompted the club to put forth a motion whereby a committee could try to get to the bottom of the county's woes. 'We asked the question in 1970, "Why are Limerick down so long?",' Cregan recalls, 'and we set up a commission to investigate it and try to improve the situation. We wanted to suss out the problems and see what could be done to improve the game of hurling in Limerick.'

The upshot of this intervention for the senior team was the arrival of Jackie Power and Dick Stokes as selectors. All-Ireland winners with Limerick on the field of play, both men were initially asked to partake in the commission Claughaun had proposed. 'When the commission came out with its findings, I approached Dick Stokes. "Dick, would you ever let your name go forward for hurling selector?" It was such a political organisation at the time you weren't even guaranteed that he would get on.'

Nevertheless, Stokes' candidacy prevailed, and Power's too. 'Now, Rory Kiely tried to take the credit for Power, but I don't care,' he notes. 'Between the two of them and three other selectors – Jim Quaid, Denis Barrett and Sean Cunningham – that started the momentum going. We had men in charge of us who had played and won in All-Ireland finals (Power had lined out with Éamonn's father, Ned) and that was a big boost.'

A development directly linked to the All-Ireland win of 1973 in Cregan's mind, he recalls the re-emergence of these respected Limerick hurling people precisely because it took the intervention of a current player and his club to initiate it. For the distinctly reactive county board, such proactivity was fine so long as it made them look good also. It was when the actions of others had a detrimental effect on how the county board were received, that the problems began.

'Some county board officials feel that you're taking a bit of power away from them,' Cregan remarks of the organisation's unwillingness to indulge criticism. 'They're not looking at the bigger picture and that kind of small, narrow mentality prevailed in Limerick for so, so long.'

As Joe McGrath quickly found out.

VI

Much criticism has been expressed about the lack of sideline attention to Limerick teams in recent years. Trainer, Joe McGrath, gave vent to his feelings in our columns over the past fortnight, and his remarks carried a great amount of commonsense. Unfortunately, some members of the County Board resented what Mr. McGrath had to say and felt that it would be more in our line to cover Gaelic games than to publish such views. We don't propose to dwell on the matter; we will not deprive any man of his right of opinion, or his right to express it. Still, it is very difficult for us not to feel bitter resentment at being told that we would be better off covering the games.

– Editorial comment, *Limerick Leader*, September 2, 1972

VII

THERE WAS RARELY an edition of the *Limerick Leader* printed that did not make mention of Joe McGrath from September 1972 on into January 1973. Since his arrival in 1969, the Limerick hurlers had contested three National League finals and a Munster decider.

Although they had only came out on top once, to win the league in 1971, four finals in three years were more than any group of Limerick hurlers had managed since the Mackey era. To give McGrath the bulk of the credit for this turnaround would be a stretch. However, he certainly played his part and by September 1973 this team had achieved exactly what he proposed it could when laying out his five-year-plan upon taking over as the team's trainer – albeit without him present.

While he has been widely credited with introducing greater professionalism to the senior set-up, it is perhaps easier to measure the impact of McGrath's tenure by the reaction of certain Limerick hurlers to news of his dismissal.

'We went on strike,' Bernie Hartigan recalls, his brother Pat, Jim Hogan, Eamonn Grimes and Joe Grimes making up the five players who declared themselves unavailable for selection following McGrath's exit. The prerequisite for their return would be his reinstatement as trainer.

According to correspondence from the Limerick County Board in early 1973, it had been *'after lengthy deliberation by the selectors'* that it was decided a new trainer was required. Although he cannot be certain, Éamonn Cregan suspects that some among the five-man panel of selectors did not appreciate McGrath's increasing tendency to weigh into hurling matters. *'Selectors... should be got rid of if it is apparent they are not doing their duty,'* McGrath claimed in the *Limerick Leader* article.

Following the shock defeat to Clare in Ennis, whereby the players were highly critical of team selection, it is perhaps unusual that those five charged with picking the team should regard the trainer with no say at all in such matters as the issue. McGrath's club Claughaun put forward a letter to the county board requesting that an enquiry into his dismissal takes place. 'We placed our confidence in [the selectors],' responded chairman Rory Kiely to this suggestion, their eventual attempt to explain their decision still some months away. 'They made a decision on the trainer and asked us to ratify it.'

As far as he was concerned, to hold an enquiry would be to undermine the county board's confidence in the five selectors. As the *Limerick Leader* reported on October 21, the blind faith afforded to the selectors' wisdom on this matter surprised a number of those present:

The Chairman was asked directly if he knew the reason why Mr. McGrath was removed from office. When Mr. Kiely said that he did not know it seemed to cause surprise and one delegate remarked that if he, as Chairman of the Board, did not know then who did and what was the reason? Mr. Kiely said that the Executive had agreed with the recommendation of the selectors. He had not asked the selectors why they had arrived at their decision.

Unsurprisingly, perhaps, it was suggested by a number of those present that McGrath's dismissal may have had something to do with his outspokenness in the *Limerick Leader* weeks earlier. The chairman roundly denied any such suggestion. 'So, you do know something about the matter,' one delegate quickly responded, given Kiely's previous claims of ignorance.

'I think you are prostituting the county board by persisting in your ruling,' railed Dan Hickey of the Na Piarsaigh club. 'It's disgraceful and disgusting if you abide by your attitude.' Abide the county board did, however, and Hickey joined a number of delegates who prematurely up and left the county board meeting.

VIII

The Limerick Hurling Club in Chicago would like to give their views on the dismissal of Joe McGrath as trainer of the Limerick hurling team. We think Mr. McGrath did a good job and played a major role in all of the teams (sic) successes. We feel that Mr. McGrath can prove what he stated – that he would bring an All-Ireland to Limerick within five years. So, why not let a man who's done such a fabulous job in the past prove what he's worth? The Limerick hurling club here have won the Chicago championship twice out of the last three years. They've done this with the help of fine selectors and officers who put on the field a fine, well-balanced team, and a manager who made key switches… We think Mr. McGrath can do the same thing if he is re-appointed – and, most of all, for the players' sake.

– Morty Scanlon, *Limerick Leader*, November 25, 1972

IX

THE DISCORDANT GROUP of players attempted to take the county board to task over their refusal to launch an enquiry. Eleven players from six clubs were reported to have co-signed a letter expressing *'their serious concern at the manner in which Mr McGrath has been treated'*. Although their primary cause for reinstating McGrath concerned his proven capabilities on the training field, it is no great secret that the personable Down native had little issue winning his players over away from the action.

'When he was manager of Molex,' Bernie Hartigan remembers (McGrath working as General Manager of the American firm's manufacturing base in Shannon), 'his Christmas parties were just legendary. He used to have a GAA table and 'Babs' Keating would be around… Ray Cummins up from Cork, myself and Jim Hogan. We had the best laughs we'd ever have in our lives.'

A Pioneer, with a 'great religious streak through him,' such fun went hand in hand with McGrath's relentless work ethic. 'Keep in mind, he was working in Shannon and driving down to Cork for training,' Cummins recalls of McGrath's time working with the Blackrock GAA club, 'and he was never late. At that time, the Cork to Mallow road was absolutely treacherous and the sugar factory in Mallow meant you had these huge lorries coming from all over the road.'

Indeed, as Cummins' clubmate John O'Halloran explains, driving was – if not

Joe McGrath's area of expertise – a task he approached with the same enthusiasm as coaching. 'There was a Sunday morning where we were going down… and I'd say it was the 1973 Cork county final,' O'Halloran explains, McGrath providing him with a lift from his own residence in Limerick. 'Joe could absolutely hit the road in spots and a Garda put the hand up in Croom. Joe couldn't stop the car for about 200 yards!' Reversing the car back up the road to court some favour from the stunned Garda, O'Halloran remembers Joe opening his window.

'The Garda pops his head in… "Joe McGrath and John O'Halloran going to Cork for the county final", he was told.' "Go on for Christ sake and don't kill yourselves!"' he says laughing.

'I used to say to Joe from then on, "We zoomed through Croom on our broom".'

The dedication McGrath displayed was never lost on the Blackrock lads. 'He used to come up to my mother's house after training then and she would have soup or a sandwich and tea ready for him,' Cummins adds, explaining the extent of McGrath's reimbursement for the night's work. 'He would be in the sitting room in front of the television and within five minutes he would have gone to sleep. He'd sit there asleep for an hour and then head back for Limerick. That alone inspired us… his commitment.'

For a significant number of Limerick's players, they understood such admiration. Yet, the dismissal of McGrath had not been solely what the selectors had decided upon in October 1972. No sooner was he pushed out the door, than Michael Cregan was drafted in as his replacement. A Limerick hurler during McGrath's tenure, the army lieutenant had called a halt to his inter-county career on account of injury.

Confounding things further, Cregan was a fellow Claughaun clubman. To make matters even more complicated, he was also, of course, Éamonn's brother. 'I wasn't asked to sign the letter because Michael was caught up in the whole thing,' Éamonn remembers, the arrival of his brother as Limerick's trainer a boost as much as he had not wanted McGrath gone.

'Michael was a qualified army physical training instructor, you know, not somebody just in off the road. He turned us into the fittest team in the country. Don't get me wrong, it was typical army stuff and there was no preferential treatment for me I can assure you. If Michael told me to do something, I did it.' He is not alone in thinking that the role Michael played was pivotal in Limerick's success in 1973.

'Joe McGrath was hard done by,' Richie Bennis allowed in *Unlimited Heartbreak*, stressing the importance of McGrath up to that point, 'but we wouldn't have won the All-Ireland unless Mickey Cregan came on the scene.' Yet, for the first few weeks after training began in January 1973, Limerick still had to do without five players – Bernie and Pat Hartigan, Éamonn and Joe Grimes, and Jim Hogan – who remained angered at the treatment of McGrath.

X

Close your ranks and strive for unity. Let nobody deny that we have problems with our county hurling team. We have a problem and it must be solved. Like everybody, the Co. Board is prone to errors, but, like men, we should admit our mistakes and work in a spirit of harmony for the furtherance of Limerick as a hurling force. It is a great honour to wear a county jersey. If our present panel recognise this, and show the proper approach to training, I have no doubt that Limerick will at last achieve the coveted ambition of an All-Ireland senior hurling crown.

– Jackie O'Connell, Limerick GAA official

XI

IN BERNIE HARTIGAN'S mind, the strike was never meant to be much more than a statement of their dissatisfaction. With the National Hurling League split across the tail end of 1972 and the beginning of '73, the five players removed themselves from consideration when play resumed in February.

'There was no GPA or anything like that around then,' Hartigan explains, refusing to play one surefire way of transmitting their frustrations to the Limerick hurling public. 'It was a big move, but we probably felt really that we were going to get nowhere with it. I don't think we were ever going to change the county board's mind at that stage.' For the five in question, their actions caused a stir, nevertheless. After regularly giving voice to the belief that Joe McGrath had been wronged, even the *Limerick Leader* now turned on these 'dissident rebels' who had gone too far. How could they consciably act in a matter that would harm Limerick's hurling hopes? On the first outing since their departure, however, it was not immediately clear that people needed to be worried.

If not for a late score to level the match, a weakened Limerick team would have beaten Tipperary. To Éamonn Cregan's mind, and a few more besides, their apparent capability to cope without the five men sat watching in the stands was an eye-opening experience that brought the strike to a hasty end. Whatever motivated its conclusion, Limerick were back in a Munster final by July and the All-Ireland decider by September. One year ahead of schedule, the players had realised what Joe McGrath believed they were capable of doing back when it seemed rather more fanciful.

Living still in Limerick but looking on from afar, McGrath contributed to the foundations of their success but reaped none of the benefits.

It is possible to appreciate the immeasurable work McGrath did for the betterment of Limerick hurling without losing sight of the fact that they continued in a similar vein of form without his direct involvement. Beaten All-Ireland finalists in 1974, they contested five further Munster finals between '75 and '81, winning two.

A member of the senior panel throughout, Cregan is the first to accept that he believes Limerick underachieved in these years. To suggest that had McGrath been kept around things might have been different is ultimately impossible to know. However, if the likes of Cregan and McGrath had had their wish, and a serious reconfiguring of the county board and its hierarchy had been carried out, it is incredibly likely that Limerick would not have been waiting until 2018 for another All-Ireland win.

XII

To my mind, one person deserves the thanks of hurling lovers in Limerick, that person being Joe McGrath. After reading his articles in the Limerick Leader, *it is clear that the dedication and eagerness of the players to win an All-Ireland can be attributed to him, for without his inspiration and total belief in their ability, we might not have seen what this team is capable of. In conclusion, let me say that within the present panel there is enough talent to win the All-Ireland hurling title. Unfortunately, all can be lost if the same dedication and eagerness is not displayed on the "sideline."*

– 'Letter to the Editor', *Limerick Leader*, November 11, 1972

XIII

RAY CUMMINS LOOKS back on his time hurling for Blackrock with all the more fondness for Joe McGrath having been involved. In the aftermath of his contentious departure from Limerick, he found a club in Cork buoyed by his enthusiasm for sport and determination to succeed.

In the years following, McGrath, who passed away in 2013 aged 77, remained passionately involved in GAA coaching and development. Having eventually left Limerick to find a new home in Cork, he was later recruited to be a full-time GAA schools coach. Friends with a number of his former players to the end, Cummins presented a poem that had been written in McGrath's honour for the tireless work he had done sharing his enthusiasm for gaelic games with a new generation.

I

The South East Board in '95
Drew up a list of names
To coach the children in our schools
In the skills of Gaelic games.
They decided on a short-list
The process it was slow
They weighed up all the options
And then appointed… Joe.

II

Joe held this post for 16 years
He travelled east and west
To the schools of our division
He never seemed to rest
He was an inspiration
And it was plain to see
That all the children loved coach Joe
With his boundless energy.

III

The children picked up many skills
To use the hurley stick

And if little ones got bumped or bruised
Joe's tissues did the trick.
Some learned very quickly
But others they were slow
But all the kids were equal
In God's eyes... and with Joe.

IV

He to schools with coloured cones
And placed them in a grid
Joe was just meticulous
In everything he did.
He lined the children up in groups
Said "READY, STEADY, GO"
And all got much enjoyment from
"Bounce – catch" and "Hand to toe".

V

The importance of "self-discipline"
And playing within the rules
"No fouling; no bad language"
Joe preached in all the schools.
So when these children graduate
And we have seen them grow
They'll all be better citizens
Because of knowing Joe.

VI

On the 2nd day of January
Just after New Year's Day
Joe felt his work on earth was done
And he quietly slipped away.
He left his family and friends
But he was prepared to go
There was a coaching vacancy
And the Lord just wanted... JOE.

*Tom Ryan surveys the action from the Limerick sideline
during the All-Ireland final defeat to Wexford in 1996.*

CHAPTER ★ SIX

1990s PART 2

Ger Hegarty

I

IT WAS A lovely warm evening in May and Ger Hegarty had a few hours to spare. Limerick's 2019 Munster Championship opener with Cork was almost at hand and he knew the final preparations were being put in place over at the Gaelic Grounds. 'I said I would pop down and see how the lads are getting on,' he explains, his son Gearóid among the group of players who had won an All-Ireland less than 12 months earlier.

'When I got there though, the gates were closed.' Although he could not see much, it was apparent that some action was taking place inside. Confused but not deterred, Hegarty opted to call a friend of his to find out what was going on and if he could come and let him in. 'He just told me, "Ger, sorry, I cannot let you in. This is a closed session,"' he recalls, 'and I thought to myself, *You can make a scene here, or you can bite your tongue*. So, I just turned around and walked away.'

The memory of that refusal sticks with him. It was not that he felt insulted, rather, Ger Hegarty just could not understand why it had happened. What difference did it make if a former county player like him, and the father of a current star to boot, sat in the stand and watched the Limerick hurlers as they trained? 'I respect that the times have changed,' he insists, 'but there was no such thing as a closed session back in my time.' Such secrecy is now commonplace across inter-county GAA. Where passersby could at one time freely wander into any county ground across the country and watch a senior team train, the denial of access is now widely regarded as a necessary measure. No backroom team wants to appear as if the work they are doing should be available for just anyone to see.

'Training for us involved going in for a warm-up, a couple of sprints and doing an A vs B,' remembers Hegarty, the effort and speed at which players carried out these tasks often determining their effectiveness. Hard work was regarded as the primary secret to success then. No opponent watching on could glean any unknown information from that, so, the gates were left open. That same basic reliance on hard work still exists, but it is channelled in various set-ups to suit particular moulds. For Limerick's modern hurlers, training requires their commitment to jump from frying pan into fire. *In the last couple of years, I found that matches were the easy part,'* former Limerick hurler Paul Browne explained to Kieran Shannon in the *Irish Examiner. 'The tough part was on the Tuesday or Thursday when you had nothing left to give and you were still being forced to have [everything] right.'*

This constant requirement for perfection in one's efforts (and ideally execution too) has manifested itself in remarkable performances and success for Limerick. In one sense, this outcome must make the excruciating effort required night after night tolerable. 'I would refuse to do it,' insists Ger Hegarty, broadly aware of what Gearóid and his teammates are being asked to do (even if he is not allowed to watch them train). Yet so many are willing to commit. The gates of the Gaelic Grounds are only kept locked because those on the inside believe they possess something worth hiding.

II

James Skehill text me on Sunday evening and asked, 'Is Kinnerk this good?' My answer was 100% yes. He was the biggest loss we ever had in Clare.

— Clare hurler Colin Ryan, *The42*

III

THERE ARE A number of individuals without whom Limerick's recent resurgence may not have occurred. Manager John Kiely, of course. There is Caroline Currid too; regularly praised by players for alerting them to the importance of mental preparation. Meanwhile, the financial generosity of JP McManus has helped in myriad other ways.

That is before one even begins to consider how essential the senior players themselves have been, who went out and won multiple All-Ireland titles. It is not so far-fetched to suggest that the most intriguing individual of all is Paul Kinnerk, however. Kiely's leadership, Currid's psychology, McManus's money, and a collection of brilliant players are all intrinsically understandable to the outsider who seeks to *understand* their worth. Kinnerk's value remains purposefully mysterious.

Players he has coached assure you that this man from Monaleen with a background in gaelic football is one of hurling's greatest minds. Between Limerick's style of play and their success, it would be difficult to argue a case against Kinnerk's brilliance. 'He incorporates game situations into your training and repeats them over and over as to how you want to deal with the situation,' the All-Ireland winning Clare hurler Podge Collins told *RTÉ Sport*; some small insight into Kinnerk's methods that does not really give anything tangible away.

Never too far from Kiely on the sideline during matches, Kinnerk manages to exert an enormous influence, while maintaining an almost elusive presence. Widely feted as Limerick's edge on other counties, he has never attempted to appear bigger than the team he coaches.

And yet, the exact nature of his work is unknown beyond the locked gates. Yes, he guides his players through situational routines at great intensity as Collins suggested, but that is not especially new. 'Éamonn Cregan would hammer us with "Speed! Speed! Speed!",' James Butler recalled to *OTB Sports* of what was expected from Limerick hurlers in training under Cregan in the early 2000s. 'He wanted everything done at breakneck speed.'

One can glean from the few interviews he has granted that Kinnerk does not regard himself as highly as many others tend to do. Furthermore, his gaelic football background precludes any suggestion that he simply has a superior understanding of hurling than any contemporary through experience. His effectiveness seems to draw on his willingness to work both hard and smart at his craft.

For all that one could try to downplay his input, however, Kinnerk's contribution has not been the result of some novel idea that he stumbled upon before anyone else. Between his involvement with Clare hurling during their success across all age-grades in the early 2010s, to what Limerick have achieved, it remains difficult to definitively say what teams coached by him do – beyond win, of course.

He is no one-trick pony. While his methods remain mysterious, some understanding of their success can be found in the players themselves. For Paul Kinnerk is inseparable from the general expectations of the modern game. To possess players willing to be driven as hard in training night after night as Paul Browne and Podge Collins have revealed, training must exist as an extension of everyday life. If you are expected to be one hundred percent committed on a Tuesday and Thursday, the remaining days of the week must be approached with a similar urgency. 'It's all about a lifestyle now,' suggests Ger Hegarty. 'From how you sleep, to what you eat and drink… everything is measured. Science and sport have met in the middle.'

An inter-county hurler across the 1980s and 90s, nothing Hegarty experienced in his playing days prepared him for the modern game as he has seen it through Gearóid's time. 'We were lucky to get a good night's sleep before a championship game,' he jokes, explaining how his son will regularly look to get a few hours of sleep in before heading off to training.

'The modern demands – and demands is the word – would not fit for me. The current players don't know any different though. What is second nature to Gearóid in that regard is alien to me.' Hegarty suspects that this increasing professionalism of the inter-county game is in no small way linked to the external opportunities now afforded to players.

Whereas he can recall leaving secondary school and heading straight out into the working world, the majority of modern inter-county players will attend a third-level institution. For Gearóid, a secondary school teacher, hurling success was contingent on the time he spent playing at university. 'I saw an athlete and probably saw him as a top class gaelic footballer rather than a top class hurler,' admits Hegarty.

'He captained the University of Limerick's Sigerson Cup team and I thought he would have a great inter-county career with Limerick's footballers. Suddenly then, he was playing Fitzgibbon Cup hurling too and I think that's where it really kicked off for him.'

A few additional years to hone one's skills before full-time employment limits what time one can spend practicing, the time spent in lectures, tutorials and seminars can also prove valuable. As much as Kinnerk is a highly effective coach, the Limerick players have proven themselves to be very willing students. For all that he has to teach them, they have spent these additional years in education becoming better learners.

This development has underpinned Limerick's resurgence. Without question, Kinnerk has proven himself to be an invaluable asset. Yet, the heights Limerick's hurlers have reached demonstrates that it is a case not only of the right coach, rather, it is the right coach with the right players at the right time. Tirelessly though all concerned have worked for this team and its success, they must surely recognise the hint of good fortune that first brought them all together in these circumstances.

It is not so surprising then that the Limerick hurlers are happy enough to keep spectators at bay until matchday. If Ger Hegarty had walked through an open gate in the Gaelic Grounds and watched the players being put through their paces among a small crowd of onlookers, one could frame the openness of Kiely and his backroom team as a decisive characteristic. *Look at Limerick, they aren't afraid of showing the world what they're doing.* Indeed, for the first 10 years of Kilkenny's dominance under Brian Cody, training sessions were kept open to the public as a rule.

When Limerick proceeded to lose their 2019 Munster opener against Cork days after Hegarty was turned away, an open gate could have been reframed as arrogance. *The gates were feckin' wide open, lads – they may as well have invited Cork in!* When Kilkenny's five in-a-row bid came asunder against Tipperary in 2010, that same openness of Cody's first decade in charge was one of the first things to go.

Training has largely gone on behind locked gates ever since. For better or worse, Limerick's determination to remain hidden will be respected – and undoubtedly mimicked by other teams – for as long as they are successful.

As others who have occupied this same terrain will confirm, however, a more transparent approach can leave you with very few places to hide when the going is not so good.

★ ★ ★ ★ ★

Tom Ryan

I

The Politburo men knew to expect harsh words and to admit their mistakes. The trick was to show contrition, limit one's guilt, and, if need be, implicate someone else. That was how Kremlin politics worked. These men advanced to the ranks of general or minister not only through hard work but also by nimble manoeuvres, making sure others paid the price for mistakes.

– Kate Brown, *Manual for Survival*

II

'I WAS DEALING with a group of Russians,' utters Tom Ryan, the political engineering within Limerick GAA an able match for the Soviet-era Kremlin. Across the 15 championship fixtures he oversaw as Limerick manager, Ryan's team won all but five of them.

In that 1994-97 tenure only Clare and Offaly, All-Ireland winners in three of the four years, won more games. Twice Munster champions, only a relative handful of Limerick hurlers from previous decades had enjoyed such success. Undoubtedly of lesser importance, the National League was still won in 1997 too.

'Ultimately, the history books will record in black and white the names of those counties that won All-Irelands,' Ger Hegarty states matter-of-factly, relative success holding little sway when he reflects on Limerick's failure to achieve their ultimate goal. It is an outlook Tom Ryan understands, if not exactly one he shares. Nevertheless, coming from a former player of his, and one directly involved in the struggle for success, Ryan can stomach it.

Nobody wants to be on the losing side, especially when you had worked so hard to come so close to winning. No, the gnarled aspect of Ryan's outlook on his years in charge owes more to those who felt entitled to share in the grief of Limerick's losses without first offering something worthwhile to the cause.

As Ryan foresaw when taking on the role of Limerick manager in late 1993, sooner or later he was bound to collide with the people whose motives he never properly trusted anyway. One of Limerick hurling's most successful managers, Tom Ryan has a few things left to say about the county board.

III

PLAYING AND COACHING have always gone hand-in-hand for Tom Ryan. 'I was managing teams from about eight years of age,' he insists, laughing at how incredulous it sounds. 'You couldn't make it up. I was always in a kind of managerial role... captain, trainer, selector... and player all at the same time.' A formidable enough hurler to represent Limerick in the successful 1973 All-Ireland final, the same tough exterior that would characterise his managerial demeanour was already there in the player.

'Ballybrown were playing Patrickswell, and Tom was a bit injured, so they threw him in at full-forward,' Liam Lenihan recalls hearing of the man he soldiered through the 1990s with as a Limerick selector. 'Now, Tom's mother happened to be in hospital at this time and the Patrickswell goalie came out just before the match started. "How's your mother getting on Tom?"'

'Well, Tom just looked at him. "If you don't stay inside in your goal you'll be within in the hospital and can ask her yourself."'

It was not toughness alone that defined him, however. If Ryan often seemed content to keep the outside world at bay, it was only because he had a lot on his mind. No more than Paul Kinnerk or his like today, coaching and management occupied an incredible amount of Ryan's thinking time. Although he has enjoyed watching Limerick win All-Irelands in recent years, he is quick to share his distrust of the 'showbiz' surrounding the modern game.

'It's not hurling at all,' he remarks of the style Kinnerk has Limerick playing. And yet, stylistic preferences aside, it is impossible to look back on Ryan's time in charge and not take into consideration how close he came to doing what Limerick have only recently managed to achieve. The extraordinary work Kinnerk has done to become an elite hurling coach has been vindicated in Limerick's success.

The same strenuous effort put in by Ryan has been largely forgotten in defeat. 'We had a supreme sports team, and we were classed as losers,' he states. 'It is a sore point for me.' Although by Ryan's own admission the county job was not on his radar in late 1993, it was a role he had spent most of his life preparing for, in one way or another. A fanatical sports fan, from a very young age he had been captivated by teams and individuals that had excelled beyond the world of GAA.

Born in 1944, he was fortunate to be coming of age during a relative flurry of high-profile rugby matches in Ireland. 'I based a lot of my own theories on the All Blacks,' he explains, the 19-year-old Ryan well-placed when New Zealand took on Munster in Thomond Park in 1963. 'I looked at them and thought to myself, *What have they got that makes them so special?* I studied them and found that their speed, their aggression, and their determination, put together with the skills that they had… that became the basis of my whole coaching and managerial concept.'

At the beginning of that same year, as England was overrun by extreme winter weather conditions, another inspirational figure of his in Matt Busby was guiding Manchester United through a series of exhibition matches in Ireland to keep his players active. Avidly researching what he could about coaching, the ability to improve a player's performance level has always fascinated him. Closer to home, Sean Boylan in Meath captured Ryan's imagination in later years.

'I love Boylan,' he admits, 'Mick O'Dwyer too. He was a rogue, but you need a bit of that as well.' Through the likes of Busby, Boylan, O'Dwyer and indeed Alex Ferguson also, Ryan identified in their longevity a shared characteristic to be prized. Each had found a way to balance the demands of managing down toward the players and up toward the decision-makers across years and years in their respective roles. The success which ultimately alluded Ryan may have helped him navigate dealings with the decision-makers better, but he may well argue that not one of Busby, Boylan, O'Dwyer or Ferguson had to deal with the Limerick County Board.

★ ★ ★ ★ ★

Ger Hegarty

I

GER HEGARTY OVERCAME almighty odds to be in a position for Tom Ryan to select him to start the 1994 All-Ireland final against Offaly. Twenty-eight years old, he had approached the rehabilitation required following his ACL tear in 1992 diligently. *In the centre, Ger Hegarty was largely anonymous,* reported the *Irish Examiner* bluntly as Limerick defeated Cork in the 1994 Munster quarter-final, before allowing, *[he] did succeed in limiting the hard-working Tomás Mulcahy.*

Hegarty's first game of championship hurling since their Munster final defeat to Cork two years earlier, things steadily improved for him as Ryan kept the faith. *Taking their inspiration from the majestic Ger Hegarty,* read the opening line of a more celebratory match report in the *Limerick Leader,* as Limerick overcame Waterford to confirm their place in another Munster final. *It was the towering Old Christians player who took the sting from Waterford as they attempted a second half comeback,* the *Evening Echo* confirmed. Praised for his involvement in a move that let Gary Kirby in to secure a much-needed score after a scoreless 21 minutes for Limerick, the county board secretary, James Hartigan suggested that Hegarty 'had kept the team together' in their moments of greatest vulnerability.

Somewhere between both extremes in the final itself, he was more modestly described as making 'his presence felt' when Limerick coasted by Clare to win the provincial championship. To cap it all off, Hegarty managed to convert a free from distance to get himself on a bulging scoresheet as Limerick eased past Antrim in that year's All-Ireland semi-final at Croke Park. Although a knock suffered in training had certain onlookers worried that he would miss the decider against Offaly, there was never truly any doubt at all that he would be starting when Limerick contested their first All-Ireland final since 1980.

In a certain light, perhaps, he would have been as well off out of the whole thing. 'It was a thought that ran through my head,' goalkeeper Joe Quaid admitted wondering in the aftermath of Limerick's defeat to Offaly, *How am I going to go back and face this?'* Although he was never subject to the same kind of scrutiny Quaid faced following the defeat, a caught ball that hopped out of Hegarty's hand sparked the move for that crucial second Offaly goal which arrived so soon after Johnny Dooley had brought his team back into contention.

'I remember the first ball that came down in that match between myself and John Troy, maybe,' Hegarty explains. 'I won the ball in the air and pushed two or three guys away, threw the ball up and hit it from about 80, 90 yards out.' The unspectacular result of his effort drifted about 40 yards wide of the Offaly goal.

'But there was just this massive roar from the Limerick crowd,' he recalls, 'and there I am running back to my position with the chest out. In the modern game, I'd have just given the ball away, but this was a different time.' Following Dooley's goal from a free, Hegarty had once again soared highest and caught Quaid's next puck out brilliantly. Once again, he had turned and charged toward the Offaly players gathered around him hoping to find a gap.

In an alternative world, Ger Hegarty may have found that space and launched a speculative shot that soared over the bar, settled Limerick's nerves, and brought their winning margin out to three points. His towering height, physical strength and unquestionable hurling ability may have been the winning of an All-Ireland.

And yet, somehow, as he engaged the players around him, the ball popped from Hegarty's hand and ultimately found its way to Pat O'Connor, who finished superbly beyond the helpless Quaid.

Ger Hegarty is not the sort to indulge those 'What if?' scenarios, really. The defeat upset him, but he was rooted enough in reality to know that no result was going to be the making or breaking of him as a person or player. Perhaps it was the time he had lost to injury, or just his unshakable enthusiasm for hurling in his county colours, but Hegarty never had cause to query his will to go… and go again.

It is all the more startling therefore that as he walked off the pitch in Croke Park, flooded at that stage by jubilant Offaly fans, Hegarty would not play another game of inter-county championship hurling for almost another four years.

II
Limerick City Championship quarter-final
Na Piarsaigh 1-13 Old Christians 1-7

With question marks still hanging over Mike Houlihan's availability for the upcoming senior hurling championship, there was more reason for concern for the Limerick selectors at the weekend when Ger Hegarty retired with a leg injury in Old Christians shock defeat by Na Piarsaigh in the League. Hegarty hobbled off in the first half and, according to a club source, tore some knee ligaments. It will be recalled that he had earlier been sidelined for over 18 months because of a knee injury. This time it is the other knee which is affected.

– Evening Echo, April 29, 1995

III

'THE CLOCK WAS ticking for me at this stage,' Hegarty concedes, the second serious knee injury he sustained a decidedly more troubling incident for his career as a whole. Had he been told then how long it would take before he represented Limerick again, Hegarty may have been forgiven for focusing his energy elsewhere. Yet only a matter of months after he had torn the knee ligaments in a fairly inconsequential club game in the Gaelic Grounds, Hegarty was plotting his comeback for the 1996 championship. *'I feel really confident at the moment that I am at last on course for full fitness,'* he told the *Limerick Leader* in January 1996, *'and I am targeting the first week of May for a return to action.'*

To his mind, this would have Hegarty back in the thick of things for Limerick's championship opener against Cork in Páirc Uí Chaoimh. Despite Limerick's superior standing at the time, championship trips to Cork generally offered nothing in return for visiting counties. Seventy-three years before Limerick travelled to Cork for the 1996 Munster opener, the home side last lost a championship game on home turf. A 6-2 to 3-2 defeat by Tipperary. Nineteen games had followed across the decades that followed and Cork were yet to be undone again.

On five occasions it had been Limerick who were defeated over their southern border. This all amounted to a general sense that however well Limerick were doing, and to whatever degree their opponent's standing had diminished temporarily, few counties ever went to Cork in the Munster Championship and won.

Liam Lenihan, one of Tom Ryan's county selectors, remembers leaving the ground on that May afternoon. 'I ran into Paddy Kelly, the former Limerick hurler,' he recalls, 'a right sound man, he said to me with tears in his eyes, "My God, I never thought I'd see the day we beat Cork in Páirc Uí Chaoimh."'

If Kelly's reaction mirrored that felt by any number of Limerick supporters that day, the margin of Limerick's victory was more surprising still. Mirroring the 2021 All-Ireland hurling final in another lifetime, Tom Ryan's team inflicted a 16-point demolition of Cork on their own patch. 'We went to Cork and beat the s**t out of them,' he succinctly puts it. Adamant that success in 1996 would have been the most difficult All-Ireland ever won, Limerick proceeded to knock out the reigning All-Ireland champions Clare in a pulsating Munster semi-final, before finally getting beyond Tipperary in a replayed provincial final.

As in 1994, Antrim stood between Limerick and a spot in the All-Ireland final. Although the Ulster champions put up a sterner test this time around, Hegarty watched on as his teammates made it all the way to the decider once again. *'I remember thinking after we beat Cork that if we kept winning I might be in shape to do something for us in Croke Park,'* he told the *Irish Examiner* the week of the All-Ireland final, any hoped-for quick return in 1996 a thing of the past. Sat in the stands of Croke Park instead, he could only watch on. *'I'd be delighted if Limerick win on Sunday and I'll be three hundred percent behind the team. I'd love to be playing but I've just learned to accept that some of us are lucky and some of us are unlucky… It puts your whole career on hold but thankfully I got over the disappointment some time ago.'*

IV
1996 All-Ireland Senior Hurling Championship final
Wexford 1-13 Limerick 0-14

Big hearts win big prizes. That's the bottom line when we sit to assess one of the most compelling All-Ireland finals it has been my privilege to witness. Wexford have the biggest hearts in hurling. That's why they're bringing Liam McCarthy home today… People will, no doubt, say that Tom Ryan's men were mentally tired after their extraordinary exertions in this year's Munster Championship. Personally, I don't buy that. I don't believe it is possible to be mentally stale going into an All-Ireland final.

– Joe Rabbitte, *Irish Independent*

On the actual field of play Wexford won because they wanted to more than Limerick. This was proven when they were reduced to 14 players and, even though playing against the win, they confined Limerick to just two points in the opening 30 minutes of the second half.

– Eugene McGee, *Evening Herald*

Men were prepared to die for the cause and it was inspiring to see. It wasn't all about heart though. It was also about using the head.

– Cyril Farrell, *Irish Examiner*

The sending-off, as often proves the case, seemed to work for the team depleted… Any hurler will tell you that it's very hard to play against 14 men. Inevitably, the team-mates of the man sent off seem to raise their dander. That said, Limerick did make a pretty poor fist of it.

– Joe Rabbitte, Irish Independent

Sure Limerick could have utilised the extra man better, but ultimately the last 38 minutes of yesterday's All-Ireland final were about Wexford's refusal to surrender... Even though Limerick were in front for a good part of that first half, they were always under tremendous pressure.

– Cyril Farrell, Irish Examiner

It was a disastrous defeat for Limerick who had convinced themselves, wrongly, that they were robbed by Offaly two years ago. There was no robbery this time. Limerick had too many players who failed to produce the goods on the day – and you cannot win All-Irelands when that happens.

– Eugene McGee, Evening Herald

And another thing – Tom Ryan cannot be blamed for yesterday. He's won two out of three Munster championships and few Limerick managers can boast that kind of record.

– Cyril Farrell, Irish Examiner

★ ★ ★ ★ ★

Tom Ryan

I

A potentially explosive situation for Limerick hurling was defused by the intervention of the county chairman, Brendan Danaher, last night. Besieged Limerick manager Tom Ryan had unexpectedly turned up at a meeting of the County Board at Claughaun and Danahar asked at the outset that it be adjourned for ten minutes to allow the county secretary and himself to meet with Ryan and his selector Liam Lenihan... Ryan was furious after being asked a series of 20 questions by the executive on Monday night which he said: "raised question marks about my personal character and integrity."

– Irish Independent, September 11, 1996

II

LITTLE UNDER ONE week after the 1996 All-Ireland final defeat to Wexford, Tom Ryan was summoned to a meeting at the Gaelic Grounds to discuss his future as Limerick hurling manager. Or so it was written, anyway. 'Nobody summoned Tom Ryan to any meeting,' he states definitively.

'I'm one man you wouldn't summon to a meeting. The *Irish Independent* had been fed this information you see, so I rang the county secretary Jimmy Hartigan. "Tell me, what's this I'm reading this morning about being summoned to a meeting? What's that about?" He replies, saying, "Well, haven't we a meeting scheduled?"

'I told him that we had, but I hadn't been *summoned* to it.'

Following Limerick's second All-Ireland final defeat in three years, tensions were fraught among county board members. Although it was routine for such a meeting between the officials and the management team to meet at season's end, the 'summoning' of Ryan to said meeting indicated that relations were now far from cordial. 'They were trying to be clever you see, but I knew who I was dealing with,' explains Ryan. 'So, I said to Hartigan, "With any meeting, the first thing we have to have is an agenda." I told him that I wanted that agenda on my desk by 5pm or there would be no meeting.

'So, they panicked. About six of them got together very quickly and they put down their thoughts in writing.

'That was a mistake. They did it so hurriedly that they even printed the mistakes just so they could have it out.'

Unbeknownst to all involved, the infamous '20 Questions' were about to be asked.

III

MIKE FITZGERALD, ONE of the three county board members who had sat with Ryan on the night he had been appointed manager in the Woodlands Hotel three years earlier, explained to Henry Martin in more precise detail how this regrettable document came into being:

'It was felt, rather than having an ad hoc discussion, that there should be an element of control to the meeting and ask the management five or six questions. Some of the officers were missing on the night and when it finished up, it was felt that they should

be consulted if they had anything to add. The list of questions finished up at 20 and some of them were sensitive. Some of them were a bit petty and should never have been put down in print. They should have been summarised into four of five questions. They were never meant to be an official document.'

The unintentional nature of these questions being put to paper is reflected in the *mistakes* Ryan referenced being printed on the final document. Dated Monday 9, September, Martin's *Unlimited Heartbreak* provides a complete run-down of the questions that the Limerick County Board wanted answered:

1. *Why did we lose the match?*
2. *Were Tom's selectors privy to all plans associated with the team?*
3. *The exact role of Dave Mahedy?*
4. *Are the hurley carriers justified when players on the panel have to go up on the stand?*
5. *Why was Mike Galligan not included in the first six after it was indicated he could not play games prior to the All-Ireland and was told by Dave Mahedy that he may be on from the start if Owen O'Neill was not fit?*
6. *Were the players given any instruction with regard to decorum and behaviour for the final? Dave Mahedy was present while it [the behaviour prior to the throw-in] was happening.*
7. *Why was it [the behaviour prior to the throw-in] allowed to happen? What happened on the Monday night prior to the final?*
8. *Players pestered for tickets – What was done about it?*
9. *Lack of punctuality during the weekend.*
10. *Why did the team come out so quickly after half-time?*
11. *When Sandra [Marsh, Limerick GAA PRO] asked Tom re: Shaws jerseys was referred to Dave Mahedy who said 'We are getting f**k all from Shaws.'*
12. *Is there a necessity for the two girls Cora and Sinéad?*
13. *Involvement of three selectors in Kilmurray Lodge: re Munster final and All-Ireland final Monday?*
14. *Was there any pre-planning done in the event of a team losing a player on the day?*
15. *Do the selectors accept any responsibility for us losing the game?*

16. *Do they think that Dave Mahedy is the right man to train the team?*

17. *Does Tom [Ryan] feel that the best interests of Limerick Hurling are served by he continuing on as Manager of the Senior Hurling Team? This bunch of players have reached and lost 2 All-Irelands. Would it not be better to make a fresh start under a new Manager?*

18. *Was there any instruction given to Joe Quaid to vary the puck-out and make use of the extra man in the 2nd half?*

19. *Do ye think the players were treated properly?*

20. *Have any monies been handed out to any member of the management that has not since been given to the Supporters Club?*

Time has not softened Ryan's outrage over this incident. 'They were a disgrace,' he declares, incredulous still at how he and his backroom team were treated by the county board. 'I walked in and the whole Politburo were there, all 14 of them sitting around a table. "If you think that I'll answer these questions, ye are making a big mistake.

You can shove them up your f*****g arse."

'That was the language I used.

'I didn't spare them.'

IV

The controversial "20 questions" presented to county hurling team manager Tom Ryan on Monday, and which sparked the latest row in Limerick GAA circles, were withdrawn by the county board 24 hours later, thus preventing what Mr. Ryan described as a "public hanging." Mr. Ryan told the Leader that he had been very upset at the contents of the document presented to him. "It was not only a personal attack on myself, but also on my selectors, Liam Lenihan and Bernie Savage, as well as trainer Dave Mahedy. Our integrity was brought into question and we had to take a stance.

– Limerick Leader, September 14, 1996

V

THROUGHOUT IT ALL, Tom Ryan has held firmly to this view.

It has less to do with personal pride than one might suspect, however.

Although his role as Limerick manager brought him joy, he has steadfastly insisted that it was never the be-all and end-all for him. Coaching was the infatuation and the chance to do it at the GAA's elite level was something to cherish. Be it Limerick, his subsequent stint with the Westmeath county team, or any of the many club sides he has worked with though, Ryan has always been at his happiest out there on the training pitch with his players. So, when the collection of county board members decided to ask him, 'Why did we lose the match?', had he the inclination to respond, Ryan may well have asked a question of his own. 'Who are 'we'?'

Rightly or wrongly, his absolute devotion has always been to those working within the camp. County board members and even supporters were not to be trusted. 'There's always this idea that Limerick have great supporters. "Oh, Jesus, Limerick, what supporters!",' he scoffs. 'They support when you're winning, which you would get anywhere. When you're struggling… then we see what support is there. I have never taken notice of those myths.'

For the Limerick hurling manager, the 'we' who were defeated in the 1996 All-Ireland final consisted solely of those who had worked tirelessly to get there across the year. 'They asked why we lost the final,' he remarks, 'but nobody asked how we got there in the first place.' The '20 Questions' constituted an attack not only on Ryan himself, but on those he had brought together for this sporting pursuit. Named in five of the 20 questions asked, the apparent attempt to undermine Dave Mahedy struck Ryan as particularly hurtful and outrageous.

The physical trainer who had made the difference during Ballybrown's heyday, Mahedy had joined Ryan when he moved to take over the county team. Educated as a Physical Education teacher in Limerick's Thomond College, he would go on to exert an essential influence on Eoin Hand's Limerick United and Munster Rugby, either side of his stint working with the Limerick hurlers. 'He was a great physical trainer,' Ryan explains, the simplicity of his praise perhaps disguising just how highly he rated Mahedy.

Before the former Limerick manager mentions any one of his players and their importance to the team's success, it is Mahedy first and foremost who is singled out. No more so than Paul Kinnerk possesses skills that set him apart in the modern coaching game, Ryan is insistent that the physical preparedness of Limerick's hurlers under Mahedy was unparalleled at the time. It is unsurprising then that Ryan would feel acutely stung by the third and sixteenth of the '20 Questions'.

The role of Dave Mahedy?

'Do [the selectors] think that Dave Mahedy is the right man to train the team?' Undoubtedly, Mahedy's role was not that of a usual physical trainer. Akin to most successful managers, Ryan appreciated what he had in Mahedy and allowed him to do whatever he believed would best prepare the team. The only caveat was that Ryan would set the bar for what was deemed acceptable. Given that they had stuck together up to that point, Mahedy was clearly well able to satisfy this tough taskmaster. In terms then of gauging the selectors' thoughts on the team's physical trainer?

Well, while Tom Ryan championed fairness above all else, if it came down to keeping Mahedy onside or his selectors, there would have been no real choice to be made at all.

And yet, 19 of the '20 Questions' may well have been all summed up as a regrettable error of judgement had it not been for the devastating twentieth: 'Have any monies been handed out to any member of the management that has not since been given to the Supporters Club?'

The finances involved in any inter-county management team tend to be submerged in murky waters. An association that prides itself on volunteerism, under-the-table payments are no stranger to the GAA. Yet, it remains decidedly unusual to see any county board demonstrating its concern for the exchange of 'monies' that it seemingly knows nothing about. If not perhaps aimed at all members of the management team, who among Tom Ryan and his staff had they concerns about?

Allowing for the possibility of a sensational coincidence, why were the county board only sharing these concerns about misappropriated funds one week after a bad result? 'Whatever bit of ability I've had has never been for sale,' Ryan asserts, the sweeping suggestion of some financial manoeuvrings going on a sore point still. In the end, Dave Mahedy announced his decision to leave the Limerick set-up a few months after the '20 Questions' had been withdrawn.

The one individual above all others that Ryan would rather not have lost, Mahedy could not go on after being subjected to what he perceived as a personal assault on his reputation.

VI

Last night Dave Mahedy closed his office door for the final time at the University of Limerick. As Director of Sport and Recreation, Mahedy has been the driving force behind the growth — and importance — of sport at all levels in UL for almost 30 years. It's hard to know which party will find it the more peculiar: Dave Mahedy without UL Sport or UL Sport without Dave Mahedy. For aeons now this place hasn't been merely his home, he's been its father, even mother, bringing into the world facilities and partnerships that not one else had even imagined.

– Irish Examiner, September 28, 2019

VII

IT MIGHT NOT have necessarily been his idea of a good time, but Tom Ryan would not have dared miss the chance to celebrate Dave Mahedy's immense contribution to the University of Limerick. 'It was a select group enough,' Ryan recalls, the retirement party taking place in a hotel close to the university itself.

'There were people there that I had never met from all kinds of sporting backgrounds.' Yet, as he walked through the main door into the lobby, Ryan was greeted by a familiar face. 'Eddie Keher!' he reveals, the legendary Kilkenny hurler who missed the 1973 All-Ireland final against Ryan's Limerick through injury.

'He rushed over to me and then called over to his wife. "This is Tom Ryan, I want you to meet him," he said. "His is the only column that we read about hurling." That was some endorsement!' If no other interest quite amounts to hurling for Ryan, the capabilities of media run it close.

The co-host of a current affairs radio show on West Limerick 102FM every Wednesday evening, Ryan has been writing newspaper columns to a local and national audience for decades. After starting a regular hurling column in *The Star* around 1997, he eventually found his way to an *Irish Daily Mail* column that is running still.

'I'd be very principled about what I was writing, and I wouldn't want anyone to be putting their input into it or editing it, you know,' he explains. 'I'd be well capable of managing that part of it myself.' Occasionally, controversial in his assessment of the modern game, Ryan rarely regards his columns as such. 'I don't follow any of the trends,' he insists. 'I have my own ideas and opinions and I express them. There is a huge reaction to that, most of it positive, but you do get fellas shouting out the windows of cars at you too. "You don't have a clue what you're writing about." It's all part of it.'

Of course, the possibility of writing a national newspaper column only became apparent because Ryan's journey with the Limerick senior hurlers came to an end. Brian Ryan from the South Liberties club had been drafted in to replace Dave Mahedy as the team's physical trainer in 1997. He may not have been able to assume the role of Ryan's veritable consigliere, but the Limerick manager was pleased to have found a physical trainer that he believed was fit to continue Mahedy's work where it primarily mattered.

Confident that the team were in good shape for another crack at the All-Ireland, Limerick impressed in the National League. Due to a convoluted structural change that did not make it beyond this trial year, the group games of the competition would take place before the 1997 championship got underway. However, the league semi-final that Ryan's team ended up qualifying for was not due to take place until the end of August, somewhere between the All-Ireland semi-final and final.

The league final they eventually reached and won was ultimately contested between themselves and Galway in October, almost a full seven months after Limerick's opening fixture in the competition. Unfortunately, the National League winners had crashed out of the 1997 championship four months earlier against Tipperary.

Although Ryan had seen off what he perceived as an attempt to oust him from his role in the county board's '20 Questions', he had some cause to believe that the winning of another trophy might afford him more time as Limerick manager. Nevertheless, within 10 days or so of Limerick's winning the National League, Ryan, after going in front of the county executive to essentially interview for the role he already held, was relieved of his duties, and replaced by Éamonn Cregan.

'To say I am disappointed is an understatement, I am shattered,' the *Irish Independent* reported Ryan saying in light of the decision. *'This is something I was not expecting, but that's what management is all about. The County Executive did not give me any reason and I did not expect them to.'*

VIII

WHERE THERE WAS no trust to begin with, there was no bond to break.

Suspicious of those charged with making the big decisions for Limerick hurling from the outset, Ryan's four-year spell in charge of the senior team only hardened his disdain. Undoubtedly, even one All-Ireland win would have altered his tenure in ways it is difficult to imagine. Although a different time entirely, the 2018 breakthrough for Limerick made the prospect of further success seem more probable than possible.

If Ryan's team had held on against Offaly and ended a 21-year wait for All-Ireland success, perhaps the 1990s would have been their decade. 'There are huge plaudits for the likes of Ger Loughnane and Liam Griffin for what they achieved and rightly so,' the former Limerick hurler, Mark Foley points out, 'but sometimes, Tom falls in between the cracks. Everyone understands that you must win the finals and there is no point saying otherwise. But he got to two All-Ireland finals, won two Munster Championships and a national league – he did a lot of things right and delivered some great days for Limerick. Yet, he is almost a forgotten man.'

Without question, Ryan believes that his own achievements and those of his Limerick team have never been properly regarded. 'RTE completely and totally ignored us,' he insists, the media more interested – justifiably so, one may suggest – in the controversies Limerick hurling became embroiled in than the team itself. 'We got no recognition, and we were never respected.'

Ask him how achieving the team's ultimate goal may have impacted his life personally though, and Ryan brushes off the idea that he is in anyway defined by the winning or losing of matches. 'My life would be no different, as such. I'm a rounded person, and I'd be a bit negative about myself, but I didn't lose any sleep over the All-Ireland finals we lost. When I got up in the morning, I had a company to run, a farm to run and you cannot cash any of that other stuff in anywhere.'

As it was then, so it has continued for Ryan.

Forever on the go, he has lost none of his intrigue for the world around him. Open to the opinions of others, he remains resolutely locked in his daily attempts to make sense of all he experiences, nevertheless. 'I do a lot of thinking to myself … and talking to myself too,' he admits freely. 'People would occasionally say I was better off talking to myself because I was only talking nonsense anyway! But look, I'm 77 years of age and still looking forward to cows calving.'

Indeed, the only regret he does have about those Limerick years is not taking up an opportunity presented to him for a behind-the-scenes documentary. Anathema to everything the current Limerick team with their closed sessions stands for, Ryan wishes they had captured some of those great and terrible days on film. 'It would have been an epic,' he says, chuckling at the thought.

'You could have sent it nearly off for the Oscars! And of course, I'd be the villain, but that wouldn't worry me either!'

IX

VILLAIN OR NOT, Liam Lenihan has one more story to tell about Tom Ryan. A few months after his dismissal as Limerick manager, Ryan was nevertheless present for a team holiday to the Canary Islands. Funded by the county board, it came after Limerick sealed National League success in late 1997.

As fate would have it, Limerick's travel plans coincided with those of the Meath gaelic footballers and both teams journeyed home on the same flight. For Ryan, it was an ample opportunity to spend some time in the company of a managerial icon, Sean Boylan. A little put out by all that had gone on beforehand, perhaps, the Limerick selector Lenihan remembers Ryan keeping a low enough profile on the flight, however.

'I happened to be sitting by Boylan on the plane,' recalls Lenihan, 'and Tom was in another seat within earshot. I was saying to Sean, "Was your job ever in jeopardy?" And he kind of told me it was at such a time when they had lost a few matches.

'Tom pipes up then. "Ask him was he ever in trouble when he won!"'

Tommy Quaid pucks out the ball in the Gaelic Grounds in the Munster semi-final against Tipperary in 1990, and his son Nickie does the same against Clare in the Munster final in 2022.

CHAPTER ★ SEVEN
TOMMY QUAID

Breda Quaid

I

2018 All-Ireland Senior Hurling Championship semi-final.
Cork 1-26 Limerick 1-26
(71:40 minutes)

Michael Duignan: 'It's just been an unbelievable passage of 10 minutes from Limerick, started by Shane Dowling taking that crucial free… great catch up here now by [Cork].'

Darragh Maloney: 'What have Cork got in reply? They're in here now Cork with Robbie O'Flynn… this should seal it… this could seal it… NO! What a brilliant stop by Nickie Quaid.'

II

THERE IS NO clarification required when talk turns to 'Nickie's save' with

Breda Quaid. It was not quite 'the touch that put Limerick in an All-Ireland final' as Michael Duignan suggested on commentary, but it unequivocally kept Cork from taking their place in the 2018 decider.

A direct puck-out by Anthony Nash had caught Limerick unawares after Aaron Gillane restored parity on the scoreboard. Not long in off the bench, Robbie O'Flynn caught the sliotar and left three Limerick defenders for dead as he bore down on goal. Although he never looked entirely in control of the ball, a lofted hand-pass across to Séamus Harnedy was well enough executed all the same.

A little too high, perhaps, Harnedy adapted superbly and was shaping up for his shot at goal almost immediately. And then the ball was gone…

Without any great certainty for those watching in Croke Park or on the television, the ball had not hit the back of the Limerick net. Everything about Harnedy's movement suggested that he would get his shot away and score. Veering to his left away from Quaid as he rushed over from where O'Flynn had been, the Limerick defenders gathered in front of Harnedy were helpless.

For all intents and purposes, Cork's full-forward did nothing wrong. In the unavoidable moment where the sliotar left Harnedy's hand to connect with his hurley, however, the Limerick 'keeper intervened.

Indeed, so quick and precise was Quaid's reaction that Harnedy's hurley was still on its backswing when the ball was stolen away. For Limerick supporters, the image of an outstretched Quaid quickly became iconic; 'Nickie's save' one of the outstanding highlights from the county's run to All-Ireland success later that same summer. That is one way to look at it, anyway. There is a more sober view of his divine intervention within the Quaid household. 'I'm nearly like Nickie now saying this,' his mother Breda admits when the save is brought up, 'but that was his job. That's what a goalkeeper does.'

It is not so surprising that she refrains from speaking about that moment in superlatives. Conscious that she sounds just like her son, it would be uncharacteristic of any modern Limerick hurler to voice a high opinion of himself. Their emphasis on the collective above all else tends now to be adopted by their loved ones too.

'It was absolutely wonderful, and a great honour for our family,' remarks Ger Hegarty of his son Gearóid being named Hurler of the Year in 2020, 'but he parked that quickly enough. That's a trait across this current squad and that's why they're as good as they are.' However technically proficient and deserving of praise Quaid's save was, Breda had additional cause to almost expect such brilliance.

Yes, it was in an All-Ireland semi-final, and yes, it catapulted Limerick into extra-time where they would see the job out. The foundations for this moment had been laid years earlier though. Unlike the unconnected onlookers bamboozled by the quickness of her son's reflexes, Breda understood what had unfolded in front of her. 'One of the key things is… never to take your eye off the ball,' she recalls her husband Tommy insisting, an essential requirement for any goalkeeper. 'Watch Nickie's face as it is happening. All he is watching is the ball. When it is played over to Harnedy, Nickie's eye is always following that ball.' Excluding all unnecessary information is a skill developed over years and years. Breda admits her son has had some natural advantages also. 'We've a lot to be thankful for that almighty God gave him good eyesight,' she insists. 'You have to be thankful for what you've been given, and he has practiced and developed that out of a pure love for hurling.' Great eyesight, thankfully, and a lineage like no other.

III

She continues to see more and more of Tommy's traits in each of them every day. Of the pride they have in their father and their desire to honour his name. They are all goalkeepers because it is in their blood. 'I like goalkeeping and it's my ambition to play in goals for Limerick like my father,' said Thomas. 'It's my ambition too to play in goal for Limerick,' said Nickie… If Thomas and Nicky ever do make it for Limerick, they may have another young goalkeeper snapping at their heels, trying to take over a position that their father occupied for eighteen long years. 'I wanted to be a goalkeeper too,' said Jack. 'I want to be like Dad.'

– Christy O'Connor, *Last Man Standing*

IV

CHRISTY O'CONNOR KNEW all about Tommy Quaid when he travelled to meet Breda and the boys in 2004. *'The coolest dude of a keeper you ever saw,'* he wrote in his essential study of hurling goalkeepers. *'He used to always chew gum that projected an image of total abandon that wasn't normally associated with GAA players.'* A fearless figure who could throw himself around the goal if it might help him keep the sliotar from sneaking beyond him, O'Connor's overwhelming memory is of a goalkeeper who seemed perfectly equipped for any situation. *'Tommy was definitely cool,'* he insisted. It is tempting to view Nickie Quaid's development into one of the modern game's finest goalkeepers with some small sense of inevitability then.

There was the lasting influence of his father Tommy and cousin Joe – two Quaids who more or less occupied the Limerick goal from the late 1970s up until the early 2000s. As O'Connor demonstrates in *Last Man Standing*, Nickie was also battling it out daily then with two other Quaids – his brothers Tommy and Jack – in the back garden day after day to determine which of them might be next in line.

No small honour, the synonymous linking of the Quaid name to the Limerick goal brought with it no small pressure too. *Joe (Quaid) remembers being over a Limerick under-16 development squad,'* ran one story which exemplified the family's stranglehold on the position. *'They were playing the county under-17s and five minutes into the match the opposition goalie had brought off two astonishing saves. One of the selectors enquired from Joe who he was. "Jack Quaid," came the reply. "Ah for f**k sake, how many more of ye are there?" the selector replied.'*

And yet, for Nickie Quaid, his first chance in senior county hurling did not come in goal at all. He made his breakthrough as a midfield player when Limerick hurling was at its lowest ebb under Justin McCarthy. One of many players drafted in to replace those that had been unceremoniously cut loose by McCarthy, or walked away in protest, his opening year on the panel brought with it nothing but a series of inevitable defeats. Relegated from Division 1 of the National League, Quaid contributed one point from play as Limerick's championship came to an end against Offaly in July 2010.

While his time as an outfield player would not last, Joe Quaid recognised in Nickie's ability to play out the field a trait shared by his father Tommy. *'They both have an unreal eye for the ball, and they are both great out the field,'* he noted of both men in that same 2015 interview with the *Sunday Independent*. In time, this comfort on the ball would be central to his effectiveness in goal. 'I think it was Donal O'Grady then who asked him to go back in the goal,' Christy O'Connor recalls, the Cork native O'Grady taking charge of the Limerick senior hurlers upon McCarthy's departure.

Limerick's starting 'keeper for the 2011 season, when John Allen succeeded

O'Grady as he had once before in Cork it had a knock-on effect that O'Connor could not have foreseen all the way back in 2004. An All-Ireland winning goalkeeper himself with St Joseph's, Doora-Barefield, O'Connor became renowned across the country as an outstanding goalkeeping coach. When Allen took charge ahead of the 2012 season, he reached out to O'Connor in the hope that he might do some work with Limerick's 'keepers.

'I'd be coming in once a week maybe,' O'Connor explains, the exact nature of his sessions designed to facilitate what a particular goalkeeper needed to work on. For those 'keepers determined to take their craft seriously, however, these sessions would additionally offer a glimpse at the amount of work they could be doing to improve themselves. Once a week might not necessarily be enough. The reputation O'Connor had cultivated as a coach often resulted in goalkeepers seeking him out for one-on-one sessions. Often located in his native Doora-Barefield or on the grounds of St Flannan's College in Clare, O'Connor tended not to organise sessions solely made up of himself and the eager 'keeper, however. 'I'd bring someone else along too,' he explains. It was in such circumstances that Nickie Quaid became well acquainted with his Galway counterpart, James Skehill.

V

In April 2007 Colm Callanan did his first session with Christy O'Connor, the pre-eminent goalkeeping coach. At the time it was a one-off appointment: 90 minutes at Doora-Barefield's old pitch outside Ennis. Callanan was ready for anything but not prepared for this: O'Connor fed him into a blender and blitzed him. When the session was over he sat in his car for 20 minutes, unable to turn the ignition; immobilised. At last he drove to the nearest shop, bought two bottles of Lucozade and 'absolutely necke''' them. "I sat there for another ten minutes and then I drove home in sheer shock. I was thinking, I never want to see that man again. I wasn't used to that. It was a totally different level.'

– Denis Walsh, The Sunday Times, *September 3, 2017*

VI

TO ALL INTENTS and purposes, Colm Callanan was James Skehill's rival.

Two goalkeepers, they had a shared dream of occupying a sole position on the Galway team. It is a small wonder then that both men got on as well as they did. 'Take 2015 when Colm got his All Star,' Skehill told *OTB Sports*. 'I pushed that man so hard in training that I could tell him in front of the group that I felt like I really got him that All Star. The same in 2017. I drove him to training early every day and I trained like a motherf****r every day. He would have to match me or exceed me.' Although he would never credit himself with engineering that blend of a competitive drive and genuine happiness for your rival's success, Christy O'Connor cultivated it in his sessions.

'I would be looking at Nickie thinking, *He's my rival and I want to best him*', Skehill recalls of the sessions they carried out together under O'Connor's eye. And yet, when the battles between their respective teams ceased, nothing but that same warmth of feeling remained. After sitting through the 2017 All-Ireland final on the bench, Skehill was named as Galway's starting 'keeper when they faced Quaid's Limerick the following year. In stopping a certain goal that would have ruled any comeback at all out in the second-half, Skehill was forced from the play through injury.

As Limerick ended their drought like Galway had the year before, the Cappataggle clubman was concussed on a medical table somewhere within Croke Park. 'I was in pain, but the worst of it had passed,' he insists now, his memory clear. 'I said to the doctor, "I have to get out onto that pitch."' Although Skehill knew the game was over and there was nothing now that could be done, his desire was not tied up in Galway's disappointment.

'I told him, "I have to go out and meet one man. That's it",' he recalls. 'So, I walked across the pitch gingerly enough and found Nickie. We shook hands, I gave him a hug and I walked back in again. That was it.'

Following the immediate celebrations on the Limerick side, when both teams were reunited in the players' lounge later that evening, Nickie Quaid made his way over to Skehill this time. Alongside the two of them was Christy O'Connor, dedicated solely to the Galway senior hurlers in 2018. 'The three of us were just sitting down at the table chatting away maybe an hour after the All-Ireland final,' explains O'Connor. 'I remember Nickie saying to me that he nearly didn't know what to do with himself now that they had actually won it.'

Skehill understood that depth of feeling. No more than O'Connor admits he was never so happy to see any player not wearing a Clare jersey win an All-Ireland, even though Galway were beaten Skehill has no problem stressing his joy on Quaid's behalf. 'I always enjoyed his company, a lovely fella,' he notes. 'Like, we might only have trained together maybe 15, 20 times over the course of a few years, but I just always thought a really nice, genuine person. I mean, I was obviously bitterly disappointed losing a final, but I was happy for him. It is strange to say that, but he is just a lovely person.' For O'Connor, Quaid's success was partly the culmination of countless hours they had put in together. In the space of seven years, he had gone from playing intermittently for Limerick out the field, to being one of the country's finest goalkeepers. His talent and the way he worked at it was never lost on his mother, either.

'Back in Tom's time, you just got the ball out,' Breda recalls, saving shots and sending it the extent of what was expected from goalkeepers. 'The stuff they do now is totally different.' Where she fondly remembers her father-in-law and his brother gently ribbing Tommy on the drive home from matches if he sent a puck-out over the sideline, such instances rarely if ever occur for their son.

'Now,' she notes, 'Nickie is almost able to puck the ball out so it lands on the sideline itself, if that's what he wants to do.' The next line in the incredible Quaid lineage, Nickie's commitment to hurling is not down to his father alone, however.

VII

1976 Munster Senior Hurling Championship semi-final
Limerick 4-12 Clare 1-13

It was tremendously gratifying, too, to see the performance of goalkeeper Tommy Quaid. Several of his saves were in the super class and he certainly outshone Seamus Durack, recognised as being one of the best goalies in the land.

– Limerick Leader, July 5, 1976

VIII

BREDA GRACE WAS a hurling fanatic long before she ever became a Quaid. Irrespective of who was playing, any match at all held the greatest potential in her mind. Growing up in Kilkenny, she was the eldest of five children. In among her three brothers and sister, hurling was a constant activity in and around the Grace household. 'We wouldn't have known what a football was,' she jokes. 'My father would have been taking us to matches from a young age and he had a great interest in the GAA. My mother had absolutely no interest at all then... wouldn't have known one end of a hurley from the other.' In this regard, Breda remained resolutely like her dad. By her teenage years, it was occasionally she who was trying to coerce him into attending matches not always necessarily involving Kilkenny. 'I insisted on going to this Munster Championship match in 1976. I don't know if it was a final, semi-final or what... but it was in Thurles on a Sunday.'

Two years shy of sitting her Leaving Certificate, she attended the convent school in Thurles and knew the town well enough. With the weather warm and a bit of hay to be saved, her father was reluctant to spurn this chance of getting some work done, however. 'He would have been slow letting me go on my own too,' she remembers, but by some means or other she was allowed set off on the 12-mile trip into Thurles for the match. Perched up behind the goals watching Limerick hammer Clare in what was in fact a Munster semi-final, her hazy recollection of the match is partially vivified by one striking memory.

'There was this small little goalkeeper in his white jersey and white togs,' she explains, the 19-year-old championship debutant easily spotted from a distance in his pristine kit. 'That turned out to be Tommy Quaid.'

They're first personal encounter was still a few years away then. After sitting her exams in 1978, Breda set out on a course in poultry management that took her to Wexford, Louth, Cork and, crucially, Limerick. 'Back in those days you would stay in digs with families,' she explains, the hatchery in Castlemahon serving as her final training base in 1980. 'The hatchery had to be managed 24 hours a day so there was a family living on site and that's who I stayed with.'

Coming from Kilkenny with a fierce passion for hurling, conversation always came easily enough for Breda. No surprise then that the woman of the house in Castlemahon believed her new tenant might get on well with her nephew, Tommy. 'That was when she introduced me to Tom,' Breda recalls, a dinner-dance the site of their first conversation, 'and sure it went from there. The GAA is a great source of conversation, and we were well able to converse on that.'

Soon enough, she was regularly attending Limerick matches with a vested interest. By September, she endured the disappointment of an All-Ireland final defeat for Tommy and the team. All in all, though, it was only the beginning of an absolutely unforgettable journey together.

IX

Tommy [once] made the point that while he never won an All-Ireland medal, he did get one thing out of the GAA, tremendous friends. I can say as a personal friend of his down through the years, he was a tremendous friend.

– Donal Fitzgibbon, former Limerick GAA chairman, October 10, 1998

X

TOMMY QUAID SHOULD have been on the Semple Stadium sideline as Limerick faced Kilkenny in the All-Ireland Intermediate hurling final of 1998. Instead, he quietly passed away in Cork University Hospital as the players he had trained rallied late on to defeat their opponents.

Sat up in the stands watching were his two eldest sons, Thomas and Nickie. Although Breda and his parents remained by his bedside, she knew the boys would get some much-needed respite heading off to the match.

Several days earlier, Tommy had fallen from a height of 14 or 15 feet while working on a building site at the Charleville Credit Union. The injuries he sustained would prove fatal; the life and young family he had with Breda cruelly transformed by his sudden and excruciating absence. Sitting there, she understood that the road their family must travel without him would be extremely difficult. Hurling, so much more than a pastime or hobby throughout both of their lives, could offer relief. A 19-year-old Henry Shefflin was the star attraction as Thomas and Nickie made the journey up to Thurles for the match. Twenty years before the nine-year-old Nickie became an All-Ireland winner with Limerick, however, it is more intriguing to note the presence of John Kiely at corner-back. At some point during the second-half, news of Tommy's passing started filtering through to Semple Stadium. 'Ten minutes into the second-half we looked to be in trouble,' the Limerick County Board chairman Donal Fitzgibbon stated in the final's immediate aftermath, 'but inspiration came from somewhere. I've no doubt that the inspiration came from Tommy above.' The players themselves would not learn of his passing until they returned to the changing room with trophy in tow.

Whatever one's thoughts on Tommy Quaid's influence over the victory, Fitzgibbon's claim tallies with an irrefutable fact about the man; he did everything he could to help Limerick hurling along.

If in death he could have had an impact, you can be sure he tried.

XI

It's part of my routine, you know. I'd always visit his grave the morning of each match. It's just, you'll say a few prayers and you'll ask him to help and get you through the day as best you can. That's been a part of my routine for the last 10 years. I wouldn't dwell on it a huge amount because we try to keep emotion out of the game… but especially in 2018 when the final whistle went, that was very emotional… knowing he had played and didn't get there, it was just very, very nice.

– Nickie Quaid, speaking to *Off The Ball*, August 24, 2021

XII

AROUND 16 YEARS after Christy O'Connor spent a day down in Effin with the Quaids, he decided to write Breda a letter. The way she had welcomed O'Connor into their home had stuck with him. 'I had a great day down there,' he admits, before recalling with a laugh, 'she cooked the dinner and all for me! I really enjoyed it there.' Following Limerick's 2020 All-Ireland win, Nickie Quaid was selected to be an All Star, 28 years after his father had won the same award while playing in the same position. 'I had always wanted to talk about that time when I went down there and how good she was to me,' O'Connor explains of his decision to make contact when he did, 'and how delighted I was for Nickie too.'

Only a boy when O'Connor first met him in 2004, he had played his own part in helping Nickie develop into the player he would become. 'I knew it used to always eat Nickie alive when they didn't win,' he notes of the goalkeeper's connection to Limerick. 'Deep down, I'd say that the fact his father never got to achieve what his team would have wanted with Limerick was a massive motivation for him.'

Yet, some half expected that Breda and her three young children might return to her native Kilkenny after Tommy's untimely passing. Truthfully, the prospect of leaving never entered her mind. Limerick GAA had played an enormous role in their married life, and she recognised in the parish of Effin an ideal community where her three sons may benefit in kind.

'The parish here is very much GAA orientated,' she explains. 'Sometimes, I do wonder if you're not into hurling or football in some of these small rural parishes, I don't know how you put down your time. You become so much a part of the community when you're involved with the games.'

Happy to stay put, she was soon joined in the house by her mother. Unfortunately, Breda's own father had passed away four months beforehand, and this arrangement made sense for all concerned. The passage of time required those present to keep on living despite the devastating sense of loss. 'He was a massive loss to the three boys,' she acknowledges, not to speak of her own feelings, 'and he is still a massive loss in their lives, I suppose.'

Her awareness of what they had particularly lost drove Breda's determination to ensure that the best of Tommy Quaid would never be forgotten, however. This was most clearly demonstrated through the GAA. Although Breda insists that she was never much of a player ('I was one of those who are one-sided'), only a matter of months after her husband's passing, she decided to give coaching a go.

On a freezing cold winter morning in Newcastle West, Breda Quaid attended an introductory coaching course. Unsurprisingly for that time, she was the only woman who had signed up, but that scarcely bothered her at all. 'I was having to get used to being on my own,' she admits. 'You become confident enough in yourself that I didn't mind at all facing into this with a group of men.' Tested on their basic hurling skills and instructed in how they may best pass them along, she wanted to play an active role in her sons' interest in the game.

After losing Tommy in such tragic circumstances, it was all Breda could do to ensure that those small rhythms of his life as a hurler did not entirely go with him. 'We were just so used to Tom training two nights a week, and then a match on Sunday,' she explains. 'The gear bag was prepared that morning, the grips were replaced on the hurleys. His boots would have been washed and polished, the socks and togs all laid out.

'The lads saw all this happening and it was a part of our week.'

As she will repeatedly stress, Breda wasn't 'fit to tie her husband's laces' on the hurling field. But she was determined to tie her own and get out there, nevertheless. 'Yeah, I suppose it was brave, yeah,' she allows, 'but you become brave.

'I wanted my lads to grow up and enjoy this game.'

*Shane Dowling celebrates in Croke Park after the All-Ireland
final victory over Galway in 20128.*

CHAPTER ★ EIGHT
SHANE DOWLING

Shane Dowling

I

Where is it then that life awaits him, in relation to his starting-point, to the point rather at which he suddenly realised he was started, above or below? Or will they cancel out in the end, the long gentle climbs and headlong steeps? It matters little in any case, so long as he is on the right road, and that he is, for there are no others, unless he has let them slip by unnoticed, one after another.

— Samuel Beckett, *'Fizzles'*

II

WHEN THE END rose to meet Shane Dowling, he did not recognise it.

Na Piarsaigh were comfortably leading Adare when Declan Hannon, an opponent for the sake of 60 minutes, urged Dowling to leave the field after he complained of a twinge in his right knee. It was not that Dowling felt any great concern really, but he decided to heed the Limerick captain's advice when the sensation was not remedied by a quick jog.

Two years earlier, in the 2017 county final between Na Piarsaigh and Kilmallock, Dowling had been forced from the game following a decidedly more severe injury to that same knee. On that occasion, the issue was initially diagnosed as a torn cartilage; easy enough to treat in the right hands. When a surgeon opened up his knee, however, the situation was found to be more complicated. 'He found a fracture,' Dowling told *OTB Sports* a few weeks after the procedure. 'There was also a big hole inside in there as well.'

By his own admission, Dowling rushed his recovery to get back playing as soon as possible. Across the two years that followed his decision seemed to show no trace of ill-effect whatsoever.

In 2018 he was an instrumental figure in Limerick's All-Ireland success. In 2019, around three weeks before he complained to Hannon about the aching in his knee, Dowling had scored another brilliant goal in an All-Ireland semi-final against Kilkenny. With only about seven minutes of normal time remaining, Limerick trailed by five points.

They seemed out of ideas after Kilkenny had hit them with an intensity that has since become Limerick's own trademark. As he had done 12 months earlier against Cork, John Kiely turned to Shane Dowling in the justifiable hope that he could upset Kilkenny's rhythm. When Cillian Buckley lost the ball to a swarm of Limerick players, it was Cian Lynch who retrieved it and popped off a pass to Kyle Hayes.

Spotting a man to his right, Hayes passed the ball along the line and Dowling, only on the pitch a matter of minutes, found himself bearing down on the Kilkenny goal. An orthodox player may have sought to shimmy left or right, attempting to evade the one defender stood straight in front of him, and get away his shot at goal.

Orthodoxy was not what inspired Kiely to turn to Dowling, however.

Dowling's idiosyncrasies set him apart. How many other players could twist expectations to the degree that Brendan Cummins, RTÉ's co-commentator on the day, let out an involuntary shout upon seeing what had just happened? With no angle to speak of or any risk-free way to turn left or right, Dowling opted to look up.

Throwing the sliotar above his head, Dowling brought the hurl down on it in a flash and buried the ball low in the right corner. Twenty-six years old and yet something of a Limerick veteran, it was further evidence of how the prodigiously talented Dowling was really starting to find his stride in a successful county team.

So, as he left the pitch in Mungret under Hannon's advice, both men would have been forgiven for thinking that they should be preparing for another All-Ireland final. Despite Dowling's brilliant contribution, Limerick had not come close to realising their potential against Kilkenny.

'*Perhaps it was the four-week lay-off since the Munster final,*' a match report in *The42* reasoned. '*Limerick started this game particularly poorly. They shot nine first-half wides and had just two points on the board inside the opening 17 minutes.*' Unusually enough, neither Hannon nor Dowling had found themselves on the pitch together that day.

The Limerick captain had started the game, but injury ruled him out of the second-half. Meanwhile, Dowling had only entered the fray in the second-half. The one-point defeat would ultimately afford Limerick a lesson they have been happy to learn. In late August 2019, however, defeat simply meant that Hannon, Dowling & Co were back playing for their clubs instead. *Death has not required us to keep a day free.* Beckett's dark humour echoes through that club match against Adare.

As Dowling jogged around trying to shift the niggly feeling in his knee, he did not think to mark that moment as perhaps his final time moving any quicker than at a walking pace. Departing the field with 10 or so minutes remaining, the 26-year-old never began to consider that he might not hurl again. It would take another year or so for that moment's significance to emerge though.

What immediately followed Dowling's exit from the pitch in August 2019 was a desperate attempt to resume his career as soon as possible. It was just a twinge, after all. Yes, he had had an issue with the right knee before, but he had played a pivotal role in Limerick winning an All-Ireland since then.

The idea that this was the end for him was preposterous. 'Literally though,' he emphasises, 'had pain every day since.'

III

IT DID NOT feel at first that he was in a race to save his inter-county career. 'I was scheduled in to get that second operation,' he recalls, the September date giving him some cause to reconsider, 'but I knew we were going over to Sandy Lane about three weeks after that for winning the All-Ireland in '18.'

The prospect of struggling around Barbados and the Green Monkey golf course on crutches did not appeal to him. 'I met John and told him that I would leave off the operation until I came back,' Dowling remembers, the suggestion being made to the Limerick manager in hope more than anything. 'He just said to me, "Shane, it is up to yourself but if you do it now, you'll have a month behind you already and you'll be ready to go again in January".

'He twisted my arm and I ended up over there on the crutches.'

Before the coronavirus could disrupt all plans large and small in early 2020 though, Dowling had discovered that something was still not right. To be ready for January, as Kiely had envisioned, he would have needed to be back running a few weeks beforehand.

When he sat down with the Limerick manager again in mid-December, joined this time by Paul Kinnerk in the Rathkeale House Hotel for a general debrief, Dowling was set a task to determine his readiness.

'I was nearly a month behind where I should have been in my recovery,' he explains, 'so John instructed me through hell or high water to go for a run on New Year's Day.'

A stone's throw from his parent's house, Dowling made his way over to the Na Piarsaigh clubhouse and out onto the pitch as instructed.

'I lasted for… no exaggeration, five seconds,' he admits, sufficiently concerned now that his first business of the new year was to seek a second opinion.

COVID-permitting, the next few weeks were made up of Dowling being told by physicians what was *really* wrong and how they could sort it out. 'One fella I went to just before lockdown,' he recalls, aware of the story's dark humour but not laughing himself, 'he wanted to break my leg and realign me… told me to retire there and then.'

Two months after his 27th birthday, he was back in with the same surgeon who had performed his initial cartilage repair in 2017 and the second procedure in 2019.

'I should have been running a marathon at this stage and I couldn't even walk right,' Dowling remembers telling him, pleading for some sort of clarity at least.

'He did a knee arthroscopy and when I woke up there was good news and bad news. The good news was that he believed he knew what was causing my pain. There were these loose bodies floating around in there and he had taken them out.

'The bad news was that there was another hole in the cartilage that had been fixed back in September… it was goosed.'

Even Dowling's good news didn't last though. Loose bodies removed, the pain in his leg remained. Although the pandemic-induced postponement of games initially worked in his favour, any hope that he might ever return seemed increasingly fanciful. 'I remember going up to some other fella in Belfast then for a look and he just wasted my time,' Dowling explains, running out of options.

'Driving down in the car at that time, I literally broke down.

Where am I going?

What am I going to do?'

IV

THE AGONY OF retirement hits every sportsperson differently. Leaving at the 'right time' just means your sport has no real use for you anymore. Ageing edges most players out of their effectiveness, eventually.

The sudden, unforeseen ending is crueller though. 'I would love to have been the oul' lad in the forwards with the club putting on the bit of weight, but being the one they looked to,' the Galway hurling great Joe Connolly once lamented, injury also denying him these twilight years. For the best GAA players, the inter-county game provides an opportunity to test your talent against the country's elite.

The lifespan of their playing days begins and ends with the club, however. Shane Dowling was one of a handful of Limerick hurlers who had enjoyed some All-Ireland senior success before the 2018 breakthrough. Na Piarsaigh broke a stubborn deadlock for the county's clubs when they triumphed in the All-Ireland club final two years earlier.

Dowling grew up practically in the shadow of the club's grounds and it was a momentous, life-affirming kind of achievement. No shortage of inter-county players would take even a semblance of that club success over whatever could be offered to them at county level.

It has never been one or the other in Dowling's mind though. For as long as he has hurled with Na Piarsaigh, he wanted to be hurling for Limerick too.

The kind of underage player that got people talking, Dowling entered the senior Limerick set-up ahead of the 2012 season with a reputation. 'We had seen Dowling, Hannon, Kevin Downes and the like coming a long way out,' Paul Browne recalls, a senior panel member since 2009. 'You would be watching what they were doing at training and it clear enough that it was only a matter of someone giving them the green light.'

A matter of days after his 19th birthday, Dowling made his first senior appearance under John Allen. It was a measure of the young forward's quick progress that Allen had no issue handing the free-taking responsibility over to him.

'You would always just turn your back on Shane when he was on the frees,' Browne explains, 'because he so rarely missed. Every free was almost like, *Lovely, get a little rest now and back into position because this is going over.*'

The opening game in Division 1B of the National League, Dowling had been outspoken in his belief that this team was about to turn a crucial corner. *'Limerick hurling is going to be right up there with the top,'* he informed the *Irish Examiner* two weeks ahead of that league clash with Clare, *'maybe this year, who knows, but definitely in the next three years.'*

Wise words in hindsight, it looked like he may have been as well saying nothing by full-time of his first senior match.

While Dowling managed to score 0-7 of Limerick's 1-13, with 0-4 coming from frees, Clare appeared any number of levels ahead of them scoring 2-24 on their way to victory in the Gaelic Grounds. 'I know Limerick are a lot better than that,' Clare manager Davy Fitzgerald commented in the aftermath, 'so we won't get carried away with that.'

When the teams met a little under two months later to see which one of them would earn promotion to Division 1A in the 1B final, the scoreline was less devastating for Limerick, but remained fixed in Clare's favour.

Going about his business all the while was Shane Dowling, however. Promotion had been denied them, but his scoring tally of 3-22 across the league told manager John Allen all he needed to know ahead of Limerick's championship opener against Tipperary.

V

2012 Munster Senior Hurling Championship quarter-final
Tipperary 2-20 Limerick 1-19

Limerick's Wayne McNamara could barely talk in the Semple Stadium tunnel after yesterday's energy sapping and heart-breaking Munster SHC defeat to Tipperary. But even in the agony of defeat, McNamara still found room for optimism. 'Absolutely gutted,' he whispered. 'So close. But at least we're on the right track. Just that things didn't go right for us at the right time. I suppose that's the way it goes – disgusted.'

– Irish Examiner, May 28, 2012

VI

ONCE AGAIN, IN a match of significance for Limerick, Shane Dowling had finished it as his team's top scorer. Once again, they had not won.

Knocked out of the Munster Championship before the end of May, Limerick welcomed Laois and Antrim to the Gaelic Grounds in consecutive qualifiers. Scoring a personal tally of 4-17 across both games, Dowling would finish the championship year sitting third in the scoring charts behind Henry Shefflin and Joe Canning; an incredible achievement in his first year playing senior, even allowing for these circumstances.

After what felt like a procession, however, the third round of qualifiers pitted Limerick against Clare, once again. At the third time of asking, John Allen got the better of Davy Fitzgerald and Limerick progressed to play – and ultimately fall short against – Kilkenny. For Dowling, the star forward scoring routinely, it is interesting to note that there was not yet unanimity when it came to judging his contribution.

The scorer of 0-8 in Limerick's defeat of Clare, each score had come from a free. Of the 0-4 he scored against Kilkenny, only one came from play. *'Quick deliveries into attacking channels brought Shane Dowling, Graeme Mulcahy and Declan Hannon into play quite regularly,'* Martin Breheny wrote in response to the Kilkenny defeat, *'and if the passing had been a little more accurate Limerick might well have got in for a few more goals.'*

To consider Dowling's year without what he managed to wrack up against Laois and Antrim, he scored an undeniably impressive 0-20 against Tipperary, Clare and Kilkenny. The only caveat worth considering, perhaps, was that three-quarters of those scores had come from dead ball opportunities. Not to be taken for granted, it may have been a caveat which troubled his manager, nevertheless.

'The Limerick line-up has attracted a lot of attention,' read a short preview of Limerick's 2013 Munster Championship opener against Tipperary in the *Sunday Independent. 'John Allen doesn't normally go in for dummy teams, or the like. He leaves Shane Dowling and Kevin Downes out of today's starting 15 which is clearly picked on form.'* Although Dowling would play no small part off the bench, scoring 0-2 from play as Limerick made their way into a first Munster final since 2007, Allen had made up his mind.

When Limerick proceeded to win their first provincial decider since 1996 against Cork a few weeks later, Dowling would once more have to be satisfied with coming off the bench. In the years that followed, Dowling would reflect on Allen's decision to drop him. *'I took that very hard at the time... John Allen was the demon, the big bad wolf,'* he revealed to the *Irish Examiner. 'We played Tipperary in the first round in Munster. I wasn't in the starting 15 and I remember driving home and pulling in around the back of the petrol station near the ground and breaking down for over an hour in my car. I genuinely thought my inter-county career was over. I was devastated.'* Given his qualities and what he would go on to achieve, it appears unlikely that Allen would have dispensed with Dowling entirely had he opted to remain in the job beyond 2013.

At what may have first appeared a crossroads for the 20-year-old forward, a change of management immediately changed his prospects. When TJ Ryan took over ahead of the 2014 season, Dowling resumed his place in the starting line-up.

There still remained some semblance of doubt among Limerick's hurling cognoscenti that Dowling may not be worth the hassle, however. Reigning provincial champions, Limerick travelled to Thurles on the opening day of the 2014 Munster Championship to take on Tipperary. The only team that had managed to compete with Kilkenny for any sustained period of time, Eamonn O'Shea, one of Liam Sheedy's coaches during the county's 2010 All-Ireland win, was in his second year as senior manager.

In a pulsating battle it was Limerick who eventually came out on top on a scoreline of 2-18 to 2-16. Given the faith placed in him by Ryan, Dowling contributed a decisive 2-9 of Limerick's total. Although 1-9 of that came from his ever-reliable dead-ball striking, the crucial goal he scored from play kick-started what would later be seen as Dowling's specialty... digging Limerick out of a hole.

Trailing by three points with a little under the same number of minutes remaining in normal time, Kevin Downes – another player dropped by Allen along with Dowling in 2013 – gathered a breaking ball before turning to run at the Tipperary goal. Attracting defenders toward him the closer he got, Downes popped a handpass off to Dowling who had found space a little further to the right of Darren Gleeson's goal.

At first glance, it seemed a straightforward finish.

By the time Dowling had the ball in hand, however, he risked being hooked by a Tipperary defender as they focused all their attention on him. Without knowing what happened next, one would be forgiven for believing that Dowling panicked.

Appearing to undo Downes' great work, he took off running away from goal. And yet, where he now had the momentum, the Tipperary defenders were helpless. Affording himself a few yards of extra space, Dowling moved away from goal so as he could find a clearer sight of it.

Standing eight or nine steps from where he had been, Dowling fired an effort over his right shoulder past Gleeson in the Tipperary goal. Drawing Limerick level, Ryan's tenure got off to the perfect start, as two more points followed and Tipperary were beaten.

The star man once more, all eyes were on Dowling in the immediate aftermath. Despite still being only 21 years old, his was a comeback story and the gathered journalists wanted to know what this meant to him. In no uncertain terms, he told them:

'Last week, the chairman of the club showed me a text message from a journalist in Limerick. I've no problem with someone voicing their opinion. Players play bad, they know they've played bad. That particular person personally abused me in that text message. I don't say that lightly.

'Above nothing else I'm just delighted I got my chance today and I hope I answered him. People have questioned a lot of things over me, fitness, ability, the whole lot. I'm not saying I set the world alight on fire. I didn't. But it's nice to show that you're still doing something good.

'One thing I saw coming out from the GPA launch during the week, we're only human. I don't know if some people know that we're only human. I go home tonight, go to bed and get up and go to work in the morning. We're only here to try our best and I *hope people realise that… I saw Andrew O'Shaughnessy saying during the week, all the abuse they got in their time and things that were questioned about them.*

'*They were unfortunate not to win anything. We're Limerick hurlers and all we want to do is hurl. It's been incredibly frustrating. I've no problem with people voicing their opinions but when people go over the top and don't show you any respect, it's not nice.*

'*Thank God, that we answered that today.*'

While John Allen's decision to drop him hurt, Dowling understood it. Or, at the very least, he accepted Allen's right to make that decision. Like any number of Limerick hurlers before him, however, Dowling was not necessarily prepared for the public judgements that can follow.

Although giving it your all might not be sufficient for a manager to pick him, he expected that it should be enough to keep the Limerick supporters on side at least.

VII

TJ RYAN'S FIRST year in charge ultimately ended in disappointment. During a torrential downpour, Limerick just fell short against the all-conquering Kilkenny in an All-Ireland semi-final. No more than what would occur five years later in his final game for county against the same opponent, at the same stage of the competition in the same venue, there was a moment of Dowling magic that Limerick supporters could look back on with fondness over the months that followed.

Once more on the receiving end of a pass from his clubmate Downes, Dowling negotiated the close attention of three Kilkenny defenders by firing off a one-handed shot that pushed Limerick's lead out to three points. '*What about that moment of pure artistry when Shane Dowling sent over a one-handed point,*' the former Waterford hurler, John Mullane enthused in the following morning's *Irish Independent.*

'*Majestic.*'

Given all that had been going wrong in Limerick hurling only a few years earlier, though they had ultimately fallen short against Kilkenny this two-point defeat signified an impressive turnaround, nevertheless. Or so it would have seemed then, anyway. All these years later, Paul Browne looks back on 2013 and

'14 and cannot but consider the team's failure to build on their development in 2015 or '16.

'We never spoke about them afterwards,' he admits, the defeat to Kilkenny a particularly sore point. To his mind, failing to deal with the seismic effort – and ultimate disappointment – resulted in an immediate drop in form.

Given what would be achieved only a few short years later, Limerick hurling in this period of Shane Dowling's emergence can only but look less sophisticated. They had travelled some distance from the nadir of Justin McCarthy's tenure and a panel in disarray. Yet, when the opportunities to achieve something truly memorable were there, Limerick could not get over the line.

It may seem rather trivial then that the players were nevertheless enjoying themselves all the same. 'Jesus, we had some craic,' Dowling is quick to insist, the quality of people that he encountered in the Limerick set-up conducive to having a good time every time. 'The laughing we would have on nights out, the messing and all that went with it. That's what I enjoyed the most really.' Citing a remark made by Browne in an interview, Dowling is fully in agreement that 'If All-Irelands were given out for the craic, Limerick would have won it every single year'.

'I can attest to that," insists James Skehill, the former Galway goalkeeper. Opponents on the field, he has nothing but the fondest memories of that Limerick team. Selected for Leinster in the 2013 Celtic Champions Classic, an 11-a-side hurling tournament in the University of Notre Dame, the travelling Munster team had a strong Limerick contingent. Although neither Browne nor Dowling journeyed to the United States, Nickie Quaid, Donal O'Grady, James Ryan, Gavin O'Mahoney, Graeme Mulcahy, Paudie O'Brien, Tom Condon, Wayne McNamara and Declan Hannon were all present.

'The first night there we were warned by chaperones of this tour not to go out,' recalls Skehill. 'We were there having the dinner and a very prominent person in the GAA stood up and told us, "Lads, we're training tomorrow. No alcohol."'

What happened next is hazy, but certain memories remain vivid. 'I'm not sure if I led the group astray myself, now,' he admits, 'or there could have been a couple of Kilkenny boys leading us astray.

'But all the Leinster team and the Limerick lads were out that night. They were just a gas group; the Limerick lads were always up for a bit of craic.'

It is not overly dramatic to Dowling's mind that they were sometimes laughing just to keep from crying though. His first few years on the Limerick panel coincided with a broader arms race, with the demands that were being made of inter-county players. 'We would be back training in November, and I distinctly recall Joe O'Connor used to do these 21-day booster programs. If your body fat was over a certain percentage, you would do this booster trying to bring it down.'

An All-Ireland-winning strength and conditioning coach with Clare in 2013, O'Connor achieved the same again with Limerick in 2018. Highly rated in his field, Dowling detested these boosters and all they represented, nevertheless. 'You were not allowed to eat after 6pm,' he notes of the rules, 'and you had to get exercise in every evening.' Hit with a booster to carry out across one Christmas period, he found himself working until 8pm on New Year's Eve. 'So, I ran home from work which was about 10km to get my exercise in,' he remarks, 'and there was a kind of family gathering going on at the house.

'But sure, I couldn't eat or drink a thing. I think if I had my time back, I would tell him to shove his booster.'

The physical demands within a team setting could be no less exhausting. 'It was always a case of, "Well, if Clare are training at 6.30am, we better be up by 6am,"' he remembers. 'You would have someone else training at 5.30am then trying to catch us out.'

Tabata workout sessions remain firmly fixed in the minds of those who started their days with them for any spell of time. 'They were horrendous,' Browne recalls, the 6am sessions consisting of a series of intense exercises that take four minutes each. 'After those four minutes, you're on the floor dead. We always had to do four, and if Joe thought the effort was alright, we wouldn't have to do a fifth.

'I would say ninety-five percent of the time, we had to do a fifth though.' The kind of early morning endeavour that did not find many fans among the Limerick players, Browne vividly remembers Dowling's own hatred for them standing out from the crowd. 'He would always speak up if something wasn't sitting right with him,' he says with a laugh. 'The Dow was a mix of the hurling life that was coming to an end, and all that was to come.

'He was old school, no two ways about that. But at the same time, the way he thought about hurling, he was very modern. The old school and the new school.'

It is little wonder then that Dowling was swept up by John Kiely's arrival and

SHANE DOWLING CHAPTER EIGHT ★

the plans that were being made for Limerick. 'John was very brave in what he did,' Dowling insists. 'With no big success behind him, he loosened things a bit. The enjoyment levels really came back into the thing again.'

Far from there being any kind of slackening off in output though, Browne believes that players had simply become more accustomed to living in a way that was conducive to the demands being placed on them. To his mind, something similar had happened a few years earlier when Dónal O'Grady took over from Justin McCarthy, following Limerick's forgotten year of 2010. With certain prominent players axed and a number of others absenting themselves in protest, Browne had been given an opportunity to play for Limerick by McCarthy.

It was a chastening experience. By the time O'Grady took over and the players were given a glimpse of how a more modern set-up operated, however, Browne recognised just how far off it they were. 'The first night in the gym we did testing inside in Young Munster Rugby Club,' he remembers, gym-work never really having been a feature of his preparation.

'I sat under the bar with 50kg, and I managed about one rep. If you asked a 16-year-old now to sit under the bar with 50kg on it, you would have to tell him when to stop, like!' With the Limerick academy still in its infancy then, Kiely's arrival ahead of the 2017 season coincided with the blossoming of numerous well coached and physically primed players.

The kind of players who could adapt to senior hurling with greater assurance, it would mean there was less room for some established players from the older guard. It would mean bad news for Shane Dowling.

VIII

A PREMATURE RETIREMENT through injury can unfairly age a sportsperson.

When the body fails in some such way as it did for Dowling, they can suddenly seem older than they actually are. His authoritative manner and self-confidence, such as we have seen during his frequent appearances on *The Sunday Game*, also informs this untimely assessment. He simply carries himself like an older man than he is.

Moreover, our perception of him is tied up in his final few years as a Limerick hurler. It was in this period that he became the county's all-time top scorer in championship hurling. While having to content himself largely with appearances off the bench, this magnificent achievement almost came to seem like an inevitable landmark that a long-serving player had reached. The reality is though that Dowling was still only 25 years old when he surpassed Gary Kirby's record in the summer of 2018.

Injuries notwithstanding, he was maybe at the mid-way point of his inter-county career. With all that he had already achieved, it can be forgotten that he had so much left to offer. To their immense credit, this is something John Kiely and his management team understood. 'When a big moment was required Shane was a player you could depend on to produce a piece of magic,' read a statement on behalf of Kiely and his team after Dowling announced his retirement. 'These moments of leadership are what separates the good player from the great player.' Despite becoming a 'super sub' years before age would have warranted that transition, Dowling remained a great player.

Although it was not to his liking then or now, he has since come to appreciate the effectiveness of Kiely's plan for him.

When the 2018 season got underway, Dowling was at the other end of his rushed recovery from that first knee injury. In February, he scored a goal of breathtaking individual brilliance in the All-Ireland club semi-final against Slaughtneil. A second All-Ireland title for Na Piarsaigh was within grasp the following month but it ultimately went the way of the Leinster champions Cuala.

These club commitments resulted in Dowling playing no part in Limerick's promotion from Division 1B in the National League. Following the first two games of the revamped round robin Munster Championship, he had yet to make an appearance. Thanks in no small part to the red card Aaron Gillane picked up against Cork in that second outing, however, Dowling was given a chance against Waterford which he seized, and another against Clare which did not quite go his way.

Hoping that he might get a chance to redeem himself against Carlow in a preliminary All-Ireland quarter-final, Dowling was overlooked in favour of the returning Gillane. 'I would get very low on a Friday night in terms of team selection,' he admits, somewhat coming to terms with what he could still do for Limerick by Saturday morning. 'I remember actually meeting John Kiely the following year and we sat down for a cup of tea together. We were chatting away, and I just said to him,

"I really thought that I would be starting against Carlow, John."'

Not sure what to expect by way of a reply, Kiely's response bewildered him. 'He just looked at me and went, "Yeah Shane, so did I,"' Dowling recalls. 'I was just like thinking to myself, *What are you on about? You pick the team!*

'But he explained that when they all sat down together, there was a trust there in me that I could come off the bench to make an impact.

'What do you say to that?'

IX

2018 All-Ireland Senior Hurling Championship semi-final
Cork 1-24 Limerick 1-18
(56:36)

Darragh Maloney: 'So here is the change, Seamus Flanagan off… Shane Dowling on. So, this is one of the big features with this Limerick team – like Cork – it is the power and the impact off their bench. They've some real quality there.'

Michael Duignan: 'Yeah, the experience of Dowling as well. He's a big-game player and at this stage you're probably going to need a goal and he's certainly a man who could give you that.'

X

SHANE DOWLING'S EXTRAORDINARY contribution to Limerick can be boiled down to about half-an-hour of hurling. When he reflects on that All-Ireland semi-final defeat of Cork in 2018, it is with the satisfaction of one who has experienced a lifetime's worth of effort rewarded in an almighty flash of brilliance.

'Everything I touched worked,' he recalls, 'and that rarely happens.'

Trailing Cork by six points, Diarmuid Byrnes uncharacteristically missed a chance to score from range moments after Dowling's arrival. 'Sometimes you need a game like this in Croke Park to learn from it for the following year,' Duignan mused on commentary, the bulk of Limerick's young panel experiencing a first big day out with major expectations upon them. One of the few who could call on 2013 and '14 to steady any pre-match nerves, Dowling had reckoned from a while out that he would be starting on the bench.

No nerves for him, not that it was ever really an issue. 'Myself and Sean Finn had gotten into a habit of heading off for a sleep before the games,' he admits, Limerick's routine base in the Crowne Plaza Hotel a hive of activity from which they were happy to take their leave. 'Everyone was different and that's where Caroline Currid was so important. She would encourage you do whatever was necessary to get in the right frame of mind.' Emerging in time to make the bus journey to Croke Park, there was no fear of Dowling becoming overawed by the occasion. 'Not starting allowed me to relax that bit more,' he admits, 'but I liked having a bit of craic and messing with lads on the bus.

'You just have to know who you can mess with... and who you're better off leaving alone!'

This was part of what made Dowling such an impactful substitute. Unquestionably talented, the luxury of calling on such a player safe in the knowledge that he was ready is obvious. 'I'd still be having the craic on the bench with whoever is around me,' he explains, keeping a close eye on proceedings all the while, 'but then I can change my mood in an instant, for good and sometimes bad.

'I remember Peter Casey saying about me that I could be acting like a three-year-old for two hours straight and then, all of a sudden, I'm a different person. Some lads need to be in the zone for hours beforehand to be ready, but I've always been able to do it instantly.' Within two minutes of his introduction against Cork, Dowling had nailed his first free taken from about the pitch's half-way mark.

The deficit became five points and a roar from Limerick's fans went up – their man was in situ. A minute later, Dowling picked up a pass from Aaron Gillane and shot over his second score of the day. 'I might have been writing them off a little prematurely,' Duignan conceded, citing Dowling's arrival as the possible catalyst for Limerick's revival.

Toing and froing across the remaining 10 minutes, Cork extended their lead back out to six points before Gillane, Kyle Hayes and Dowling contributed a flurry of scores to ensure things were even by the time referee Paud O'Dwyer blew the full-time whistle.

'The fact that there was extra-time then just gave me more time to try and get on the ball,' Dowling explains with a laugh, the most important part of his day's work yet to come.

XI

Joanne Cantwell: 'Was there any debate over who'd take the penalty?'
Shane Dowling: 'There was. I looked at Paul [Kinnerk]. Paul had come in and his words were, "This is how championship games are won. Go for it." And I did.'

XII

THE FIRST-HALF OF extra-time was understandably cagey.

A goal should have followed when Dowling played in Gillane for a one-on-one with Cork's Anthony Nash, but a point was all the Patrickswell forward managed. Cork managed two scores of their own, but Dowling responded with two more of *his own* that gave Limerick a slender lead heading into the second 10-minute half.

The nip and tuck of a game that neither county really wanted to contemplate losing then changed in a heartbeat. Quicker than the television cameras could capture, and equally bewildering for many watching on in Croke Park, a long Nickie Quaid puck-out landed in among a body of players from both teams.

No sooner than it seemed as if a Cork player had the sliotar... and Shane Dowling was bearing down on goal with the ball in hand. Overly eager Cork defenders were determined not to give him any opportunity to shoot, however, only to give away a penalty in the process.

'It has to be a penalty if it's a free,' Michael Duignan stressed on commentary, a contradiction in terms that everyone understood all the same.

A penalty it would be.

Sitting on the Limerick bench still was Paul Browne. A teammate of Dowling's since 2012, a cruciate injury had cut short his playing time in 2018. Such was the collective spirit within this team, however, Browne, who was still awaiting surgery at the time, had been kept around the camp by Kiely. 'That group just had a huge impact on me,' he recalls, the All-Ireland semi-final taking place shortly before his partner Niamh was set to run in the 100m sprint final at the National Championships later that evening.

'She was running at about 6pm, but when the match went to extra-time things became a lot tighter for me getting from Croke Park to Santry.' All hands to the pump, Browne was commandeered by the county board secretary Mike

O'Riordan to run some water bottles out to the lads. 'I was actually standing beside Declan Hannon on the field when Dowling won that penalty,' he recalls, the atmosphere among those frenzied Limerick supporters primed to reach a crescendo.

'I was just saying to Dec, "What's going to happen here then?" Mike Casey was in behind us and just before Shane hit the ball he went, "Top corner, kid!"

'Christ, and then Shane absolutely stitched it! Mike knew exactly what the Dow was going to do.'

Four points ahead and in control, the final few minutes went as planned. In a way that the All-Ireland final a few weeks later would not allow, here they could enjoy themselves. 'I remember just looking across at one stage to Peter Casey,' Dowling recalls, two of the four Na Piarsaigh players on the pitch in that moment alongside Peter's brother, Mike and William O'Donoghue.

'We just gave each other the biggest smile.'

Somewhere out there watching too were his parents. Thrown into a difficult situation with his team trailing by six points, Dowling had been pivotal in the comeback. He could only imagine what they were feeling. 'My parents lived week-to-week for the hurling with me,' he explains, 'and it had been a tough journey at times with all the ups and downs. I just loved having them there on that journey with me though.'

When the match finally ended and Limerick were victorious, it was Dowling who made the call for calm. This group had more to give, as they would go on to demonstrate. Inside in the dressing-room, whatever cool detachment he had pre-match had been consumed by his elation. Making time for a quick phone-call in the bathroom to his parents, he undoubtedly held hope that this performance would earn him a starting spot for the final to come.

'It's not that I've ever been comfortable or uncomfortable with the 'super sub' tag,' he insists, Dowling's effectiveness from the bench ensuring that he ultimately stayed there against Galway. 'I'm proud to be able to say I did what I did.

'The long and short of it is that I wanted to win an All-Ireland, I wanted to be a part of it. I was a part of it and for that I'll be forever grateful.'

XIII

WHEN WE SEE Shane Dowling now there is still some enjoyment in what he is doing. *The Sunday Game* has given him an opportunity to showcase nationally what most in Limerick already knew about him. Through presence alone he encourages you, the viewer, to enjoy yourself too.

He delivers honest assessments with a relatable wit or damning forthrightness bolstered by the eye of one not long removed from hurling at the elite level. 'You wouldn't know if you were at a party or a funeral with him,' he memorably remarked of his close friend, Declan Hannon, praising the Limerick captain's unflappable balance in any situation. Never hurtful or mean for the sake of it, his closeness to this Limerick team has prompted him to defend and celebrate their cause at every opportunity – objectivity on this front will take time. He embodies the kind of tribalism and pride of place that fuels GAA supporters. Even those who undoubtedly loathe him as a cocksure Limerick man basking in all this new success would love a 'Shane Dowling' of their own.

Although his serious insight and reading of the modern game is the essential foundation of his effectiveness as a pundit, Dowling's humour, passion, and the personable way he communicates his expertise suggests he will remain an appealing pundit for some time. Yet, there is a reliable uncertainty to what he might say that provides a curious kind of comfort in itself.

As when John Kiely once turned to Dowling and beckoned him from the Limerick bench, everyone knows that something exciting is about to occur.

The tragic circumstances which have shaped this adeptness for punditry are inescapable though. Standing alone in freezing December conditions as his former teammates celebrated their second All-Ireland win in 2020, the other side of this bargain was captured on the mobile phone camera of Des Cahill. *'This is Shane Dowling, forced by injury to quit hurling with Limerick at the age of 27,'* The *Sunday Game* host wrote on a Twitter post sharing the video. *'Two years ago he was in the middle of the celebrations. Yesterday he watched the game with me, but stood alone at the end.'*

With *Limerick You're A Lady* ringing out across the empty stands, Dowling, still a few years shy of his 30th birthday, could be seen bringing up a hand to wipe the tears away. It briefly overwhelms him, trying to balance his unshakeable love for those successful Limerick people with the fact that he should still be out there with them. He knows that the 2018 breakthrough win will never be forgotten. Yet, watching this team develop year on year in his absence, Dowling is aware that beating Galway was only the beginning.

The team he watched defeat Waterford were better again. When they met Cork in the following year's decider, Limerick had somehow managed to find even more room for improvement. They will slow up with time and Dowling may one day have cause to criticise Limerick on television, but nobody can foresee it yet.

Although he would have had to face retirement eventually, the clear path Dowling had laid out in his mind as a Limerick hurler disappeared prematurely. In high demand following the 2018 All-Ireland win, Dowling agreed at one point to join a five-person panel of Irish sportspeople. In front of a gathered audience, each would answer questions about their career, their successes, their challenges, and the like.

Talking – even in front of a room full of strangers – has never been an issue for Dowling. Ask him what you want, and he will give you an answer. 'A question came up from the floor for me,' he remembers, 'and this person asked, "How do you deal with disappointment?" Well, I just said, "You're going to have to ask the other four panellists here because I still don't know to deal with it."'

When he jokingly praised the emotional steadiness of his former teammate and friend Declan Hannon, he was not being facetious. When a moment calls for an emotional response, Dowling feels every inch of it. 'I'm a very bubbly, outgoing person,' he insists, 'but within my own four walls the bad stuff impacts me. I used to go too high and too low. Declan is the kind of person I would like to be, but there's no point in me even trying because I can't do it.'

Hurling has frequently pulled his emotions one way or another. Joyful moments are there to be shared and he has taken the greatest pleasure in seeing his family enjoy the successes he has been involved in. Between them, Dowling's parents run the post office in Cahirdavin and no conversation with passing customers goes too long before turning to hurling.

'To give them that sense of satisfaction when things were going well,' he notes, 'that was everything for me. Really, one of the most difficult things about having to retire was that I knew the journey was gone for me... but it was gone for my family as well.'

The journey was always going to end, however.

What Dowling managed to pack into it remains timeless. 'History is going to be so kind to Shane,' insists Ger Hegarty, a Limerick hurler painfully familiar with the circumstances of Dowling's injury anguish.

'When we measure his time, his input will be held right up there. Shane Dowling was phenomenal… *phenomenal.*'

Stephen Lucey chases Eoin Brosnan of Kerry in the Munster Championship in 2002, and fields the ball in front of Eoin Kelly of Tipperary in the Munster Championship in 2005.

CHAPTER ★ NINE
THE ACADEMY

Shane Fitzgibbon

I

Everything about their story now can be traced back down a logical, unemotional path. To a carefully structured development pathway, to feeding chains like Ardscoil Rís, Castletroy College, Doon CBS, to the prolific harvesting of Fitzgibbons by the city's third-level institutions, to elite athlete conditions on the north campus of UL. There is a permanency to this story, the feel of something organic.

— Vincent Hogan, *Irish Independent*, August 7, 2021

II

THE DARK DAYS of Limerick hurling appear increasingly strange and regrettable. *To win just once,* supporters of Mayo's beleaguered footballers continue hoping year after year. For a long time, the same Saw Doctors song captured the central motivation of Limerick's summers too.

To win the Liam MacCarthy Cup just one more time, *that would be enough.*

Inconsistency is rarely prized as a characteristic of champions. For generations of Limerick hurlers, however, it has been an unfortunate tag that fit too well. "One thing about Limerick that time,' Ollie Moran recalls of his own days representing the county across the 1990s and 2000s, 'we were a great team to spring a surprise. Teams didn't know what they would get.' It brought about some truly great days.

Unforgettably, Moran shone as a heavily unfancied Limerick travelled to Páirc Uí Chaoimh in 2001 and defeated Cork. And what about 2007 when both Ollie and his brother Niall hit the two concluding points to give the county a famous victory against Tipperary in the third game of a thrilling series.

The six years in-between that, Limerick went without so much as a win in the Munster Championship though, that's the cruel reality of inconsistency.

To Win Just Once has more to do with losing than anything.

We are captivated by tales of the underdog having its day, but it is hardly a role any team wants to regularly fulfil. *To never have considered losing/As if to win is by your choosing.* This is a frame of mind certain sports teams actively cultivate for themselves. In the alternative world of soccer, *You'll Never Walk Alone* rings out across Anfield before Liverpool play in front of their home supporters. A show tune from the musical *Carousel,* its importance for Liverpool fans transcends this initial purpose. It is an expression of identity.

That identity is the foundation upon which their team's success is built. In the frenetic world of professional football, the song is symbolic of the fans' constant presence. In the right circumstances, their presence – as Liverpool fans will gladly inform you – can be harnessed to create a 12th man of sorts for their team. Over at Manchester United the message is different, but the purpose remains the same. *This Is The One* by the Stone Roses plays out at Old Trafford as the teams emerge onto the field.

Whatever club they are up against, the expectation is clear: this is Manchester United, *this* is the game you need to win. If Real Madrid were there the week before, or Rotherham United are due for an unglamorous cup tie the week after, those matches will similarly adopt this oneness. Combatting the relentlessness of football's endless run through season after season, the song focuses minds on what's occurring right now.

Respectively, *You'll Never Walk Alone* and *This Is The One* reflect how both of English football's most successful clubs consider themselves. With strong foundations, their next win is always right around the corner. *To Win Just Once* is the antithesis of this sporting outlook.

Of course, Limerick hurling never adopted the song as any kind of anthem. It is just a symbol for how the county has tended to conduct its business. *To win just once against the odds/And once be smiled on by the Gods.* Luck and good fortune are prized over careful planning and effective structures. Eventually, we are told, favour will fall on us, and we'll be the winners. Until then, just grin and bear it.

Yet, even if that win does arrive, it will only offer fleeting relief. Limerick's hurlers of 1973 won just a single All-Ireland title when it was within their capabilities to claim a few more. In ending a 33-year wait, however, winning just the once was enough for a number of players involved in that team. 'We were willing to be killed in training that year,' Éamonn Cregan recalls, the exhausting sessions his brother Michael put the team through a small price to pay if it would help them win an All-Ireland in 1973. 'The following year, not all of us were ready to be killed anymore.' It would be another 45 years until Limerick won the Liam MacCarthy Cup again, although chances arrived along the way.

Good teams that sprung up in the county every few years, it rarely seemed that Limerick were on the precipice of doing what has been achieved following the 2018 breakthrough in terms of sustained success. Yes, the team of the 1990s have cause to think they left multiple winners medals behind them, but would wins in 1994 or '96 have kick-started further success in the 2000s?

Were there any plans in place to build for the future away from the immediate success of the senior team? *To Win Just Once* is romantic folly.

Limerick hurling required rational thinking.

III

WHEN SHANE FITZGIBBON envisioned changes in Limerick's development of young hurlers, it was not in the hope that a team down the line might win an All-Ireland. It was not even a case where the county may claim several All-Ireland wins as this current generation of Limerick hurlers have done.

What he wanted to do was eradicate any reliance on hope. *To Win Just Once* requires things to fall into place for a few months in a single year. Fitzgibbon wanted what Liverpool and Manchester United possess; a strong foundation upon which generations of hurlers could continually reach their potential. Winning was not itself the point exactly; as Mayo's footballers will attest, the ultimate prize can remain just out of reach no matter how many times you come agonisingly close to it. The Adare clubman's thinking was more long-term than that.

'This Hurling Development Plan for Limerick GAA aims to build up the quantity and quality of hurlers and coaches in Limerick,' reads the opening line of 'Lifting The Treaty', an essential document Fitzgibbon was instrumental in presenting toward the end of 2008. As journalist Vincent Hogan correctly outlined over a decade after the instructions within 'Lifting The Treaty' were heeded and senior success had arrived, it ignited a process rooted in logical thinking. To describe it as unemotional, however, goes slightly too far.

It was Shane Fitzgibbon's emotional attachment to Limerick hurling that had him pick up the phone in the first place. Similar feelings of frustration were shared by those who answered and joined him in his new endeavour. During the early years of their work, when one could not yet tell whether it would reap any dividends, it was emotion that kept them all going. 'I've been through it… oh Jesus, I've been through it,' Cregan stresses, one of the first former players to acknowledge the wisdom in Fitzgibbon's plan and get involved.

'Like, we played Cork in a league final and 2-17 to 0-7 we were beaten. We've played Kilkenny in matches, and they've beaten us well. Tipperary… oh holy God, Tipperary… they love beating you.

'This is what I grew up with. We were always the underdogs.' Limerick's logical revolution has been fuelled by emotion.

★ ★ ★ ★ ★

Stephen Lucey

THE FRUSTRATING CYCLE of boom and bust that characterised Limerick hurling can be traced back to innumerable parties. Nevertheless, Limerick's hurlers and management teams have always been soft targets for culpability.

Successive generations have often looked around and wondered if greater support could have been provided by those more elusive figures on county boards. When the senior team made it all the way to the All-Ireland hurling final against Kilkenny in 2007, Stephen Lucey could not believe the additional and unnecessary expectations put upon the players' shoulders. 'Ten days before the final,' he recalls, 'I had 53 tickets to give out.

'I was driving around meeting people and giving them their tickets. That was insane. There's no way I should have had to deal with loads of people ringing me over and over again to sort that out.' Eleven years since the county's last appearance in an All-Ireland final, it appeared that the excitement surrounding the event had thrown best practice out the window.

As everyone attempted to soak in what could be a once in a lifetime experience, there seemed a distinct lack of concern for the players' own well-being comparable to their Kilkenny opponents. Be that on the county board, management or the players themselves, Lucey acknowledges that the build-up was a fiasco.

'There was a supporters night then, which I think is pretty common,' he remembers, the event taking place around one week before the final, 'and I'd say there must have been at least 10,000 people there... an enormous amount. Underneath the stand in the Gaelic Grounds there is a big corridor where they had lined out a load of tables and chairs.

'Thirty of us were lined up there and everyone queued with the hurleys and jerseys to be signed. It was a lovely idea, but we had trained for 40 minutes beforehand and were there then another two-and-a-half hours. I didn't get home that night until about 11:30pm!'

Along with some ribbon-cutting at shop openings and two suit fittings for what could be the big night after, there's no telling what would have happened if Limerick had won the match. It was not for nothing that Shane Dowling called for the players to be left alone following Limerick's semi-final defeat of Cork 11 years after the chastening experience in 2007.

Given the strength of their opponents, the 2007 All-Ireland final does not possess the same sense of regret as other deciders Limerick have thrown away. Objectively speaking, anyway. For Lucey, it was his one chance across a 17-year association with Limerick's senior hurlers and footballers to achieve what he had ultimately set out to do.

A supporter in Croke Park witnessing the defeats of 1994 and '96, there was nothing you could tell him and his teammates about Brian Cody's team that would have convinced them they could not beat Kilkenny. 'Even during the game after those two early goals went in against us,' Limerick's star forward Andrew O'Shaughnessy has explained, 'I still felt we could have won.' Although the weeks building up to the match had not been ideal, the arrival of Richie Bennis as manager had revitalised a team that was heading in no clear direction.

More than any other individual, perhaps, this man who had scored 0-10 in the victorious 1973 final provided Limerick with an edge. He was the right man in the right place at the right time, Lucey believes. 'We loved Richie,' he explains, 'and he would tell you straight if you were doing something stupid or something he didn't like too. He would cut you in two, but he would have the craic with you as well.'

Since making his way onto the senior panel in 1999, Lucey had already played under four different managers by the time Bennis arrived. While they all possessed certain characteristics suitable for the task at hand, no one man suited this particular group of players quite so effectively. 'We would follow Richie. We knew that he had green blood… the man bled Limerick.

'He united us so strongly and we were so determined."

Through the unforgettable summer of 2007, their devotion coincided with some incredible results. Beyond the pulsating three-game series against Tipperary, Limerick's ability to turn the tables on Waterford and beat them in an All-Ireland semi-final was characteristic of that classic inconsistency at its very best. Comfortably beaten in the Munster final weeks earlier as Dan Shanahan grabbed a hat-trick of goals, Limerick went two better and hit their opponents for 5-11 in a result few had seen coming.

'I think Waterford underestimated Limerick slightly,' reckons Eddie Brennan, one of the Kilkenny hurlers who expected to be facing Shanahan & Co. in that year's All-Ireland final. 'Limerick were the big underdogs, but they came with a plan, and it worked.' Devising a plan that could similarly halt Kilkenny was a more considerable challenge. Reigning All-Ireland champions, although the likes of Brennan, Henry Shefflin and JJ Delaney were all still in their twenties, most of the players Limerick were coming up against had already won multiple All-Ireland winners medals.

'We were comfortable with what came in an All-Ireland final at that stage,' explains Brennan. 'We knew the drill. I remember that day when we were out doing our warm-up and Limerick came out onto the pitch. I swear to God… Croke Park shook when Limerick came out. I've never experienced anything like it. The supporters must have outnumbered Kilkenny five to one.'

A momentous day where Limerick might end the county's long wait for success, no Kilkenny hurler was getting too caught up in the event. Though they did not know it then, many of those players would be back here with Brian Cody on All-Ireland final day for the next five years in succession. They went about their business as usual, whereas Limerick's hurlers may be forgiven for feeling the magnitude of what would be many of these players' only chance.

'A friend of mine was there watching the match and he told me afterward that Limerick's warm-up broke down about three or four times,' Brennan notes, putting any lack of concentration down to the raucous atmosphere. 'That's nothing bad or sinister, it is only natural. Generally, you need to go there to come back, you know.'

Within the game itself, the defeat Limerick suffered almost mirrored what had happened in 1994 – albeit at opposite ends of the match. Whereas Offaly scored an improbably 2-5 to snatch victory away from Limerick, Kilkenny started the 2007 final with a similar bang, scoring 2-3 before their faltering opponents could register a single score.

Instrumental in this start was Kilkenny's full-forward line, particularly Brennan and the captain Henry Shefflin. Two points to the good, the serendipitous angling of a camera just behind James 'Cha' Fitzpatrick as he prepared to take a sideline cut captured the incessant movement of Brennan, Shefflin and Aidan Fogarty as they await the sliotar's arrival.

Tasked with marking this trio, Damien Reale, Seamus Hickey, and Lucey in the centre on Shefflin were constantly kept going. 'My philosophy always for playing inside was that you could never just stand still,' insists Brennan, the Young Hurler of the Year in waiting; Hickey his direct opponent that afternoon. 'Every time a defender had his eye on me, I was off somewhere else. We always had that with Kilkenny.'

Famous for the fluidity of their six forwards, it had been Brian Cody's plan from the off that Brennan would face off with Hickey. 'I was looking forward to it,' Brennan admits, his own performances in the year up to this point scarcely spectacular by his standards. 'I knew he was after cleaning every quality corner-forward in Munster, including John Mullane, and there was all this talk about a potential All Star… and he had done an awful lot of media.' No more than Lucey's regrets about how Limerick handled the run-in to the final, Brennan's perspective from the outside was that things should have been handled differently.

'I thought at the time even that that was naïve of the Limerick management team to allow a young lad be so up front and centre for the media,' he suggests. 'This was his first All-Ireland and I thought that would be an advantage for me.

'I'd been there, knew what to expect. He had never played in an All-Ireland final in his life. There's bound to be a level of nerves. On top of that, I don't think I had really performed in a final up to that point, so I was really driven going into that match.'

As Fitzpatrick's sublime cut made its way toward the Limerick goal with eight minutes on the clock, it is Brennan, wearing the No 10 jersey on his back, who races out in front of Hickey. 'One thing I had a decent skill for was gauging the flight of a ball straightaway,' he remarks, the left-handed catch at first appearing to take Brennan away from Brian Murray's goal. 'Once I caught that ball, I felt that Seamus Hickey had over-committed by just a step and I had the room to wheel him. Sure, once you get inside him then it is just a case of slowing things down and thinking about what you need to do.'

'The 'Goal King' as Ger Canning refers to him on commentary in the aftermath, what Brennan needed to do was quite often exactly what he did… score a goal.

In the 1994 final, those watching Offaly's resurgence on television memorably missed the sequence of events that led to Pat O'Connor's crucial goal. Coming so soon after Dooley's strike, a replay of the first goal was still being shown when Joe Quaid took his puck out and Offaly won the ball back. There was no such blind spot in 2007, albeit a very close run thing.

No sooner had Murray's next puck out down onto the Kilkenny half-back line broken free, it was picked up once more by 'Cha' Fitzpatrick. Spotting Shefflin in front of the Limerick goal with only one man on him, one Ballyhale Shamrocks man fed it into the other and Stephen Lucey's best efforts were not enough to keep Shefflin from scoring.

A second Kilkenny goal in around 60 seconds, Limerick were effectively kept at arm's length for the remaining 60 or so minutes of play.

'We got very close to things under Richie,' Lucey insists, Bennis ultimately deciding to vacate the role in 2008 after some of the magic had been lost. At around the mid-point of his inter-county career with Limerick's hurlers, Lucey would have another three managers in the years that followed. A shrewd operator in Justin McCarthy was the first man in and the Croom clubman has no trouble saying that however much Richie Bennis was adored, McCarthy was as good a replacement as they were likely to get.

'We were in awe of Justin. We definitely had the bounce you get with a new coach too. There was an enthusiasm there with everyone trying their hardest.' Into his 29th year, Lucey had given more of his life than most over to Limerick GAA.

Things may just have fallen short in 2007, but McCarthy's arrival and a more developed panel of players brought hope for greater chances down the line.

Shane Fitzgibbon

I

TO HAVE A clear idea of what could be done to help Limerick hurling, Shane Fitzgibbon first needed to identify exactly what was wrong. 'We were producing inter-county hurlers, but just not enough of them,' was how he eventually summed it up. What constitutes an inter-county hurler though, if hurling for your county alone is not the definition? Not since Éamonn Cregan recalled four fellas turning up to county training in the mid-60s has any Limerick manager had an issue wrangling up enough hurlers to play for their county. Furthermore, how were those players whom he regarded as sufficiently talented hurlers being produced in the first place, and could that system not just be rolled out across the county?

In short, Limerick weren't producing enough of the *right* kind of inter-county hurlers. When a Cregan, Carey or O'Shaughnessy did come along, it owed more to circumstance, talent and usually an astute coach or two somewhere along the line. The emergence of any great hurler in Limerick wasn't lucky; hard work had gone in along the way. It was almost random, however.

Prior to the establishment of the current development pathway for young hurling hopefuls in the county, there was no coherent plan in place. The prevailing wisdom taught that one, two or maybe even more talented players would come along every few years and take Limerick to where they wanted to be. It is no surprise the county so rarely got there.

It was not a revolution that Shane Fitzgibbon and his new group of volunteers brought about then. That typically requires some semblance of a system to overthrow. When he started making calls, he sold those he spoke to on the idea of creating something where there had been nothing. A former county player, Fitzgibbon knew where the pitfalls were in the development of young hurlers.

Individuals like Éamonn Cregan, Ger Hegarty, Anthony Carmody, Brian Finn, Ger Cunningham, Frankie Carroll and Mike Galligan were acutely aware of this also. It made Fitzgibbon's phone calls that bit easier. Even for an All-Ireland winner like Cregan, any experience in Limerick hurling had a chastening aspect to it, a brutal realisation that other counties were always doing something better than you were. It was time to do something different.

'Our standards of preparation were lower than the counties around us,' Fitzgibbon suggests. 'We were behind the curve, most of the time.' The Cork hurling great Gerald McCarthy had made as much clear to Fitzgibbon when he travelled up to coach Adare for a year in the 1990s. After asking McCarthy what differences there were in coaching players from Limerick as opposed to Cork, McCarthy, five times an All-Ireland winner in red, told Fitzgibbon that Limerick hurlers relied on 'eighty percent brawn and twenty percent brain'.

Cork hurlers, as you might expect, were the inverse of that. 'Hurling in Limerick was more physically demanding than it was in those counties,' Fitzgibbon admits in hindsight. 'That may sound strange now, but back in the 1970s and 80s, the hurling was very tough and not necessarily reliant on skill.'

To develop a better standard of hurlers, the brain would need to be brought up to speed with brawn.

II

IT CAN BE difficult to discern if an individual is open to criticism or has the willingness to change. If the plan was to alter how young hurlers were being developed in Limerick, an argument could have been made that the likes of Fitzgibbon and others so deeply rooted in the county's hurling culture were poorly equipped to drive that transformation.

Emotion played a significant role in their determination to take on a task that guaranteed little or no personal payback. Yet, it was this group's openness to look beyond their considerable wealth of hurling knowledge and experience that truly defined their effectiveness. 'Was there a blueprint for us? No,' Fitzgibbon admits. 'Did we figure it out as we went along? Yes.'

Dr Áine MacNamara was one of the first outside figures drafted in to help this group figure out what they wanted to achieve, and how it could be done. A lecturer in Sport and Exercise Psychology in the University of Limerick, Fitzgibbon made the first move and sought MacNamara out for help. A Limerick native, her career has since taken her to the UK and back where she has worked with numerous high-profile teams and sporting organisations.

As a young academic given the chance to explore intriguing theories in practice, however, her memories of working within Limerick GAA remain precious to her. Crucially, MacNamara's involvement remains absolutely central to what was achieved also. 'My expertise were around what good development pathways and good talent environments look like,' MacNamara explains, now working in Dublin City University as an Associate Professor in Elite Performance. 'I was trying to get people to recognise that coaching young players is different to coaching senior players. I wanted them to reevaluate how they coach and become a critical friend for them in those situations.'

For this group of men rooted in competitive sport, MacNamara's proposals did not always appear feasible at first glance. 'I remember one individual throwing down a pen,' she explains, 'and just going… "I've been a coach all my life and I've been judged on whether I win or lose. Now, you're telling me that it's not important. Well, what is important?!"'

Of course, winning and what it could enable a coach to do was still vital. The more games a coach won, the more time they would get with their players, especially at underage level. From MacNamara's perspective, however, winning should not be an end in and of itself. 'At a developmental level,' she notes, 'I want teams to win doing the right thing to help younger players to get better.' To be successful, this message had to be taken on board by coaches at every level.

One session MacNamara undertook with every Limerick hurling manager, from John Allen of the seniors down to the under-14s boss, illustrated the collective importance of this primary responsibility. 'She asked everyone in the room, "How many of you here have winning your championship as the number one priority?"' Fitzgibbon recalls. 'Almost everybody put their hand up. She pointed out then that the only person there who should be judged on that is John Allen.

'Everybody else was here to develop players for John Allen."

Even this had its unseen challenges, though. Before Fitzgibbon and the new team of coaches could hope to seriously work with young players, they first had to make playing for Limerick an attractive prospect again. Too many players seemed more concerned with scoring some of the clothing gear than actually hurling for the county. 'Young fellas didn't particularly see going in hurling with Limerick as a great thing,' Fitzgibbon explains, the allure of alternative sports compounding the ill-effects of a sub-standard underage inter-county experience that was losing Limerick players.

'We knew we had to raise the standards so that when they came out they'd think, *This is way better than what I do with my club.* It had to be better than the club.' One way of achieving this was to centralise all of the underage training activity. Across four hours each Saturday morning on the University of Limerick grounds, players from all age grades were gathered together. In the auspicious sporting surroundings of UL, young hurlers were given a glimpse of where their journey may lead if they were determined enough.

'There were always role models around,' MacNamara explains. 'Strategically, the under-14s would train beside the under-15s, who were training beside the under-16s, who were training beside the minors.

'The next step on the pathway was there. There were goals and role models around to drive behaviour and promote aspirations for the kids.' Furthermore, the location generally provided parents and guardians with a more suitable place to drop their children off for training. *'They could go for a walk around the campus… or head off for a cup of coffee or a bowl of soup in one of the cafes and restaurants nearby,'* recalled Anthony Daly, the former Clare hurler and Limerick GAA's Director of coaching, in the *Irish Examiner.*

The use of UL's astroturf pitches also ensured that the weather would hold little risk of disturbing any sessions. A series of small decisions in only one aspect of the overall plan, this serves as a symbolic representation of how things were now being looked at on a wider scale. As with the short, sharp and precise passing game that would come to define Limerick's successful senior team in years to come, the Limerick hurling academy owes its success to a series of small decisions executed with little fuss.

Stephen Lucey

I

STEPHEN LUCEY NEVER required any encouragement to go hurling. From a young age, he found himself gravitating toward Croom GAA's pitch a short way from his home. 'We only had a junior club back then, so even on the nights when we weren't training ourselves, I would be up at the pitch with the junior team standing in for training,' he explains.

'They didn't have great numbers, maybe 10 to 15 lads at training. So, I would be standing in near the goals playing a little part with these men. I was only 9 or 10 like, but I loved it so much.' A child of the 1980s, his interest in Limerick hurling blossomed just as the team itself became a formidable force under Tom Ryan in the mid-1990s. It was not that long after Ryan's departure in 1997 that Lucey was making his name as a senior hurler – and gaelic footballer, for that matter.

A dedicated player of two games, he emerged at a time when juggling both at the elite level was barely doable. By the time Lucey finally called a halt to the inter-county game in 2015, the dual player was all but extinct. On and off, he had somehow persevered.

II

Stephen Lucey is currently enjoying a few days at home in Limerick. The UCD student should enjoy the break while he can because, over the coming weeks, he faces a schedule from hell. Lucey is perhaps the most extreme example of a young GAA star who is punished for his talent, versatility and powers of endurance. And now, he will be punished on the double because of foot-and-mouth. As the GAA season resumes after its enforced hibernation, the dual player from Croom will be answering to several masters at once. He will be playing for the UCD hurlers, the UCD football team, the Limerick U21 footballers and the Limerick senior football team. Just consider the following potential schedule for an amateur player who, somewhere in between, has to find study time for looming examinations:

- *Tuesday, March 27: Lucey travels to Sligo for a Sigerson Cup quarter-final against Sligo IT.*
- *Thursday, March 29: He's in Nenagh for a Fitzgibbon Cup semi-final*

against NUI Galway.
- *Saturday, March 31: Another day, another big game beckons.*
  The Munster Council has provisionally pencilled in the U21 football
  semi-final between holders Limerick and Tipperary for the last day of March
  in Mitchelstown.
- *Wednesday, April 4: A Sigerson Cup semi-final against St Mary's or Trinity,*
  presuming UCD have qualified.
- *Friday, April 6: Again, presuming UCD advance, Lucey can look forward to*
  a Fitzgibbon Cup final against Waterford IT or UCC in Parnell Park.
- *Wednesday, April 11: Another potential D-Day – this time the Sigerson Cup*
  final.
- *Sunday, April 15: Limerick's concluding NFL fixture against Wicklow.*

You might expect Lucey to bemoan the crazy schedule that now awaits him. But perhaps typical of his generation, he simply wants to play now and not worry about the consequences.

– Evening Herald, March 16, 2001

III

OWING TO ITS rarity among inter-county players, perhaps, or the obvious time constraints such a career entails, it seems preposterous that Stephen Lucey balanced his dual inter-county status with becoming a doctor. 'I wanted to be a doctor since I was about five years old going with dad to do house calls,' he recalls. 'I thought it looked like a nice life and I liked what he did.'

Hurling and medicine were twin ambitions of his from that young age. The business of attaining a positive outcome in both took some doing, however. A minor on both Limerick panels, Lucey attended Limerick Tutorial College to repeat his Leaving Certificate and acquire the necessary points for a spot in University College Dublin. 'I got away with murder because I wasn't supposed to be playing any sport,' he explains. 'There was zero sport there, it was all academia.' As would be the case again and again in the coming years, however, Stephen tended to find a way over, under or around any barrier.

'I used to bring the gear bag in with me and hide it in South's Pub,' he says, the bar only a short walk from the college. 'We were off between 5pm and 7pm, so I would grab the bag then and head off up to Mary Immaculate College.' Covering all angles, he had an inside man with some sympathy for his plight. 'Leonard Enright was the caretaker up there and he used to let me in to get changed and do a bit of training,' Lucey says with a laugh, one former Limerick senior hurler helping a prospective player out.

'I'd head back down then afterwards to study from 7pm to 10pm.'

The discipline for this had not come naturally to Lucey. Always on the go, the previous few years he had spent as a boarder in Cistercian College Roscrea were crucial for his ability to spin so many plates. 'I became very, very, very organised with my time,' he explains. 'As a 12-year-old in first year I was already doing the same hours studying as a Leaving Cert student. We had school from Monday to Saturday and it finished at 12:15pm on Wednesday and the Saturday. Your tea was at 5pm… and then you studied from 5:20pm until 10pm. Like, studying until 10pm on a Saturday night from 12-years old! That discipline stuck with me.' When he eventually made it to UCD, Lucey had refined his system somewhat. With college football and hurling to play now too, a greater amount of work had to be done in even a more finite amount of time. 'I got very good at studying and just crammed like mad,' he explains, the general preference then for end-of-year exams over continuous assessment a grading mechanism that worked in his favour. 'A lot of it was just time-management. I always knew looking ahead with calendars and fixtures, but I doubt I was ever in on Friday afternoon during six years studying Medicine. I missed every single Friday afternoon lecture due to sport.'

When so many of his contemporaries were enjoying a more traditional third-level experience, Stephen Lucey just remained doggedly focused on those twin ambitions. Hurling and medicine, above all else. 'I had the will to do it and a lot of people just don't have that,' he states matter-of-factly. 'They couldn't be arsed and would want to go for pints or a weekend away or have their summers off.

'I just wanted to play. That's who I was.'

Shane Fitzgibbon

I

For any real progress to take place in the development of Hurling, we must look at the current structures in the county and seek to revise them where necessary in order to ensure the smooth implementation of this plan. It must not be allowed to break down because of the non-cooperation of any unit of the Association and if it is to work it must be implemented as a whole. There is an urgent need to co-ordinate all underage activities in our County. There are a huge number of committees and people working to improve the standard of hurling in this County, but it needs to be more co-ordinated, and we need all units working towards the same plan. We need to co-ordinate the initiatives run in our County so that an under 10 or under 12 hurler is given sufficient time for coaching and skill development. The focus from 8 to 12 years of age should be on quality coaching, skill development, small-sided conditioned games and non-competitive tournaments or blitzes. We must go back to basics and ensure the fundamental skills are being taught properly in Clubs from 6 to 12 years of age.

– 'Lifting The Treaty'

II

SHANE FITZGIBBON'S INTER-COUNTY career with Limerick came to an end when he concluded that the work going into it was no longer worth the reward. There is no question that the timing of his decision bothers him slightly.

Walking away after a disappointing end to the 1993 season, he wonders if he could have been of use to Limerick as they fell agonisingly short in '94. It would be easy enough then to read Fitzgibbon's recent service to Limerick GAA as an act of atonement. That just is not how he sees the world though. The work he has done to *'prepare the Limerick rocket for moon landing'* as Kieran Shannon brilliantly put it had nothing to do with how it may redeem Shane Fitzgibbon.

Beyond the joy it brought him as a Limerick supporter watching the senior team eventually winning All-Ireland titles, he would happily have it left unsaid that he contributed anything at all. He cannot have everything his own way, however. Dr Áine MacNamara singles out the humility of Fitzgibbon and the coaches he brought together as a fundamental characteristic of the academy's success. 'You're allowing someone else get the plaudits later on,' she explains, this selflessness the antithesis of what competitive sportspeople tend to be striving for. The effectiveness of this first group of coaches owed much to their hunger for hard work with no immediate reward whatsoever.

There are small victories along the way, however. In trying to establish a hurling culture that would ideally be embraced right across the county, Fitzgibbon recalls certain eureka moments when he felt the whole thing was coming together. For the likes of those Saturday morning training sessions to take place on the UL campus, they had had to first achieve the inconceivable. With 'Lifting The Treaty' in hand, Fitzgibbon and Éibhear O'Dea, then a games development officer in Limerick, who had worked on the document also, gathered the four divisional boards of Limerick GAA together.

The kind of coordinated thinking required for the development pathway to work was impossible with each board doing their own thing. To their credit, however, each eventually recognised the value of what was being proposed and threw their lot in with the plan. A positive result owing to the hard work of many hands, Fitzgibbon insists that without Carmel Ryan and Tony Roche from Bord na nÓg things would never have gotten to that point. Another significant moment came a few years into the project when Fitzgibbon fell into conversation with Joe McKenna.

Another All-Ireland winner from 1973, who carried that cement block on his shoulders that Éamonn Cregan spoke about, McKenna was keen to know how the work with Limerick's underage hurlers was going. Straight-forward as ever, Fitzgibbon explained that money was an issue. Be it nutritionists, specialist coaches or facilities, their elite ideals could not be run on volunteerism alone.

McKenna proposed that he would get in touch with some South Liberties friends of his, JP and Gerry McManus. 'It was when the money came into it and Joe McKenna got involved that the county board thought, *Oh, these lads might be onto something here,*' remembers Fitzgibbon with a laugh.

A more precious victory to Fitzgibbon's mind was something far more fleeting than either of those significant moments. Standing in front of 30 young lads who shared a dream of doing what he had once done in hurling for Limerick, he understood that the future might be safe yet. 'We were talking about confidence and belief,' he recalls, the presence of both not to be taken for granted among even this talented group of young Limerick hurlers.

'How could they have confidence? How could they have belief? Sure, they were beaten every time they went out. They were coming from zero.'

To change the hurling culture in Limerick, Fitzgibbon & Co had to change the mind-frame also. In later years, supporters would look on agog as Limerick's senior hurlers bounded through the likes of Tipperary and Cork despite the county's poor historical record against these opponents. Cian Lynch, Kyle Hayes, Seán Finn and any other beneficiary of the development pathway couldn't care less about that past, however. They had beaten these counties at underage level, and they would do it again at senior. 'But how do you build confidence?' Fitzgibbon recalls asking this group of young lads. 'One young fella put his hand up and said, "Hard work". He was right. Through hard work. Inch by inch… they got better.

'That's the story of Limerick hurling now. Lots of people going in the same direction trying to improve the thing.' He could hardly have known it then, but that combination of inches has taken Limerick hurling through lightyears.

Stephen Lucey

I

STEPHEN LUCEY THRIVED on hard work.

He does sometimes wonder if he spread himself too thin trying to remain an inter-county footballer and hurler, however. Occasionally, a new manager would arrive in with negative impressions of the dual player concept and Lucey would have to choose one sport over the other. It might not have been his ideal scenario, but the increased specialisation of gaelic football and hurling across the course of his career suggested that it might be the more sensible course of action.

It rarely remained the case for long though and Lucey more regularly found himself balancing his personal life with work and two county panels. He was a starter for the Limerick footballers as they fell one point short of Cork in the 2009 Munster football final. With the exception of the 2007 All-Ireland hurling final, life in Limerick football tended to be more charmed than hurling. Although he never got over the line, Lucey experienced four Munster football finals, compared to just the one hurling decider. Yet, he is certain that the additional responsibility of playing gaelic football negatively impacted his hurling ability. 'You need to spend more time with hurling,' he admits. 'Football is not as skilful as hurling but there is more athleticism involved. You really need to spend time working with the skills of hurling and performing those skills under pressure.'

This was never made more apparent to Lucey than a few weeks after Limerick's footballers had been beaten in Munster by the eventual All-Ireland finalists, Cork. With Justin McCarthy at the helm, an All-Ireland semi-final against Tipperary was all that stood between Limerick and another shot at the Liam MacCarthy Cup.

II

I stood on the Hogan Stand on the steps that day when we were beaten very comprehensively by a phenomenal Tipperary team on the day. For some strange reason I turned around at the top of the steps and looked out over the pitch and I said to myself 'I am going to do something to try and make sure this doesn't happen again.' I said it to my wife Louise, but she didn't realise I was serious. I rang Liam Lenihan (Limerick GAA chairman) the next day to tell him I wanted to get involved and help out at any level.
— John Kiely, Limerick hurling manager

III

FROM START TO finish, Limerick never came close to Tipperary in 2009. 'We had just got through that year and I'm not sure how we really got as far as we did,' suggests Lucey. 'We were waiting to be beaten.' Defeated soundly by Waterford in a Munster semi-final replay, Limerick fairly narrowly overcame Wexford, Laois and Dublin to earn their spot in the final four. On a score-line of 6-19 to 2-7, Tipperary left Limerick in no doubt that they had travelled a little bit further than they should justifiably have come.

The starting full-back in Croke Park that day, a 29-year-old Lucey is certain that his divided commitment to hurling and gaelic football came back to haunt him. 'John O'Brien caught a puck out,' he vividly recalls, the Tipperary man playing left-half forward. 'I've known Johno because I'd played in Roscrea with him since we were 12 or 13. Johno would always catch the ball, and then turn inside to try and feed it to Eoin Kelly. Himself and Eoin were thick as thieves.'

The Tipperary full-forward Lucey had a job of marking, he knew exactly what was going to happen next and what he needed to do as the defensive player. 'I ran out in front of Eoin, about five or six yards,' he recalls, preempting the low pass into Kelly that was sure to arrive. 'I put down my hand to catch it and missed the ball completely. It went under me, and Eoin was standing there on the '21' to collect it and absolutely bury it in the back of the net.' Where the speed and fluidity of hurling can sometimes spare the blushes of an individual error, it was blatantly obvious what had happened here. I wanted the ground to swallow me up,' he explains. 'It was such a basic mistake. I do wonder if I had been playing hurling only would I have done that? Would I have put the hurley down instead to control the ball?

'That's just a small moment in the game, but it stuck with me.'

IV

THE LIMERICK HURLING academy was up and running by 2009.

John Kiely, the manager who would bring its hard work to fruition at senior level years later, was about to begin that journey by taking over the county's intermediate team. Incredibly though, that All-Ireland semi-final defeat to Tipperary was not even the lowest point of Limerick hurling's *annus horribilis*.

'All manner of shit went on at the end of 2009,' Lucey recalls, the Limerick hurling 'strike' just about the one aspect of his inter-county career that causes him discomfort to think back upon. 'Best practice was all we wanted, to create the best chance for Limerick to succeed.' One of two representatives for the Limerick hurlers along with Niall Moran, Lucey was keenly aware of what the panel believed was required to actually challenge the likes of Tipperary. 'We just wanted to bring in some of the stuff that we had been doing in 2007,' he recalls, training and a notable lack of tactical work two primary areas of concern vocalised by Lucey and Moran to management on a number of occasions across 2009. 'Basically, it went, "We're the management, you're the players. Shut the f**k up and do as you're told". 'That was it. Nothing changed.'

Adamant that the county board were aware of the issues raised by players and management's flat refusal to address them, things came to a head when McCarthy opted to drop a number of players from the Limerick panel. The Croom clubman was among a dozen or so players cut. 'He didn't want to be listening to us, we were annoying him. To me, that was completely and utterly wrong. There was a complete sense of injustice.'

Before the 2010 hurling calendar got underway, a number of Limerick hurlers walked away in solidarity with the likes of Lucey, Moran and O'Shaughnessy who were cut. While others chose to remain and new players were called in to fill the vacant slots, the 'strike' was underway. 'It was civil war there for a while,' Lucey remembers, the worst in some ways yet to come. Speaking in the build-up to Limerick's 2021 All-Ireland final clash with his native Cork, McCarthy reflected on the events of 2009 and '10 with a different point of view. *'I was with Limerick at a time when there were a lot of fellas I thought weren't serious inter-country hurlers,'* he told the *Irish Examiner. 'And even if they were good enough to be a decent inter-country hurler, I felt a lot of them weren't serious about what was required. There was a lot of messing going on.'*

Citing the strong involvement of the Gaelic Players Association within the county and its apparent emboldening of Limerick players, it was this that McCarthy identified as cause for culling so many members of his senior panel. *'But obviously, there were too many 'palsy-walsy' there, backing one another up,'* he commented, *'and they wouldn't go forward. That was okay. That happened.'*

Throughout the county people were busy taking sides. After events in Cork over previous years, the situation in Limerick was regularly cited as yet another example of player power. Where did they get off thinking that they should have a say in how Justin McCarthy runs his team? For those sympathetic to the players' plight, the evidence of what had occurred in Croke Park against Tipperary told its own story; Limerick had fallen some way shy of the country's best teams.

On the ground, however, to be a Limerick player – or player in exile – was not easy. *'I remember going through the county championship and I was getting abused by people on the sideline,'* Paudie McNamara told *OTB Sports*, one of the emerging Limerick hurlers who opted to play on during the strike. *'You would often be hearing people on a night out, and they'd be calling you a scab because you stayed.'* For those on the outside, the pressure to break ranks with the striking players was enormous.

'There were county board officials and club men trying to go into fellas' houses to convince them to join the panel and go against teammates they had left in solidarity with,' Lucey insists. 'One lad came home one evening and there was a county board official sitting in his kitchen with his parents.

'There were people trying to coerce players, turning families and clubmates against each other. This was a really dark time for Limerick hurling.'

An easy-going kind of individual despite his chockablock schedule, this dark side of inter-county hurling greatly troubled Lucey. From a gaelic football perspective, playing for Limerick was an overwhelmingly positive experience. Munster champions once and once only in 1896, he played during a relatively successful era for the county.

Although they never quite got over both Cork or Kerry when it absolutely counted, four provincial deciders in eight years (2003-10) meant they were as good as any Limerick team in living memory. Across that same period there was only one year (2003) in which one of Cork and Kerry did not reach an All-Ireland final. Between them, they won five of the eight on offer.

This made life that bit easier when Limerick ultimately fell short of their lofty ambitions. Things were never the same for Limerick's hurlers, however. Although there was often no logical reason why they should be beating Kilkenny, Tipperary, Cork or Waterford, defeat rarely came with a caveat.

Limerick supporters might not fall into the 'f***ing animals' category Páidi O Sé infamously put Kerry football fans into, but there were times when Stephen Lucey could not understand why players were treated with such hostility. The advent of internet forums had something to do with the openness by which county players became targets for abuse.

Whereas most would not dare criticise a player to their face, behind this shroud of anonymity the most cruel and undeserving comments were routinely made. For a period of time, Lucey could do nothing but look at what they were saying about him.

'You become addicted to reading what people say,' he explains now, the years following Limerick's All-Ireland final appearance in 2007 an unadvisable time for those who may feel the effects of these comments to be seeking them out. 'Every manner of thing was being written – untrue and really hurtful stuff – (but) I couldn't take myself away from it really and I don't know why. If I never had access to that stuff, it would have made my life much easier.'

He did not have a smartphone for such purposes so Lucey would keep track of what was being said on his laptop. Before work, during his lunch break and in the evenings at home, it became all-consuming. 'My wife knew about it, and she would be trying to get me to stop looking at it,' he says, 'but it was like an addiction, really. It would absolutely ruin my day too.

'It would darken my mood and it would impact those around me. I would become completely distracted and that just radiates from you.' The flippancy with which individuals could make such comments online was not reflective of their staying power. This relatively moderate selection of views surrounding the 2009/10 'strike' which is still accessible on the boards.ie internet forum demonstrates their permanence:

> **'buck65', October 30, 2009:** *Good to (Justin McCarthy) trying to sort out this mess of a Limerick hurling team. Andrew o Shaughnessy (sic), Niall Moran, Steve Lucey, D O Brien all dropped from the panel. Discipline definitely being hinted at as the problem. Good riddance.*
>
> **'grenache', March 17, 2010:** *Stephen Lucey likes to think he's the leader of the pack, talks and shouts a lot, and if Stephen doesn't get his way then he throws his toys out of the pram. Anyone who knows anything about Limerick hurling knows that he's the main instigator in the camp, the guy who upsets things. Who you do you think McCarthy was referring to when he talked about a couple of "trouble makers" in the squad?*
>
> **'soccymonster', March 24, 2010:** *And what would happen if Justin Mc did get ousted out? The likes of Stephen Lucey and Co come back and we're back at square one again?*

Although he was far from alone in terms of what he sacrificed to give Limerick hurling what he could of himself, to see his character so callously questioned and degraded hurt Lucey deeply.

The general turmoil and absence of so many significant senior players resulted in 2010 becoming an utterly regrettable year on the field for Limerick hurling. Relegated from Division 1 of the National Hurling League after losing all seven of their games, Limerick's championship exit was a similarly foregone conclusion. After losing to Offaly in the All-Ireland qualifiers in July, McCarthy vacated his role as Limerick hurling manager.

The man that followed him would have a task on his hands to drive the county forward without being crippled by recriminations. 'When Dónal O'Grady came in,' Lucey recalls, O'Grady's appointment coinciding with his return to the senior panel, 'it was the cleanest of slates. That whole scenario was the turning point for Limerick...the reset button.' Likening the new manager to the thaw that follows an ice age, Lucey was content to discover that many of Limerick GAA's dinosaurs had been wiped out along the way. Yet another All-Ireland winning manager from Cork in John Allen followed O'Grady's single year in charge. In 2013, Allen would lead Limerick to a first provincial win in 17 years.

Lucey, however, had been cut adrift by then.

After impressing in a collective fitness session that took place in late 2011, the 31-year-old Lucey had been assigned a training programme to stick with over the winter until inter-county training properly restarted. 'I was dropped the next day,' he remembers. 'I don't know what went on, but I knew that was the end of my hurling career with Limerick then. That was very, *very* hard.'

Denied what he believed was a fair opportunity to earn his place in Allen's plans, Lucey's time in Limerick hurling ended with a predictably cruel whimper.

Shane Fitzgibbon

I

There is no true club ethos in pro football. There never was. It is therefore ironic in 1986 to hear clubs bitching about the cavalier way modern footballers exercise the freedom of contract that has revolutionised the player/club relationship. In the past you could be a great player and never become rich; now you can get rich without being a great player. Equity has never been achieved and never will be now.

– Eamon Dunphy, *Only A Game?*

II

TO ADVANCE AS Shane Fitzgibbon believed it could, Limerick hurling had to adopt a more professional approach to player development. Through JP McManus and his considerable contacts, Fitzgibbon was among a group of Limerick coaches who visited Arsenal Football Club in England to get a closer look at what a leading academy looked like.

The former Irish international footballer Liam Brady was heading up Arsenal's youth development at the time and Fitzgibbon remembers the experience vividly. 'We spent a full day there getting an idea of how they structured things,' he recalls, the respect with which their fellow countryman, Brady was treated something that stuck with him. 'He was a God there. You had Robin Van Persie coming over to say, "Hello, Mr Brady", before he was introduced to us.'

The practical side of things was ever more slightly unnerving. Player development on an industrial scale, Fitzgibbon was staggered by the number of players who would be on Arsenal's radar at one point or another. 'They start at under-6s and have about 50 academy schools around London,' he explains, the tour taking place around 2013. 'Then they have a Head of under-6s, under-7s, under-8s... all the way up to under-18s.

'At the end of each year, they have to tell certain under-6s, "No, you're not going any further". Now, that must be tough.' Not present for that trip, Dr Áine MacNamara is familiar with these development pathways and how they operate. Increasingly, the homogenised development of footballers through such academies leaves very little room for the late developer. Whereas an Arsenal legend like Ian Wright could become one of the club's greatest goal-scorers despite not playing professionally until he was 21 years old, it is now practically impossible for a player to succeed via an alternative pathway.

To a certain extent, Limerick hurling is feeling the effects of a similar division between those players on the academy pathway and others who are not. The standard of coaching and preparation are now so great that MacNamara wonders if a young hurler who has not experienced it could last in the county game. 'If I'm a young lad and I've only played club up to minor level,' she suggests, 'if the club environment hasn't been good enough I don't think I'll ever make it in a county set-up. I wouldn't be able to leapfrog the kids with a few years' experience of it. If I don't get on the pathway early, I'll never be able to pull on a senior Limerick shirt.' Given the high number of young players that do experience the academy training at some time or other, MacNamara is really not even sure whether the club game is at all complementary to inter-county matters anymore.

As with professional football clubs in England, little time is spent combing non-league football for hidden gems or players that have been overlooked for some reason or another. Although it is scarcely limited to Limerick hurling alone, the increased separation of club and county has left Shane Fitzgibbon feeling similarly disenchanted with elements of the GAA. Years after he last had any direct involvement with events at county level, he has found the prioritising of the county game dispiriting at times.

'This is still amateur sport,' he insists. 'It saddens me now that the inter-county lads leave their friends and schoolmates at 14 or 15 and spend more and more time in development squads. When I see young players not being made available to their club, I struggle with that.'

It was within his own club of Adare that Fitzgibbon laid the groundwork for what he would later attempt on a wider scale with Limerick. Shortly after retiring from the county game in 1993, he began conducting Sunday morning training sessions with young children from the club. Alongside his friend Ger Hickey, they spent every Sunday coaching upwards of 60 kids in different skills of the game. Read it however you want, Adare were county champions for the first time seven years later. By the end of the 2000s, the club had won the senior title four more times with a number of players having come through Fitzgibbon's Sunday morning sessions. A leader whose reluctance for personal adulation makes him all the more effective, he is even troubled now by the growing sense of sacrifice that is required and championed within the club game. 'I think it is madness... *madness*,' he notes, disheartened by a game he does not remember as once being so serious.

'The GAA should be about every young person getting a chance to play and enjoy the game. We're losing that.' It was not Fitzgibbon's work initiating the Limerick hurling academy that triggered this change. Beyond all comprehension when he drafted the decisive 'Lifting The Treaty' document, its success has nevertheless contributed greatly toward Limerick hurling's leading position in this ever-escalating race. This may one day capitulate not with a whimper, but a bang.

Stephen Lucey

IN WHATEVER FORM it takes, gaelic games run strong through Stephen Lucey's veins. 'Be it the county, UCD, Roscrea before that... or my club,' he explains, 'it is deeply ingrained in me. Before I was a player and now after that part of my life is over, I'm as proud to be from Limerick and see them doing well.

'When I'm 95, I'll want to watch the match... gaelic football or hurling, I don't mind. I'll want to be there.'

★ EPILOGUE ★

I
2017 All-Ireland Senior Hurling Championship Qualifiers
Kilkenny 0-20 Limerick 0-17

Limerick failed to translate their possession control in the first-half to the scoreboard and were left to rue the fact that they were two points adrift. Kilkenny didn't hit full speed in attack thereafter – both Richie Hogan and Colin Fennelly were held scoreless – but they defended heroically and survived in a tense finale. They'll be keeping a close eye on Monday morning's qualifier draw while Limerick are left to reflect on a disappointingly short summer.

– Fintan O'Toole, The 42

II

HOW LONG WOULD the summer of 2017 have had to run for it to be anything other than a disappointment?

Limerick had fallen decisively short against Clare in a Munster Championship opener that had not managed to half fill the stands of Semple Stadium in Thurles.

Joyous and all as Munster success had been in 2013, as Limerick overwhelmed Cork in the Gaelic Grounds, this 'breakthrough' was beginning to appear more of an aberration. Yes, they had worked their way back into the provincial decider 12 months later – Cork getting their own back on that occasion. In the grand scheme of things though, Limerick still seemed the kind of team that could surprise you, but usually didn't.

Three Munster titles across three decades since Tom Ryan's team had won in 1994, in a competition consisting of five counties? Limerick's record was not great. When they took the backdoor out of Munster there rarely seemed to be any greater certainty about how they would fare. It had been Clare who knocked them out in a 2016 qualifier. They had been beaten by Dublin at the same stage one year before that. Even when things seemed to be going well (2013 and 2014, particularly), Limerick remained equally adept at losing decisive games in a glorious or hugely frustrating manner.

The county's well-being and competitiveness in hurling seemed almost random. Maybe, if things fell just right, they could eventually sneak an All-Ireland win. No more than Clare in 2013, it was possible for an unfancied team to burn brightly, albeit briefly.

For Limerick to replicate what Clare had achieved, I'd have given anything for one such summer by 2017.

It had been five years since I moved to Dublin permanently. Although it did not feel like it then, I was halfway through a doctoral thesis the reality of which bore little resemblance to how I had hoped academia may shape my life. 'I'm doing a PhD,' had some gravitas to it as conversation starters go. No more than the teaching degree I had earned as an undergraduate student, however, what in God's name I would do as 'Dr Arthur O'Dea' was beyond me. Perhaps if I had spent my childhood mornings before school reading books or the newspaper instead of old match programmes, the university environment may not have been so daunting.

'I'm doing a PhD,' suggests some intellectual heft on the speaker's part. The apotheosis of a life spent learning, stubbornness – and some lingering naivety – kept me going in spite of other shortcomings. A series of hotel jobs and a few months working in Tommy Hilfiger subsidised what was an inescapably modest lifestyle. On the whole though, I was happy enough. Hurling still dominated the conversations I had with my father, but if I was beginning to feel jaded by our attachment to Limerick, he was going full Éamonn Cregan.

'"Yeah," he told me when I first explained to my father that Éamonn could barely bring himself to sit down and watch Limerick hurling for fear of how a defeat may leave him feeling, "I understand that".'

While we travelled to neither of Limerick's championship outings in 2017, we were in rapt attendance at both All-Ireland semi-finals. A 22-year-old Austin Gleeson appeared to have inter-county hurling sussed as Waterford defeated Cork on the second Sunday of August 2017. We may well have believed that Derek McGrath's team were about to end a famine of their own. Unfortunately for Waterford, however, our close proximity to Joe Canning the Sunday before, as he pulled off a match-winning shot of incredible proportions, had us in no doubt that Galway would not be losing another All-Ireland final.

Hurling, we quickly discovered, tended to be a lot more enjoyable when Limerick weren't playing.

It tended to be that bit more enjoyable when Kilkenny weren't around, either. As the draw for the first round of qualifiers in 2017 was being made, John Kiely needed a favour. His first year as manager of the senior team, that first outing against Clare did not inspire major confidence. On the one hand, Limerick's team was young, and these players boasted an impressive record of underage success. On the other, Limerick had been here before.

A promising group of young players, it nevertheless assures nothing of what the future might bring. And anyway, Tipperary, Galway, Kilkenny and Waterford could all point to minor success in recent years. No serious hurling county was ever without a raft of exciting new talent for very long. So, one thing that Kiely's team could have done with to push things in the right direction was a championship win. In a draw where Offaly, Westmeath and Laois were potential opponents, Kiely's second game of championship hurling as an inter-county manager would be against Brian Cody's Kilkenny instead.

On a Saturday evening in Fagan's Pub, Drumcondra, I sat and watched as a Kilkenny team shy of the county's more iconic sides overcame Limerick. It was close, but not close enough.

The prospect of Limerick enjoying the full breadth of a hurling summer seemed years away, if not unimaginable entirely.

III
Email sent to 'The Gaffer', Balls.ie:
February 1, 2017

Afternoon,

Without taking up too much of your time, how can I get involved with Balls?

I have been attempting (and hopefully improving) to write about sport (football primarily to be honest) for years now, and, have had the good fortune of featuring in The Blizzard footballing quarterly (attachments below, taken from Issue 19 and 22 respectively) as well as a host of other online and occasional print publications. Of a year I spent living in London (2013/14) I also found myself spending a few weeks in The Guardian newspaper's sports department, which was needless to say a really tremendous experience.

Ultimately, I'm looking to garner experience working within an organisation that understands the nature of contemporary sports journalism. While the prospect of eventually working professionally in this field is exciting, I am more than happy to simply be involved. First and foremost, I want to learn more about the day-to-day aspect of this industry.

IV

MY ALMOST AGGRESSIVE humility aside *('more than happy to simply be involved…'),* cold emailing Balls.ie changed the course of my life. Within a few weeks of meeting Mick McCarthy, Brian Reynolds and Donny Mahoney for the first time, I had left Tommy Hilfiger and started working in a freelance capacity for the website. The PhD was ongoing, but for the first time in my life I had a job that felt like a road to somewhere I was interested in going.

Oddly, sports journalism had never crossed my mind as a potential career path. I enjoyed writing about sport, trying where I could to incorporate aspects of it into my academic work, but never once did I really try to figure out how I might make a living out of it.

I didn't know any journalists. I had no idea how the industry worked, and even less of a clue about how you break into it. (After spending some time working with the brilliant journalist Maurice Brosnan, I later discovered that I'm probably not even *that* interested in sports journalism – such is his astonishing ability and willingness to consume material from all over the world, all of the time)

Under the assumption that I would one day finish that doctoral thesis and make use of it in some academic setting or other, I initially viewed my time at Balls.ie as an opportunity to explore my shallow understanding of what a sports journalist does: write flowery pieces of prose to show off how smart you are, watch a lot of sport, and occasionally talk to some sportspeople past and present. I was a victim of Con Houlihan's dangerous example.

I have never heard the word 'doyen' used to describe an Irish sportswriter of high esteem. It seems to be a title reserved for their British and American counterparts only. There remains a certain deference to the well-regarded sportswriters of Ireland, however, and if we did dish out doyen status, Con Houlihan would have been among the most popular recipients.

A native of Castleisland in Kerry, Houlihan did not truly enter the national consciousness until the early 1970s (as he was approaching his late forties) when he decided to accept an offer to write for the *Evening Press*. A well-educated, well-read individual with an unshakeable grasp of what was happening in the real world around him, Houlihan epitomised what the legendary British writer Brian Glanville described as the measure of a sportswriter's mastery of their craft: '[a] columnist who can be read by intellectuals without shame and by working men without labour'.

Yet, it was not until I heard reports of Houlihan's death in 2012 that I first encountered his work. Acquiring a few books of his collected articles on sport - literature, art, rural and city life - he seemed something to aspire to be. *If he can talk about Thomas Hardy, a train journey, and a Republic of Ireland international all within a paragraph, why can't I?!*

It was an entertaining style of writing and Houlihan's references to literature often pointed me toward books that would be worth my while reading. Yet, it was all too deceptively easy. The problem with Con Houlihan is how many aspiring writers he inspired to be just like Con Houlihan.

At its best, Houlihan's writing deserved a more permanent home than a daily newspaper:

> *When Arkle stormed up the hill to his first Gold Cup, few of his myriad admirers realised that nibs of snow had started to come with the wind; yesterday it was very cold in the Cotswolds but in retrospect most of those who were on*

Cheltenham's racecourse will remember the time between about half past three and four o'clock as a fragment of Summer. Such was the enormous outburst of emotion that for a little while the thin wind seemed not to matter. And no doubt there are decent men and women who will dip into their imaginations at some distant date and say that they were there – and they will be right.

Although the references to John Clare's poetry or Vincent van Gogh's art sometimes seemed superfluous, I never got the sense that he was trying to impress the reader. Yes, he read widely and deeply, but bringing attention to that was not an end in and of itself. For Houlihan, it was of the utmost importance that his sporting columns reflected the seriousness with which sport and its outcomes were felt by his readers.

If an occasionally overbearing run of metaphors was how he believed this could be best translated, then this is what he would do. Beyond the colourful language, however, Houlihan's true gift as a writer was to arm himself with the distinction of saving his simplest words for when a moment really required it.

It was never a matter of style over substance for Houlihan. *It isn't long since every village had its Joe McCarthy,* he wrote in 1989 of the GAA's ban on foreign games and the *mesmerising ignorance* of those who upheld it. *It is an astonishing fact that now on the run-in to the 21st century we still have people in our midst who are convinced that if you play Rugby or Soccer you are an inferior Irishman.*

Engaging sport without prejudice, Houlihan despised those who sought to impose an otherness or inadequacy on people. *If you asked me to name mankind's greatest curse, I wouldn't hesitate,* he continued, *I would like to bury nationalism at a crossroads and drive a stake through its heart. Now read on.*

This kind of rhetoric had an undeniable influence on how I viewed the world.

As a Masters student in Trinity College Dublin, Houlihan's outlook prepared me for what I would read of Edward Said – his work becoming central to my doctoral thesis a few years later. CLR James, the Trinidadian writer responsible for writing the best sports book perhaps ever written, *Beyond A Boundary*, was another whose work preached an openness of mind and outlook that I related to.

Considering his introduction to Britain, a coloniser that had set about taking control of Trinidad in the late 18th century, any frustration James harboured for the institutions of power did not necessarily stretch to its people. When he first encountered *the working people of the North* of England, James felt a kinship that was not impeded by nationality. Born only a few years after the Irish War of Independence, Houlihan shared a similar outlook on his eastern neighbours. *In his youth [my father] had worked in the Welsh coalfield,* he recalled in a later article. *He learned to love the miners – and the Welsh people in general. From listening to him, I began to believe that the Irish were not the only great people in the world.* This was the basis for Houlihan's writing; a willingness to engage in cultural exchanges full of hope for what you might find.

It was with this message in mind that I at some stage or another ceased imagining myself to be another Con Houlihan. Although I still admire how he successfully dissolved the line dividing sport and the arts in his columns, Houlihan's stylistic approach is too equally mimicked. Flowery prose that sounds good to the ear, those who try to follow him too closely rarely appreciate how rooted his work was in meaning.

V

2017 All-Ireland Under-21 Hurling Championship final
Kilkenny 0-11 Limerick 0-17

Limerick are a hurling force on the rise.

– Kevin O'Brien, *The 42*

VI

IN A BUSINESS that tended to be at its busiest when there was sport to cover, I had watched Limerick defeat Tipperary, draw with Cork, hammer Waterford and lose to Clare all from the Balls.ie office in Phibsborough. Limerick waltzed past Carlow the weekend of the FIFA World Cup quarter-finals in Russia, and then came a quarter-final of their own against Kilkenny.

Whatever hope there might have been of travelling to Thurles was dampened by what was going on in Moscow; the World Cup final between France and Croatia. The ball had been thrown in between Kilkenny and Limerick at 2pm. France and Croatia kicked-off one hour later.

Located in what was the company boardroom with Maurice Brosnan and

PJ Browne, the main office had been given over to an event involving some competition winners, a raft of food and drink… and Tony Cascarino. With the television we had to work with showing the World Cup final, and streaming the match too unreliable an alternative, I suppose we can only have been keeping up to speed with the hurling via Twitter updates from journalists in Semple Stadium.

It is difficult to say how much of this feeling was informed by what has happened since, or by subsequent viewings of the game, but something had changed from a Limerick perspective since they had bowed out of the championship to Kilkenny 12 months earlier. Three points ahead at half-time, Limerick's advantage was relinquished in the second-half. Yet, even when Richie Hogan scored a goal to put Kilkenny in front not long after the 60-minute mark, Limerick, as they have come to do so often since, calmly rattled off points until they reclaimed the lead.

Although things may have been far more conclusive if Eoin Murphy in the Kilkenny goal was not putting in his All Star-winning performance, Limerick's steady belief in spite of that was different.

Perhaps it was fitting that a hurler from the Ahane GAA club scored the decisive point that afternoon. Two of the three All-Ireland titles Mick Mackey and his Limerick team won required them to beat Kilkenny in the final. This was only a quarter-final and nobody was quite comparing Tom Morrissey and his teammates to Mackey and his men just yet. All the same, Limerick had not beaten Kilkenny in championship hurling since the 1973 All-Ireland final.

This felt like a watershed moment for the team, and for those who followed them. If this was possible, what else might they be able to achieve? With France looking as if they had met the general expectations and would win another World Cup, I walked out of the office building into the drizzly rain to phone home.

From the outset, it first felt like 2018 represented a leap forward as Limerick won promotion from Division 1B of the National Hurling League. To make it out of the revamped Munster Championship ahead of Waterford and Tipperary was a pleasant bonus. Topped off with a place in an All-Ireland semi-final at Kilkenny's expense, any notion of a disappointingly short summer had never materialised.

What my father and I discussed during that brief call escapes me now. Neither of us would have dared consider aloud the possibility that Limerick might win the All-Ireland, however. Whatever we did talk about, plans would certainly have been made for the semi-final to come a fortnight from then.

Of the numerous opportunities writing this book has provided me to speak with people for whom Limerick hurling means everything, listening to Shane Dowling as he discussed the 2018 championship season game-by-game was one of the greatest pleasures. Although he dealt with his personal frustrations that year, throughout the All-Ireland semi-final against Cork he became Limerick's main man once more. Similarly, I felt as if I was being let in on something as Breda Quaid downplayed the excitement surrounding her son Nickie's save in the final few moments of normal time.

As she explained it, all Nickie had done was his job. Even in a moment of such intensity as that, Nickie had done the one thing his father Tommy would tell anyone about goalkeeping: 'Keep your eye on the ball.'

We were sitting in the lower Hogan Stand that afternoon, somewhere approaching midway between the halfway line and the goals at the Hill 16 end. As such, Quaid's magnificent save only became properly apparent to us via the big screen in the stadium. If we might have regretted our position in that moment, we had no cause to complain in extra-time.

When Limerick upped the ante one final time and took control of the game, when Dowling powered through on Anthony Nash's Cork goal… we watched it all unfold directly in front of us.

It can be difficult in the aftermath of such an occasion to remember the particulars in any great detail. You might remember a decisive score being converted, but do you remember how you reacted? Have you any recollection of what you said to the person beside you, or whether you thought the game was really won in that moment? What distinguishes the Cork game in my mind is how easily I can answer those questions – for one particular moment, anyway.

Realistically, Limerick secured the win in a two or three minute burst in the second-half of extra-time. Dowling's penalty put them 'in the box seat,' as I have subsequently heard Darragh Maloney describe it on RTÉ's coverage of the game dozens upon dozens of times. That gave Limerick a four-point lead with about six or seven minutes left to play.

The next couple of minutes were frantic enough without either side making much of a breakthrough. When Richie English found himself with a bit of space in his own half then, launching the sliotar up toward a corner of the field on Cork's half seemed a sensible decision.

Get rid of it at all costs! Pat Ryan took up the challenge of chasing it down, bolstering English's efforts of keeping the sliotar out of a Cork player's hand. From our vantage point in the stand, we were surprised then as Ryan shifted the dimension of play back toward the Cork goal. Where a hurler chasing down a ball into the corner will usually double back to get a pass or difficult shot off, Ryan explored what little room lay ahead of him instead. Leaving hurling to one side in search of a more appropriate comparison, there were shades of Lionel Messi in how he identified the space around him and exploited it.

No more than Cork's Damien Cahalane who was chasing the same ball, you just were not expecting Ryan to go where he went. Catching up with what he had executed, it was already too late for Cahalane to react. Indeed, there was no small bit of Gareth Bale in how Ryan temporarily left the confines of the Croke Park pitch to get his body beyond Cahalane while keeping the sliotar in play. One-on-one with Anthony Nash in the Cork goal, Ryan still had not even brought the ball to hand.

It is only when Ryan has nobody but Nash ahead of him that we remember why players tend to double back in the corner. With Cahalane now behind him, Nash running toward him and no time or real angle to speak of where he might get in a shot, Ryan doubled down on his ingenuity. We had been up off our seats from the moment Ryan turned Cahalane on the end line.

As Ryan opted to lob the ball up over the on-rushing Nash, I had reached out to grab my father's shoulders. From our viewpoint, I remember this moment before the ball hits the net with an unusual clarity. Owing to the speed at which hurling is played, it is rare enough in a goal-scoring scenario for the sliotar to move so slowly.

Taking Dowling's penalty minutes earlier as an example of a more ordinary score, by the time we could celebrate its conversion the ball was already on its way back out of the goal. Often times, I have found, celebrations are ignited as much by the movement of the umpires toward their flags than what I can see of the sliotar itself. So, as Ryan's shot hung in the air it suddenly felt like everyone in Croke Park had the opportunity to hone their attention on this particular moment in real time.

Travelling through that arc from Ryan's hurley into the net, the ball's flight provided us Limerick supporters with one last moment as our usual selves. To be entirely accurate, true relief would not arrive until Limerick overcame Galway in the All-Ireland final a few weeks later. And to be fair, even if Ryan had popped the ball over the bar or hit it wide, Limerick were likely to see out the victory from that point anyway.

These two factors do not influence my reading of Ryan's goal, however. As the looping sliotar travelled, before the reality of a final descended and the frenzied search for tickets began, in that split second before Ryan's shot became a goal, we can identify the moment where one iteration of Limerick hurling ends, and another begins.

The greatest game of hurling my father and I attended, we embraced as Ryan ran off celebrating in the knowledge that Limerick had done it.

Life has never been the same since.

VII

I HAD BEEN working at Balls.ie for little over a year when they presented me with a ticket to the 2018 All-Ireland hurling final. Somewhere in the week building up to the match my father had managed to procure a ticket from a Mayo man he knew through the hotel. Although it was usually a case whereby both of us went to these matches or neither one of us did, that custom went out the window here.

If it was a case of him going to the match as I walked up and down Clonliffe Road listening to the crowd and the radio, so be it. Once he had his ticket, anything else would be a bonus. I may be mistaken then, but I believe it was as late as the Friday afternoon before Sunday's final that Mick and Donny brought me into the multi-purpose meeting room for a chat.

To this day, I still do not really consider myself a sports journalist. I work in sports journalism, for sure. But having worked alongside or in close enough proximity to some of the best sports journalists we have in this country, I have known for a while that I am on a slightly different path in this industry – whatever that may be.

I like to think that I had settled in nicely at Balls though, and that I had given the lads no great headaches since coming on board. I was learning a wealth of information and felt grateful to be involved with what was a brilliant group of people. I do not remember if I sensed what this impromptu meeting was about.

I recall asking Mick to keep an eye and ear out for any tickets, but that was in hope more than expectation. When they did reveal what they had brought me in to discuss, that I would be going to the All-Ireland final too, it felt like I had arrived in a way.

Or that I had been accepted in, anyway.

VIII

An exchange of text messages in Croke Park, August 19, 2018:

Father: In my seat and no WiFi. Enjoy (3.06 PM)

Son: Not too bad. Lot of wides, but look, you'd have taken 4 point lead before throw in (4.10 PM)

Father: Fingers crossed now sitting beside 2 lads from Kilmallock (4.12 PM)

Son: God Almighty (5.16 PM)

IX

SUCH WAS THE extent of our conversation during the 2018 All-Ireland final. Whatever manner of ticket dad procured had him hobnobbing at a more exclusive level than my lower tier seat allowed.

Fortunately, we were both in the Cusack Stand at least. As we parted company at around a quarter to three to head for our seats, we planned to meet when the match ended by the statue of the man lending his name to the stand. It would be the first time we had ever watched Limerick play together, but apart.

A few hours earlier Donny had cycled to meet us just down from Drumcondra railway station. He handed over my ticket and it would be beside him in the stand where I would sit. Easy company at any time, that he had Galway connections I hitherto knew nothing of did not dampen my extreme gratitude. If it was not to be Limerick's, Galway were about the only other county I could bear to see enjoy this success at Limerick's expense.

Donny to my right then, there was an older gentleman from Patrickswell to my left. There in 1973 when Limerick had last won the All-Ireland, he had been there in 1974, '80, '94, '96 and '07 too. So used was I to having someone to grab a hold of during these matches, this man and I would share a good number of hugs before we became strangers to one another again at full-time.

A row or two down to my left then sat Mick and his wife, Sue. A Galway native, it had been her county who came out on top in the other, equally compelling All-Ireland semi-final against Clare. Given Mick's allegiance to the Banner, it could so easily have been him who was eaten alive by the nerves of the day. Instead, he was one of only a few there who might actually enjoy the match.

Beyond maybe Graeme Mulcahy's bungled goal, Joe Canning's laser-like goal of his own, James Skehill going off injured after sacrificing his body to keep Galway alive, and Canning's final free falling short, I honestly do not remember much of the All-Ireland final at all. I have watched it back any number of times and can discuss other major talking points, but these are not memories in the true sense of the word.

What I do remember most vividly of all is the dreadful feeling that Limerick were going to lose. In a certain regard, I think it is that lingering sensation (even though it did not materialise) that makes me prefer Limerick's defeat of Cork in the semi-final to the final itself. For a few minutes anyway, it seemed a foregone conclusion that Limerick would be lucky to escape with a draw.

When Breda Quaid explained to me how that same sense of dread filled her mind as Canning's final free started falling short toward Nickie's goal, I was not surprised to hear how it had not disappeared until long after Tom Condon broke away from goal with sliotar in hand. It is not like any asterisk hangs over Limerick's victory; they won it fair and square.

The manner of that victory, however, remains incredibly hard to enjoy even from the relevant comfort of a rewatch.

When the tears first arrived, I am not sure. By the time *Dreams* was coming across the tannoy, however, they were flowing freely. Motionless, I just stood there.

Somewhere up above me was dad.

To my right, Donny, buoyed by Galway's late comeback until it just fell short, offered his heartfelt congratulations, and went on his way. The man to my left, here the last time Limerick were All-Ireland champions 45 years earlier, was overcome with joy. And I just stood still. I did not say much until Declan Hannon eventually made his way to the Hogan Stand to lift the Liam MacCarthy Cup.

At this point I said goodbye to those around me and made my way up the steps myself. Dad had been a few beats ahead of me and I saw him before he could spot me as I skipped down the steps toward the statue of Michael Cusack. On numerous occasions since, I have considered this moment in my mind.

Coherence was a few minutes away yet as we settled into an embrace that continued on and off from there to Connolly railway station. I had never seen my father as happy as in that moment. A man for whom even life's greatest satisfactions are meaningless beside the family's general well-being, this outlook generally keeps him balanced when a moment appears to demand an outpouring of some sort or other.

Yes, he had always been moved to shout and roar and jump up out of his seat by the hurling, but it was momentary; he never took it personally.

As we walked to Connolly where he would take the train back to Sligo, it felt immensely personal. I suppose on some level he was transported back to his own youth. He had been about three weeks shy of his 18th birthday when Limerick last won the All-Ireland, but work precluded him from going to Croke Park. It was also around this time that he ceased to call Limerick home.

Hotel work would bring him everywhere from Munich to Mayo, before finally settling in Sligo. He set out into adulthood with Limerick as the reigning All-Ireland champions. Forty-five years on, though he prefers to consider retirement a choice that others make while he continues on like the star hurler whose legs are going but whose mind is sharper than ever, the emergence of what has probably become Limerick's greatest team at the moment where he can pause and truly enjoy it has been serendipitous to the extreme.

Had this team never materialised and Limerick's hopes of success remained bound by randomness, his life would have been no worse. They did materialise, however, and while success has flown freer than ever since that 2018 breakthrough, that immediate aftermath whereby we all knew the wait was over uncovered a kind of happiness none of us had really imagined possible.

X

IN THE MIDST of all this my mother had somehow managed to make it through the unyielding stress of the match on her own. With my sister Helena watching with friends in the Croke Park Hotel, and my father and I in the stadium, she sat and stood and paced and left, only to return and begin all over again from our living room in Sligo. Without question, I am sure she endured the greatest level of pressure that day.

Born in Sligo, hurling only came to her through my dad. The sliotar being that bit too small and fast to really get a sight of, she remains true to those Sligo roots in probably preferring to watch a brilliant game of gaelic football over hurling. No manner of personal preference matters when Limerick are playing, however. On her own or in our company, she has a knack of finding a job that needs doing elsewhere when Limerick are on the television.

Whatever personal toll it takes on her, she will come and go from one room to another sitting down for a few moments to get the score and a feel for the game. Be it a consequence of viewing the games in these small chunks, or something more intuitive, my mother always seems to grasp what the moment requires and how to relieve some tension, however.

Given that virtually no lead is so conclusive that my dad will believe Limerick have won until the cameras return to the RTÉ studio, her brief messages of support ('Sure they've this won,' coming earlier than we were willing to accept in the first-half of the 2021 All-Ireland final – right though she was in the end) tether us safely to reality.

This counts for little when you are on your own though. As Galway chipped away at Limerick's lead with the final whistle seemingly never going to be blown, I can only imagine the concern. Approaching 40 years of being married to one another, I would not assume to know what Limerick's eventual winning of that All-Ireland meant to mum given how she knew it would make dad feel. On three previous occasions she had been back in Sligo as he travelled to and from Dublin only for Limerick to lose an All-Ireland final.

Do not get it wrong, ours is not a house where a week of mourning follows such defeats. It is sport, ultimately. There are things to be done and a job to get back to. Indeed, when my dad returned to work the day or so after the 1994 All-Ireland hurling final, a banner had been raised for him. 'We're Offaly sorry,' it read, the staff of the Sligo Park Hotel not in the business of humouring any lingering disappointment. Nevertheless, it matters. A lot.

I sometimes wonder how close she came that afternoon to going full Éamonn

Cregan herself and heading off out of the house for fear that she could in some way influence things. The brutality of sport, in some ways, is that it never ends. When Limerick reached the top of that mountain in 2018, the joyous few weeks and months that followed basking in it only served to precede their being kicked back down to the bottom to start again in 2019 with everyone else.

XI

A text message from my father, August 22, 2019:
Listened to the montage you sent to Mum with the commentary and Dolores in the background. It was magic, but our meeting at the statue after the match was a moment to cherish forever. By the way, Helena will get the Limerick Leader OK.

XII

BEFORE THE CORONAVIRUS pandemic altered everything, Limerick's hurlers made their way through the 2019 championship as if the previous year's success had allowed them to loosen up and enjoy things a little more. Although Cork had beaten them well in their Munster Championship opener, Limerick responded by hammering Waterford and Clare. If the final round defeat to Tipperary gave any cause for concern, Limerick's 12-point dismantling of Liam Sheedy's team in the Munster final seemed to suggest they had sorted any potential problems out.

Kilkenny awaited. The first All-Ireland semi-final between the pair since 2014 in the rain, it was a fitting precursor. Although the weather was nicer, Limerick's performance showed the deficiencies of old. Reigning champions Limerick were better than Kilkenny that day. Nevertheless, they came up short in slightly controversial circumstances. Should Limerick have had a '65' that would have afforded them a chance to level the game late on? Yes, without question.

As narratives go, however, if this was to be the rude awakening Limerick required to sharpen their minds for the championships that followed, we'll take it. Anyway, it is more so the fact that my father and I were joined high, *high* up in the Cusack Stand that day by my partner Erica that keeps that game fresh in the mind. Her first such exposure to hurling, I think she enjoyed the temporary disturbance of behaviour a match at such proximity encourages.

Two times removed from Limerick, by the time Shane Dowling's brilliant goal appeared to have given his team a foothold in the game she had gone native. In the midst of such an unusual period whereby Limerick are hurling's dominant force, it was nevertheless fitting that her first experience should begin with a defeat. This team of hurlers has a funny way of wearing their mortality without fear that it makes them more vulnerable.

By this stage in my own life, I had left Balls.ie for Off The Ball. A similar job within a bigger organisation, it felt like the correct step to take. Almost four years after first joining, I now work as the assistant producer on the nightly radio show. Only a few months into my new role, the show's brilliant producer JP Gilbourne decided that it was time for a change (Ray Foley was getting the band back together). An understandable phenomenon in a country as small as Ireland, it came to pass then that his replacement would be none other than Mick McCarthy.

The person who first gave me a chance at Balls.ie, his arrival assured there would be no drop off in quality or standards. Of course, it was Mick's second time around as Off The Ball's producer.

Truthfully, before joining OTB myself I had not appreciated the show's continuing legacy. Once in the door, it took all of five minutes to recognise that what sets Off The Ball apart is its complete unwillingness to dwell on that legacy anyway. An astounding place to call 'work', as there are simply too many dedicated people working there to name individually for what they contribute, I will not name any.

Shortly after I joined OTB, I managed to complete my doctoral studies too. There has yet to be an occasion where I have felt the need to refer to myself as 'Dr O'Dea', but the day will come, I'm sure.

XIII

LIMERICK'S CROKE PARK disappointment in 2019 paled in comparison to the fear, grief and frustration of 2020 on a wider scale. There is no succinct way to summarise the havoc wreaked by the coronavirus pandemic. From a personal standpoint, we were fortunate to suffer no loss of life on account of COVID-19.

The restrictions did not always make life easy, however, especially as both of my parents suffered the loss of a beloved sibling (my father's sister Anne, and my mother's sister Eileen) in this period. All things considered, while I remained in Dublin with Erica and my family stuck it out in Sligo, we were in constant contact and had no real cause for complain, thankfully.

As we hoped it would, the return of some small semblance of normality had inter-county hurling back on our television screens before too long. It has been within this environment that Limerick have reached heights we would not necessarily have considered possible beforehand. Sitting in our Dublin home watching the All-Ireland hurling final of 2020, Erica and I watched Limerick – who had only been leading Waterford by three points at half-time – run-out 11-point winners in an unfortunately desolate Croke Park.

A phone-call followed, tears were fought back, and then as if to elevate higher what had been an incredible few hours in this coronavirus nightmare, RTÉ aired an episode of their revamped *The Den*. Replete with Dustin, Zig and Zag, and Ray D'Arcy, it seemed like the realisation of some childhood wish that Limerick could be winning All-Irelands and *The Den* was back on television.

If that defeat of Waterford had felt Kilkenny-esque at times, nothing prepared us for what was to come in 2021. Against Cork of all counties, I sat with my family in Sligo to watch the final. While one All-Ireland win was brilliant, and the second two years on rubber-stamped Limerick's greatness, winning back-to-back titles felt like another landmark this team were desperate to reach.

Unlike any championship from 2018 onward, this was the first time that I felt Limerick were definitively the best team in the country. When they defeated Waterford by 11 points in the All-Ireland semi-final this time around, it just felt like anything other than a win against Cork in the decider would be a disappointment. To go and win by 16 points was a touch surreal, nevertheless.

The performance against Cork was heralded as this team's peak in some quarters. A third All-Ireland title for Limerick in four years, even Kilkenny had never managed to look as fearsome again following their 2008 decimation of Waterford. Although the likes of Gearóid Hegarty, Cian Lynch and Seán Finn were still only in their mid-20s (Kyle Hayes had just turned 23), even the very best teams cannot maintain their highest point of excellence indefinitely. At some point life beyond hurling would exact a toll on this group of Limerick hurlers who had hitherto dedicated everything to their team. At some point, certainly, but not yet.

Before they defeated Cork in a half-full Croke Park, no Limerick team had ever won two All-Ireland titles in-a-row. At a local level, these guys were already legends. Historically, the seven All-Ireland wins Limerick recorded between 1897 and '73 ensured their status as the best of hurling's rest. With the exception of Galway in the late 1980s, no other county beneath Limerick in the roll of honour had ever managed to back one All-Ireland win up with another. There is a special place reserved in GAA folklore for those counties who have successfully managed to meet the next logical challenge, however. Three All-Ireland wins in succession has only ever been achieved by the elite. In 2022, Limerick stopped looking over their shoulder to measure how far they had travelled.

XIV

Tommy Rooney: 'Have you ever seen a team like Limerick that are so physically dominant?'
Paddy Andrews: 'Yeah, us.'
Tommy Rooney: 'Oh, were ye that physically dominant?'
James O'Donoghue: '…Financially dominant'
Tommy Rooney: 'You didn't tog out as big as Gearóid Hegarty, Paddy.'
Paddy Andrews: 'No, we got jerseys that fit us.'

– *The Football Pod*, April 19, 2022

XV

IF KILKENNY REPRESENT hurling's benchmark for brilliance, Limerick's superiority in recent years has always had more of a Dublin football feel to it. Without question, Kilkenny's constant production of incredible hurlers is the product of hard work carried out by volunteers in primary schools and clubs right up to the county set-up.

And yet, it has always had something of an organic feel to it. From DJ Carey to Henry Shefflin and TJ Reid, no county has such a knack for producing generational talents in such a linear, almost inevitable manner. Theirs is a seamless enterprise – on the surface, anyway. Limerick, like the Dublin footballers, leave behind traces of their stitching.

In both cases, these modern giants of gaelic games have been constructed along very carefully plotted lines. While the inter-county game and professionalism still make for an uneasy alliance of terms, few shreds of amateurism linger in the processes surrounding Dublin and Limerick. Far from the only two counties to have envisioned and executed long-term plans for senior success, theirs have thus far yielded the greatest return.

As Limerick prepared for their fourth All-Ireland final in five years, it was notable then that questions regarding the money behind such a highly functioning operation were few and far between. *There are people in Limerick GAA circles sensitive to the idea that JP McManus's money has bought success,* wrote Matt Cooper in the *Sunday Business Post* following Limerick's 2021 All-Ireland win. *It hasn't, in itself, but it surely has to have helped.* While there is a general acceptance that McManus's financial contributions have aided Limerick's ascent, the lack of any specific knowledge on the matter has rendered questioning rather futile.

Of course, patience had worn thin with Dublin long before they had started to exert such dominance. Throughout the managerial tenures of Pat Gilroy and, perhaps more notably Jim Gavin and Dessie Farrell, the suggestion that their success somewhat relied on the game being rigged in their favour was never too far away.

'*This perception that Dublin GAA is rolling in money is just not there,*' an agitated Farrell insisted in late 2020, around one week before he managed the county's senior footballers to an eighth All-Ireland win in 10 years. '*And anyway, money doesn't help Stephen Cluxton kick the ball out better, or Jonny Cooper mark someone better.*'

It does not, to be certain. And yet, Dublin, whose financial clout admittedly differs in kind and origin to whatever amount JP McManus provides Limerick, cannot escape the reality of their good fortune. It would be similarly churlish of those people in Limerick GAA circles whom Matt Cooper references to pretend that their county's success would have been possible without McManus.

In an ideal world, each county would operate from an equal footing. In this world, no such standardisation across the GAA has ever been in place. Different counties have always benefited or struggled on account of population, expertise and the emphasis that is often placed on football over hurling, or vice versa. Before taking up its annual residence in Limerick recently, the Liam MacCarthy Cup – and its predecessors – had spent over 90 years in one of Kilkenny, Cork or Tipperary as they almost ceremonially shared the tag of All-Ireland winners between them.

Dublin's dominance of gaelic football is perhaps that bit more galling due to their historical successes. Prior to their 2011 breakthrough, only Kerry had managed to win` more All-Ireland titles; a hierarchy that remains intact despite Dublin's eight All-Ireland wins in recent years. Limerick, for the time being, remain something of a novelty at hurling's top table.

While the extent of McManus's generosity is ultimately unknown, it is not seriously believed that he is hurling's answer to Roman Abramovich, either. *It has been claimed that the McManus money is actually less than what Dublin gets from AIG or Cork gets from Sports Direct, although it should be noted that the population of Limerick is a lot smaller and therefore the money goes further,* Cooper explained. *It has been suggested that the largesse is of a similar size to what Teneo provided for Tipperary, the last All-Ireland winners other than Limerick.* According to John Fogarty in the *Irish Examiner,* this figure was *worth north of €225,000 a season to Tipperary GAA.* Nobody but McManus and those others who need to know will likely discover the exact nature of these dealings, however.

An undoubted source of frustration in counties that lack one or both of the structural vision and financial capabilities open to their bigger rivals, the foundation for Limerick's success owes more to money well spent, than money for its sake alone.

XVI

THE NOUVEAU RICHE in competition with hurling's aristocrats then, it was fitting for any number of reasons that Kilkenny stood in Limerick's way as they set about demonstrating their credentials to join the elite.

The last team to beat Limerick in a meaningful game of championship hurling since the 2018 breakthrough, analysts alternately held up the 2019 All-Ireland semi-final as a case for Kilkenny's ability to defeat Limerick, and as additional fuel that would fire Limerick to victory. A devoted Mayo GAA man had provided my dad with his ticket in 2018; one county that could surely empathise with Limerick's plight up to that point.

It was fitting then that an equally devoted follower of Dublin's footballers should sort all of dad, myself and Erica out with tickets for the 2022 final. No longer a hard-luck story, we were as my cousin's husband Niall remarked a few hours before throw-in, 'travelling to Croke Park in expectation rather than hope'.

Seated once more in the Cusack Stand, two of the three seats we had procured were beside one another. The other, adamantly taken by Erica so dad and I could sit together, was a few sections down the way. Her first All-Ireland final, she feared her presence at the 2019 semi-final had been a bad omen.

No more than the Limerick hurlers since that defeat, however, we all trusted in the process and believed any misfortune had been washed away when the three of us sat together and watched Limerick get over the line against Galway a few weeks earlier. The events of the All-Ireland final itself then bore out our optimism. What happened on the field those reading this book will likely already know. It needs not to be retold by me. Indeed, what I can say of my own experience throughout a final that became a classic in the very act of its occurrence may be strikingly familiar to those who were nowhere near me and my dad. The nerves were excruciating. In the extreme heat of that Sunday in mid-July, a sweaty permanence hung on my forehead. A sensation so incredibly irksome to me in any other situation, it seemed oddly fitting here.

Those Limerick hurlers were down there on the pitch playing for us as much as for themselves. The least I could do was sweat for them. I clutched and I clawed at my bare knees. I wrapped my arms around my stomach only to roar up from my chair in approval for even the slightest incident that went in Limerick's favour. Professionally, it is suggested I suppose that those working in sports media should retain some sense of neutrality.

Personally, I felt guilty sitting back down for exposing such rabid one-sidedness at the expense of a young Kilkenny couple sitting beside me. I know why this team means so much to me, however, and it had everything to do with my father sitting to the right of me.

It surprised me then that as I turned to him in minor moments of excitement or despair, he appeared so calm. Even as Kilkenny levelled the game, setting up one of what might have been Brian Cody's finest All-Ireland win as a manager, he sat and watched what was unfolding with a certain detachment. John Kiely and his players are not the first great team nor the last to make use of those sporting clichés that highlight the importance of the next ball, the next game.

It must help them in some way or another, focusing their minds on what can be controlled without falling foul of the greater stakes at play. I never really considered that those of us who are listening on the outside take much from it, however. We know ourselves to be powerless, really, and let our minds wander through each possibility without fear of disturbing the flow of things.

As I clocked my dad's steadfastness, it dawned on me that he had been listening intently.

Those Limerick hurlers were down their playing for us, but he felt himself to be down there with them.

In the aftermath of the 2018 final, the playing of *Dreams* across the stadium's PA system had caught me unawares. I was waiting for it four years later as a victorious Limerick team celebrated and yet, once it started, the tears flowed in an uncontrollable way. Job done; my dad allowed himself to celebrate now. A few inches taller than him, I put my arm around his shoulder and marvelled at what we had witnessed... were witnessing, again.

Limerick supporters have generally loved hurling more than hurling has loved them back. One revelation that stuck with me from the conversations I had for this book was Éamonn Cregan's insistence that he could not watch the 2018 All-Ireland final, the 2020 final, or even the 16-point hammering of Cork in 2021 (he may have allowed himself to watch a few minutes at the end live).

Through his father and through himself, Cregan remains intrinsically linked to the great Limerick team of Mackey's era and the only Limerick team to break the deadlock between then and now in 1973. His life has been lived from the very beginning with Limerick hurling in mind. Countless hours have been given over to the betterment of Limerick hurling; be that during his playing days, as a coach, or in any other number of voluntary roles across the years. He devoted his time and expertise for the betterment of this current team when Shane Fitzgibbon made the call, and the academy came into being.

And yet, Cregan struggles to watch these same county hurlers playing at the highest point for fear that they might fall off. It is a rare predicament, certainly, but not entirely unique.

As my dad and I were celebrating together, Éamonn celebrated in front of his television at home. Both cars had been washed while the action was underway, of course. A radio update had given him reason to believe that Limerick were beaten, but when he eventually returned indoors and saw what was unfolding on the television, he felt the same relief all Limerick supporters had that evening. At one point, I had assumed that he and my dad and countless others suffered with this same sensation that no matter how good it got, Limerick would eventually lose, and the feeling would be catastrophic.

As I stood there in Croke Park though, watching a Limerick team who had achieved something only a small number have ever managed, it felt closer in kind to 2018 than anything else. It may have been Limerick's fourth All-Ireland title in five years, but it may as well have been the first.

I sincerely hope that someday Éamonn will feel comfortable enough to sit down and watch this team play. But if he does not, I hope the rest of us remember that this modern colossus of a team is only so big because it stands on the shoulders of giants like him.